97~101年

英文科

統測/學測

等歷屆試題解析

應考破題技巧大公開

English

黃惠政 著

序

擔任英文教學工作數十年，尤其在年歲漸長時，更會感到「經驗傳承」的必要。

不論從事任何行業，如果能將所學的菁華重點記錄下來、編輯成冊、出書，可讓讀者「分享好的經驗、少走冤枉路」，那也是美事一樁。

本人在「各層級英語考試教學」與「英語領隊與導遊帶團實務」等兩大專長領域裡，多年來出書多冊。此次，蒙五南圖書出版股份有限公司相邀，撰寫「英文科指考‧學測，歷屆試題解析——應考破題技巧大公開」、「97～100年，英文科統測‧學測，歷屆試題解析——應考破題技巧大公開」二書，希望能在學校一般英語文教學方法之外，提供考生另一種有助得分的解題方式。

作者出版過的英文考試用書，主要目的都是在幫助考生得分過關，本書也不例外。

不論任一層級的英文考試，必包含若干的「試題題型」，包括字彙測驗、語詞測驗……等。所以，考生在準備考試時，必須先了解有哪些試題題型？不同題型的試題怎麼計分？有沒有倒扣？

本書在〈題型分析學測指考篇〉裡，詳細說明了：在不同題型裡有不同的解題技巧與策略、各種題型需注意的地方。

另外，在本書的〈重點文法篇〉裡，也詳列多項文法重點，特別是在不同層級英文試題裡常出現的文法試題。並放入作者的「重點提醒」，請考生一定要多看幾遍「重點提醒」的內容，因為它才是要告訴考生該如何答題的重點。

本書〈附錄〉裡，也收錄了統測、學測、指考等三大考試，考生的必備字彙、俚語＆片語等。請考生在閱讀這些資料時，儘量利用「線上詞典」等的翻譯軟體，快速看出某字當名詞時會有哪些例句，當形容詞時會有哪些例句……等。

當然作者也不忘在此建議考生幾件事：

1. 在做選擇題時，每題的做題時間最好不超過一分鐘。大多數的考生都會為了一個好像會，但一時想不起來的字詞、片語，而浪費太多時間在同一題上，以致延誤了做其他題目的時間。

2. 考試的前一天晚上必須要有充足的睡眠。千萬不要在考前一天的晚上還在熬夜讀書，否則第二天到了考場，就比較會因為睡眠不足，而有忽然間大腦一片空白的情況，那就得不償失了。

3. 到了考場後，要有「一切順其自然」的應考態度，答題時只要憑直覺應答即可。反正考前該準備的都準備了，到了考場後著急也沒有用，所以，你為什麼不以放鬆的心情、愉快應考呢？

最後，在準備相當的字彙量（含片語、俚語）、充分了解各種試題題型的特色，以及應考之道、勤做歷屆考古題、熟練解題技巧與策略等的多管齊下下，想得高分並不難。

作者在此預祝——認真研讀本書的考生，考得高分、金榜題名！

黃惠政

於新北市2011年9月26日

學測、統測歷屆試題解題技巧

一、詞彙題（15分）

> 說明：第1題至第15題，每題4個選項，其中只有1個是最適當的選項，畫記在答案卡之「選擇題答案區」。各題答對得1分，未作答、答錯、或畫記多於1個選項者，該題以零分計算。

例題1

All the new students were given one minute to _____ introduce themselves to the whole class.

(A) briefly　(B) famously　(C) gradually　(D) obviously

題型解題技巧：

1. 本題屬於一般的「字彙題」題型，在題句裡有一空格，而從 ABCD 四選項擇一作答。

2. 這種「題內有空格」的字彙題，快速答題的關鍵字通常是在空格左、右兩邊各三個字內。如果在這 6 個字內找不到它的關鍵字，不要浪費時間，趕快作下一題，等一下如果有時間再回來看這一題。

3. 以本題為例，關鍵字就在空格左右兩邊的「one minute to _____ introduce themselves」（用一分鐘來_____介紹他們自己），只要考生看懂這幾個關鍵字的中文意思，就可立即判斷 (A) 項的「briefly（簡短地）」才是正確選項。

二、綜合測驗（占15分）

> 說明：第 16 題至第 30 題，每題一個空格，請依文意選出最適當的一個答案，畫記在答案卡之「選擇題答案區」。各題答對得 1 分；未作答、答錯、或畫記多於一個選項者，該題以零分計算。

例題—部分短文

　　When it comes to Egypt, people think of pyramids and mummies, both of which are closely related to Egyptian religious beliefs. The ancient Egyptians believed firmly in life ___16___ death. When a person died, his or her soul was thought to travel to an underworld, where it ___17___ a series of judgments before it could progress to a better life in the next world.......

選項

例題16

→(A) for　(B) by　(C) after　(D) into

例題17

→(A) went through　(B) made up　(C) changed into　(D) turned out

題型解題技巧：

1. 「綜合測驗」與「字彙測驗」兩者的解題方法基本上是一樣的，只是字彙題是一題題單獨列出，且兩題之間毫無關聯；而綜合測驗則是在一段短文裡劃分出幾個加註題號的空格，看起來像有了題號的填空題。

2.考生在作答綜合測驗時要特別小心，你在答案紙上的題號與試卷上的題號必須一致。換言之，假設試題卷上的第 16 題你會寫，千萬不要誤用第 17 題的 ABCD 四選項作答。誤用不同題號的四選項作答經常發生，這樣會造成骨牌效應，其後的試題有可能都會答錯。

3.建議考生在作綜合測驗時，與其要看懂整段文章的每一個字，不如重點式的只看每一題的單獨「題句」就好，（其範圍是以「題號空格」為基準，往前與往後，看到「逗點」、「句點」或「連接詞」之處）。以上述第 16、17 題為例，可單獨列出兩題的題句如下：

| 題句16 | The ancient Egyptians believed firmly in life _____16_____ death. |
| 題句17 | where it _____17_____ a series of judgments before ...in the next world |

4.近年來，不同種類英文考試裡的克漏字測驗、文意選填、篇章結構、綜合測驗等，都是同一類的測驗題（即「在文章裡劃有若干標有題號空格」的題型）。建議考生：平常要多多練習，碰到這類型題目時，先快速的將每一題看成單獨題句即可答題。

三、文意選填（10分）

說明：第31題至第40題，每題1個空格。請依文意在文章後所提供的(A)到(J)選項中分別選出最適當者，並將其英文字母代號畫記在答案卡之「選擇題答案區」。各題答對得1分，未作答、答錯、或畫記多於1個選項者，該題以零分計算。

Popcorn is one of the snacks that rarely fail to make watching a movie more fun. However, the modern way of preparing this _____31_____ snack may carry an unhappy secret. Research by the U.S. government now reports that microwave popcorn may contain substances that can cause health _____32_____ .

(A) chemical 化學　(B) amount 數量　(C) popping 突出 爆出　(D) popular 受歡迎的
(E) comes 來　(F) healthy 健康　(G) needed 有需要　(H) responsible 負責　(I) remove 移開
(J) problems 問題

題型解題技巧

1.文意選題的題目與綜合測驗題型幾乎相同，不同的是，文意選填 ABCD 四個選項，都列在該題號，等於是「四選一」作答。綜合測驗，則是從整段文章後的 A～J 10 個選項中擇一作答（有些試題是 A～L 12 個選項，不一定），難度增加。

2.考生在應此類解題法與「二、綜合測驗—題型解題技巧第 3 點」說法一樣，與其看懂整段文章每一個字，倒不如重點式的只看每一題單獨「題句」就好。以上文為例，第 31、32 句的單句範圍如下：

| 題句31 | the modern way of preparing this _____31_____ snack may carry an unhappy secret |
| 題句32 | that microwave popcorn may contain substances that can cause health _____32_____ . |

3.如果考生看懂第 31 題句關鍵字的「preparing this _____31_____ snack」（準備這種 _____ 的點心）中文意思，就知道要選(D)「popular（受歡迎的）」。

四、閱讀測驗（占 32 分）

說明：第 41 題至第 56 題，每題 4 個選項，請分別根據各篇文章之文意選出最適當的一個答案，畫記在答案卡之「選擇題答案區」。各題答對得 2 分；未作答、答錯、或畫記多於一個選項者，該題以零分計算。

There is a long-held belief that when meeting someone, the more eye contact we have with the person, the better. The result is an unfortunate tendency for people making initial contact-in a job interview, for example-to stare fixedly at the other individual. However, this behavior is likely to make the interviewer feel very uncomfortable. Most of us are comfortable with eye contact lasting a few seconds. But eye contact which persists longer than that can make us nervous.

題型解題技巧

1. 閱讀測驗的題型，是在一篇文章後列若干問題，每個問題後也會跟著 ABCD 四個選項，讓考生擇一作答。

2. 這類試題文章長度與內容難易，依不同層級考試不同。但至少每篇文章都需花幾分鐘才看得完，再根據該文內容的了解答題。對字彙量不多的考生是一大考驗。

3. 這類測驗題目，常會問到像「What is the passage mainly about ?」、「What does the word」、「mean ?」、「What is the best title for this passage ?」等。

4. 以第 42 題為例請見本書 P.174，題目是問「What is true about fixing your eyes on a person when you first meet him/her ?」（與某人第一次見面時就直視對方的後果，下列哪一說法為真?）考生從文章裡的「to stare fixedly at the other individual. However, this behavior is likely to make the interviewer feel very uncomfortable」可看出，(C) 才是正確選項。"

第貳部分：非選擇題（占 28 分）

一、中譯英（占 8 分）

說明：1. 請將以下中文句子譯成正確、通順、達意的英文，並將答案寫在「答案卷」上。
　　　2. 請依序作答，並標明題號。每題 4 分，共 8 分。

例題1　臺灣的夜市早已被認為足以代表我們的在地文化。

題型解題技巧

1. 先將題句內相關字詞寫出中譯。

臺灣的夜市 night markets in Taiwan

早已被認為 has been long recognized

足以代表 to represent

我們的在地文化 our local culture

整句中譯：The night markets in Taiwan has been long recognized to represent our local culture.

2. 本句主詞 The night markets in Taiwan 是指一件事，一件事是一整體單位，所以其動詞用「has」而非 have。同理，「Five million dollars is a big sum of money」，因 500 萬是一個整體單位，所以必須用單數動詞。

二、英文作文（占 20 分）

說明：1. 依提示在「答案卷」上寫一篇英文作文。
　　　2. 文長約 100 至 120 個單詞（words）。

例題1

提示：請仔細觀察以下三幅連環圖片的內容，並想像第四幅圖片可能的發展，寫出一個涵蓋連環圖片內容並有完整結局的故事。

題型解題技巧：

1.這種「看圖說故事」的作文很容易發揮，它並沒有固定的格式要求考生怎麼寫，只要寫出來的文章不
　離圖意太遠，加上語句通順、文法不要錯，都可得高分。

2.接下來，把每一幅圖畫的細節寫出來，例如：圖 1

圖 1　　那是一場化妝舞會　a boy and a girl were in a costume party

　　　　男生帶著眼罩　the boy is wearing a blindfold

　　　　女生化妝成選美女王　the girl is playing a role of beauty queen

　　　　丘比特愛心之箭射向女生 Cupid's arrow is shooting toward the girl

　　　　酒杯裡還剩有酒　there was still some wine left in the glass

100年統測

　　統測的二技與四技試題題型完全相同，都包括字彙、對話、綜合、閱讀等四種測驗。本篇
所引用之例句皆源自 100 年度四技試題。

I.字彙題：

第 1 至 7 題，每題均有一個劃底線的字詞，請在四個選項中選擇一個與劃底線的字詞意義最接近的答
案。第 8 至 15 題，請選擇一個最適合的答案，以完成該句。

例題1

　　Don't park your car here because it is reserved for the handicapped.

　　(A) fascinated　　(B) twisted　　(C) disabled　　(D) endangered

題型解題技巧：

1.這種試題內某字劃有底線（有時會以粗體字的形式出現）最容易作答。只要考生先看懂該底線字／粗
　體字的意思，就可直接在 ABCD 四選項裡找出該底線字的同義字即可。如果時間不夠，不必看完整個
　題目也可作答。

2.以上題爲例，底線字 handicapped 中譯爲「有缺陷的、殘障的」，而 ABCD 四選項之中譯，分別爲著迷
　的、古怪的、殘廢的、瀕臨絕種的等意思。只有(C)才是正確選項。

例題10

　　Whenever I am in trouble, he always helps me out. I really _____ his assistance.

　　(A) accomplish　　(B) associate　　(C) achieve　　(D) appreciate

題型解題技巧：

1.本題屬於一般的「字彙題」題型，在題句裡有一空格，可從 ABCD 四選項擇一作答。

2.這種「題內有空格」的字彙題，快速答題的關鍵字，通常是在空格左、右兩邊各三個字內。如果在這 6
　個字內找不到它的關鍵字，不要浪費時間，趕快做下一題，等一下如果有時間再回來看這一題。

3.以本題爲例，關鍵字就在空格左右兩邊的「I really _____ his assistance」（中譯：我眞的
　_____ 他的援助）。只要考生看懂這四個字的中文意思，就可立即判斷 (C) 項的「achieve感
　激」，才是正確選項。

第16至25題，請依對話內容選出一個最適合的答案，使其成為有意義的對話。

例題16

Paul: Hi, I wonder if you could help me. I have a fever and a sore throat. Can you give me something for it?

Pharmacist: _____

Paul: Thank you.

(A) Did you want to try our delicious doughnuts?

(B) Smoking or nonsmoking?

(C) OK. You can take these medicines twice a day.

(D) That's very kind of you.

題型解題技巧：

1.這類對話試題，不外是甲乙甲三句、甲乙甲乙四句、或甲乙甲乙甲五句等的對話型態，其內容都是一些日常生活用語，絕少會用生澀難懂的字句。

2.作答時，每句對話的意思大概看懂即可，如果碰上句內某字詞看不懂，千萬不要浪費數十秒或更久的時間，硬要想出某單字意思。考生只要按照整題的大意與你的直覺作答即可。

3.對話題的關鍵字和字彙題一樣，也是在空格的前一句或後一句。因為有了前句的「我發燒，可以給我些藥嗎？」(C)項的「這些藥你一天服兩次」才是正確選項。

III.綜合測驗：

以下三篇短文，共有 15 個空格，為第 26-40 題，每題有 4 個選項，請依各篇短文文意，選出一個最適合該空格的答案。

　　Strolling through the streets in Taiwan, people often see a convenience store within a short walking distance. Taiwan is _____26_____ first in the world for having the greatest number of convenience stores, which reflects Taiwanese's craze _____27_____ immediacy and convenience. The shelves in the stores are fully stocked for consumers to pick up _____28_____ day or night.

題型解題技巧：

1.「綜合測驗」就是以前所稱的「克漏字測驗」。這類題型是將一段短文劃分出 5 或 10 個標有題號的空格。

2.如果把這 5 個或 10 個題句分開看成單句，就跟一般的字彙題沒兩樣。

3.考生平常就要自我訓練，很快看出每一個標有題號的單句起訖點在哪裡？

4.說穿了非常簡單：從有題號的空格往左或往右，看到有句點或逗點的範圍就是該題的單句。

例題26

它的單句是「Taiwan is _____26_____ first in the world for having the greatest number of convenience stores,」

(A) ranked　(B) famous　(C) popular　(D) favored

5.本題的關鍵字只有「Taiwan is _____ first in the world.」等 6 個字。因為，ranking 或 ranked 都有「排列、順序、等級」之意，空格右邊的 first 當然是「第一」的意思。 所以，「Taiwan is ranked first」這幾個字才是重點。至於 for 之後的 having the greatest number of convenience stores 幾個字詞，看

不懂或沒看完也沒關係。這就是自我訓練，每一題只看「空格兩邊的少數幾個關鍵字」的重要性。

IV.閱讀測驗：

以下有三篇短文，共有 10 個題目，爲第 41 至 50 題，請於閱讀短文後選出最適當的答案。

Everywhere we look there is color, from the blue sky to the green grass, from the gray concrete of a city to the black of a moonless night. Colors have a direct and powerful impact on the way we feel and react to our surroundings. When we decorate our homes, we choose colors that welcome us and make us feel good. Some colors excite us while others soothe and calm us. For example, when the Blackfriar Bridge in London was painted green, suicide jumps from the bridge decreased by 34 %.

例題42

According to the passage, what color has a soothing effect on people?
(A) Red　(B) Blue　(C) Green　(D) Gray

題型解題技巧：

1.「閱讀測驗」的題型格式，是在一篇文章之後列有若干問題，每個問題後也會跟有 ABCD 四個句子選項，讓考生擇一作答。

2.這類試題的文章長度與內容之難易，依不同層級的考試有所不同，但至少每篇文章都需花幾分鐘才看得完，再根據對該文內容的了解答題。這對字彙量不多的考生是一大考驗。

3.這類測驗題目常會問到，像是 What is the passage mainly about? What does the word「」mean? What is the best title for this passage? 等。

4.以例題 42 爲例，題目是問「what color...soothing effect on people」（什麼顏色對人有慰藉的效果？）考生可從文章的「....when the Blackfriar Bridge in London was painted green, suicide jumps from the bridge decreased by 34%.」（橋樑漆成綠色後，跳橋自殺減少了34%）看出，(C)項的「綠色」才是正確選項。

目錄

統測（二技）

97 年統測（二技考試）

I. 字彙測驗

共有 15 題，第 1-7 題，每題均有一個劃底線的字，請在四個備選字中，選擇一個與劃底線的字意義最接近的答案。第 8-15 題，請選擇一個最適合的答案，以完成該句。

1. This museum is proud of its many <u>ancient</u> paintings collected through generations.

    （這家博物館以收藏歷代古畫聞名。）

    (A) old 老舊　(B) valuable 有價值的　(C) important 重要的　(D) modern 現代的

    解析

    (1)先看底線字的中文意思為「古代的」。

    (2)在四個選項中，只有(A)項的「老舊」才是與底線字意思最接近的正確選項。

2. J. K. Rowling is the author of the <u>famous</u> *Harry Potter* books, which have been published in 28 languages.

    （若玲是著名的《哈利波特》一書的作者，該書已有 28 種語言的版本。）

    (A) healthy 健康的　(B) wealthy 財富　(C) unknown 未知　(D) well-known 出名的

    解析

    (1)先看底線字的中文意思為「著名的」。

    (2)在四個選項中，只有(D)項的「出名的」才是與底線字意思最接近的正確選項。

3. Many people find it hard to keep up with the <u>rapid</u> development of modern technology.

    （多數人認為很難追得上快速發展的現代科技。）

    (A) slow 慢　(B) fast 快　(C) new 新　(D) high 高

    解析

    (1)先看底線字的中文意思為「急速的」。

    (2)在四個選項中，只有(B)項的「迅速的」才是與底線字意思最接近的正確選項。

4. About 3,000 police will be deployed to help <u>maintain</u> law and order in the election.

    （選舉期間將會部署大約 3,000 名警力來維持秩序。）

    (A) abandon 遺棄　(B) keep 保持　(C) take 採取　(D) eliminate 排除

解析

(1)先看底線字的中文意思為「維持」。

(2)在四個選項中，只有(B)項的「保持」才是與底線字意思最接近的正確選項。

5. This company was <u>founded</u> in the 60's and has been running successfully since.

　　（這家公司於 60 年代所設立，且一直經營得很順利。）

　　(A) discovered 發現　(B) communicated 溝通　(C) grounded 根據　(D) established 設立

解析

(1)先看底線字的中文意思為「成立」。

(2)在四個選項中，只有(D)項的「設立」才是與底線字意思最接近的正確選項。

6. The government now allows food made from <u>cloned</u> animals to be sold to the public.

　　（政府現已同意複製動物的食品公開銷售。）

　　(A) original 原先的　(B) copied 複製　(C) primary 主要的　(D) claimed 要求

解析

(1)先看底線字的中文意思為「無性繁殖」。

(2)在四個選項中，只有(B)項的「複製」才是與底線字意思最接近的正確選項。

7. All teenagers under the age of 16 must have the <u>consent</u> of their parents to drive a car.

　　（未滿 16 歲的少年必須有家長的同意才可開車。）

　　(A) ban 禁止　(B) prohibition 禁止　(C) permission 允許　(D) band 樂隊

解析

(1)先看底線字的中文意思為「同意」。

(2)在四個選項中，只有(C)項的「允許」才是與底線字意思最接近的正確選項。

8. Before printing any document, you need to _____ the printer to the computer.

　　（在列印文件之前，你需要先 _____ 印表機到電腦。）

　　(A) confuse 混淆　(B) contact 接觸　(C) connect 連接　(D) conduct 引導

解析

(1)答題關鍵在題目空格左、右方的「需要」與「印表機」。

(2)四個選項中，只有選(C)項的「連接」，才可有意義連成「需要連接印表機到電腦」。

9. The exact _____ of that woman's death couldn't be determined.

　　（該婦女之死的確切 _____ 還無法斷定。）

　　(A) cloth 布料　(B) clause 文章條款　(C) cause 原因　(D) calf 小牛

解析

(1)答題關鍵在題目空格左、右方的「確切」與「該婦女」。

(2)四個選項中，只有選(C)項的「原因」，才可有意義連成「婦女之死的確切原因……」。

10. I hit a wrong button on my computer and ＿＿＿＿＿＿ deleted all the important information.

（我按錯鈕而 ＿＿＿＿＿＿ 刪除了所有的重要資料。）

　　(A) accidentally 不小心　(B) traditionally 傳統上　(C) peacefully 和平地

　　(D) conventionally 依慣例

解析

(1)答題關鍵在題目空格左、右方的「按錯鈕而」與「刪除了所有的……」。

(2)四個選項中，只有選 (A) 項的「不小心地」，才可有意義連成「按錯鈕而不小心地刪除了……」。

11. Billy was ＿＿＿＿＿＿ by the judge to three days in jail because of drunk driving.

（比爾因酒駕而被法官 ＿＿＿＿＿＿ 入獄三天。）

　　(A) paid 償付　(B) sentenced 判決　(C) injured 傷害　(D) defended 防禦

解析

(1)答題關鍵在題目空格左、右方的「was」與「被法官」。

(2)四個選項中，只有選(B)項的「判決」，才可有意義連成「因酒駕而被法官判決入獄三天」。

(3)was sentenced 為「判決」的被動語態。請考生注意，被動語態的公式永遠都是 be 動詞 + 過去分詞。

12. The children showed their ＿＿＿＿＿＿ by giving their mother a gift.

（兒女們送給母親一份禮物以表達他們的 ＿＿＿＿＿＿。）

　　(A) limitation 限制　(B) calculation 計算　(C) occupation 職業　(D) appreciation 感激

解析

(1)答題關鍵在題目空格左、右方的「表達他們的」與「送給母親一份禮物」。

(2)四個選項中，只有選 (D) 項的「感激」，才可有意義連成「孩子們送給母親一份禮物來表達他們的感激」。

13. More and more people are ＿＿＿＿＿＿ about security on the Internet.

（越來越多人 ＿＿＿＿＿＿ 網路上的安全。）

　　(A) concerned 關心　(B) compared 比較　(C) combined 聯合　(D) continued 繼續

解析

(1)答題關鍵在題目空格左、右方的「越來越多人」與「網路上的安全」。

(2)四個選項中，只有選(A)項的「關心」，才可有意義連成「越來越多人關心網路上的安全」。

14. His parents are celebrating the fifteenth ＿＿＿＿＿＿ of their marriage.

（他的雙親正慶祝他們婚姻的第 15 ＿＿＿＿＿＿。）

(A) ancestor 祖先　(B) anniversary 週年的　(C) university 大學　(D) competition 競爭

解析

(1)答題關鍵在題目空格左、右方的「第15」與「他們的婚姻」。

(2)四個選項中，只有選(B)項的「週年的」，才可有意義連成「他的雙親正慶祝結婚15週年」。

15. The World Wide Web has made a huge ＿＿＿＿＿＿ on modern business and communication.

（全球網路對現代商務與通訊造成極大的 ＿＿＿＿＿＿ 。）

(A) import 重要　(B) imitation 仿造　(C) impact 衝擊　(D) immune 免疫

解析

(1)答題關鍵在題目空格左、右方的「極大的」與「對現代商務……」。

(2)四個選項中，只有選 (C) 項的「衝擊」，才可有意義連成「全球網路對現代商務與通訊造成極大的衝擊」。

II. 對話測驗

共有 10 題，為第 16-25 題，請依對話內容選出一個最適當的答案，使其成為有意義的對話。

16. Judy：May, would you like some tea?

（梅，妳要不要喝些茶？）

May：＿＿＿＿＿＿

Judy：Here you are.

（這是妳的茶。）

(A) Is that all? 就這些？　(B) I don't think so. 我不認為如此。　(C) How do you want it? 你要加糖或奶精嗎？　(D) Yes, please. But not too much. 好的。但不要太多。

解析

(1)答題關鍵在第一句。

(2)在四個選項中，第二句只有選(D)項的「好的。但不要太多」才是回應第一句的正確選項。

17. Sally：Hi, Ben. What did you think of your finals last week?

（嗨，賓，你上週的期末考考的如何？）

Ben：＿＿＿＿＿＿

Sally：I'm glad to hear that　（我很高興聽到你這麼說。）

(A) Not bad. 還不錯。　(B) I flunked my math. 我的數學不及格。　(C) I didn't have time to study. 我沒時間準備考試。　(D) I have too much homework. 我的功課太多。

解析

(1)答題關鍵在第三句。

統測（二技）

（97～100年統測）

97 年統測（二技考試）

I. 字彙測驗

共有 15 題，第 1-7 題，每題均有一個劃底線的字，請在四個備選字中，選擇一個與劃底線的字意義最接近的答案。第 8-15 題，請選擇一個最適合的答案，以完成該句。

1. This museum is proud of its many <u>ancient</u> paintings collected through generations.
   （這家博物館以收藏歷代古畫聞名。）
   (A) old 老舊　(B) valuable 有價值的　(C) important 重要的　(D) modern 現代的

   解析
   ⑴先看底線字的中文意思為「古代的」。
   ⑵在四個選項中，只有(A)項的「老舊」才是與底線字意思最接近的正確選項。

2. J. K. Rowling is the author of the <u>famous</u> *Harry Potter* books, which have been published in 28 languages.
   （若玲是著名的《哈利波特》一書的作者，該書已有 28 種語言的版本。）
   (A) healthy 健康的　(B) wealthy 財富　(C) unknown 未知　(D) well-known 出名的

   解析
   ⑴先看底線字的中文意思為「著名的」。
   ⑵在四個選項中，只有(D)項的「出名的」才是與底線字意思最接近的正確選項。

3. Many people find it hard to keep up with the <u>rapid</u> development of modern technology.
   （多數人認為很難追得上快速發展的現代科技。）
   (A) slow 慢　(B) fast 快　(C) new 新　(D) high 高

   解析
   ⑴先看底線字的中文意思為「急速的」。
   ⑵在四個選項中，只有(B)項的「迅速的」才是與底線字意思最接近的正確選項。

4. About 3,000 police will be deployed to help <u>maintain</u> law and order in the election.
   （選舉期間將會部署大約 3,000 名警力來維持秩序。）
   (A) abandon 遺棄　(B) keep 保持　(C) take 採取　(D) eliminate 排除

解析

(1)先看底線字的中文意思為「維持」。

(2)在四個選項中，只有(B)項的「保持」才是與底線字意思最接近的正確選項。

5. This company was <u>founded</u> in the 60's and has been running successfully since.

　　（這家公司於 60 年代所設立，且一直經營得很順利。）

　　(A) discovered 發現　(B) communicated 溝通　(C) grounded 根據　(D) established 設立

解析

(1)先看底線字的中文意思為「成立」。

(2)在四個選項中，只有(D)項的「設立」才是與底線字意思最接近的正確選項。

6. The government now allows food made from <u>cloned</u> animals to be sold to the public.

　　（政府現已同意複製動物的食品公開銷售。）

　　(A) original 原先的　(B) copied 複製　(C) primary 主要的　(D) claimed 要求

解析

(1)先看底線字的中文意思為「無性繁殖」。

(2)在四個選項中，只有(B)項的「複製」才是與底線字意思最接近的正確選項。

7. All teenagers under the age of 16 must have the <u>consent</u> of their parents to drive a car.

　　（未滿 16 歲的少年必須有家長的同意才可開車。）

　　(A) ban 禁止　(B) prohibition 禁止　(C) permission 允許　(D) band 樂隊

解析

(1)先看底線字的中文意思為「同意」。

(2)在四個選項中，只有(C)項的「允許」才是與底線字意思最接近的正確選項。

8. Before printing any document, you need to ＿＿＿＿＿＿ the printer to the computer.

　　（在列印文件之前，你需要先 ＿＿＿＿＿＿ 印表機到電腦。）

　　(A) confuse 混淆　(B) contact 接觸　(C) connect 連接　(D) conduct 引導

解析

(1)答題關鍵在題目空格左、右方的「需要」與「印表機」。

(2)四個選項中，只有選(C)項的「連接」，才可有意義連成「需要連接印表機到電腦」。

9. The exact ＿＿＿＿＿＿ of that woman's death couldn't be determined.

　　（該婦女之死的確切 ＿＿＿＿＿＿ 還無法斷定。）

　　(A) cloth 布料　(B) clause 文章條款　(C) cause 原因　(D) calf 小牛

解析

(1)答題關鍵在題目空格左、右方的「確切」與「該婦女」。

(2)四個選項中，只有選(C)項的「原因」，才可有意義連成「婦女之死的確切原因……」。

10. I hit a wrong button on my computer and ＿＿＿＿＿＿ deleted all the important information.

　　（我按錯鈕而 ＿＿＿＿＿＿ 刪除了所有的重要資料。）

　　(A) accidentally 不小心　(B) traditionally 傳統上　(C) peacefully 和平地

　　(D) conventionally 依慣例

解析

(1)答題關鍵在題目空格左、右方的「按錯鈕而」與「刪除了所有的……」。

(2)四個選項中，只有選 (A) 項的「不小心地」，才可有意義連成「按錯鈕而不小心地刪除了……」。

11. Billy was ＿＿＿＿＿＿ by the judge to three days in jail because of drunk driving.

　　（比爾因酒駕而被法官 ＿＿＿＿＿＿ 入獄三天。）

　　(A) paid 償付　(B) sentenced 判決　(C) injured 傷害　(D) defended 防禦

解析

(1)答題關鍵在題目空格左、右方的「was」與「被法官」。

(2)四個選項中，只有選(B)項的「判決」，才可有意義連成「因酒駕而被法官判決入獄三天」。

(3)was sentenced 為「判決」的被動語態。請考生注意，被動語態的公式永遠都是 be 動詞＋過去分詞。

12. The children showed their ＿＿＿＿＿＿ by giving their mother a gift.

　　（兒女們送給母親一份禮物以表達他們的 ＿＿＿＿＿＿ 。）

　　(A) limitation 限制　(B) calculation 計算　(C) occupation 職業　(D) appreciation 感激

解析

(1)答題關鍵在題目空格左、右方的「表達他們的」與「送給母親一份禮物」。

(2)四個選項中，只有選 (D) 項的「感激」，才可有意義連成「孩子們送給母親一份禮物來表達他們的感激」。

13. More and more people are ＿＿＿＿＿＿ about security on the Internet.

　　（越來越多人 ＿＿＿＿＿＿ 網路上的安全。）

　　(A) concerned 關心　(B) compared 比較　(C) combined 聯合　(D) continued 繼續

解析

(1)答題關鍵在題目空格左、右方的「越來越多人」與「網路上的安全」。

(2)四個選項中，只有選(A)項的「關心」，才可有意義連成「越來越多人關心網路上的安全」。

14. His parents are celebrating the fifteenth ＿＿＿＿＿＿ of their marriage.

　　（他的雙親正慶祝他們婚姻的第 15 ＿＿＿＿＿＿ 。）

(A) ancestor 祖先　　(B) anniversary 週年的　　(C) university 大學　　(D) competition 競爭

解析

(1)答題關鍵在題目空格左、右方的「第15」與「他們的婚姻」。

(2)四個選項中，只有選(B)項的「週年的」，才可有意義連成「他的雙親正慶祝結婚15週年」。

15. The World Wide Web has made a huge ＿＿＿＿＿＿ on modern business and communication.

（全球網路對現代商務與通訊造成極大的 ＿＿＿＿＿。）

(A) import 重要　　(B) imitation 仿造　　(C) impact 衝擊　　(D) immune 免疫

解析

(1)答題關鍵在題目空格左、右方的「極大的」與「對現代商務……」。

(2)四個選項中，只有選(C)項的「衝擊」，才可有意義連成「全球網路對現代商務與通訊造成極大的衝擊」。

II. 對話測驗

共有 10 題，為第 16-25 題，請依對話內容選出一個最適當的答案，使其成為有意義的對話。

16. Judy：May, would you like some tea?

（梅，妳要不要喝些茶？）

May：＿＿＿＿＿＿

Judy：Here you are.

（這是妳的茶。）

(A) Is that all? 就這些？　　(B) I don't think so. 我不認為如此。　　(C) How do you want it? 你要加糖或奶精嗎？　　(D) Yes, please. But not too much. 好的。但不要太多。

解析

(1)答題關鍵在第一句。

(2)在四個選項中，第二句只有選(D)項的「好的。但不要太多」才是回應第一句的正確選項。

17. Sally：Hi, Ben. What did you think of your finals last week?

（嗨，賓，你上週的期末考考的如何？）

Ben：＿＿＿＿＿＿

Sally：I'm glad to hear that　（我很高興聽到你這麼說。）

(A) Not bad. 還不錯。　　(B) I flunked my math. 我的數學不及格。　　(C) I didn't have time to study. 我沒時間準備考試。　　(D) I have too much homework. 我的功課太多。

解析

(1)答題關鍵在第三句。

⑵在四個選項中，第二句只有選 (A) 項的「還不錯」，第三句才會接著說「我很高興聽到你這麼說。」。

18. Woman：The bed was dirty, the TV didn't work, and there was no hot water.

（床鋪很髒，電視不能看，也沒有熱水。）

Man： ＿＿＿＿＿＿＿ , ma'am, I will speak to the manager and try to return your money.

（ ＿＿＿＿＿＿＿ ，女士 我會跟經理報告，看看可否退費給妳。）

Woman：You also charged me for some drinks I never drank

（你們也多收了我根本沒喝的飲料費用。）

(A) That's great 那太好了　(B) I am sorry 我很抱歉　(C) I can't afford it 我付不起　(D) I will fix the sink 我會去修水槽

解析

⑴答題關鍵在第一句。

⑵在四個選項中，第二句只有選 (B) 項的「我很抱歉」，才是回應第一句的「床鋪很髒，電視……」的正確選項。

19. Woman：How may I help you?

（我可以幫你忙嗎？）

Man： ＿＿＿＿＿＿＿

Woman：If you need any help, please let me know.

（如果你需要幫忙，請告訴我。）

(A) I'm just browsing. 我只是隨便瀏覽一下。　(B) I'm sorry to hear that. 很遺憾聽到你這麼說。　(C) I'm lost. 我迷路了。　(D) The total are $ 110. 總價是 110 元。

解析

⑴答題關鍵在第三句。

⑵在四個選項中，第二句只有選 (A) 項的「我只是隨便瀏覽一下」，第三句才會接著說「如果你需要幫忙，請告訴我」。

20. Man： Evis' Car Rental Service.

（這裡是艾佛斯租車中心。）

Woman：I'd like to rent a trailer for a couple of days, please.

（我要租兩天的拖車。）

Man： You will have to call a moving company for that, ma'am.

（妳應打給搬家公司才對。）

Woman：＿＿＿＿＿＿＿

(A) You have dialed the wrong number. 你打錯號碼了。　(B) Do you have their number? 你

有他們的號碼嗎？ (C) Sorry! They are all sold out. 抱歉，都賣光了。 (D) What did you do to it? 你怎麼弄的？

解析

(1)答題關鍵在第三句。

(2)在四個選項中，第四句只有選 (B) 項的「你有他們的號碼嗎？」才是回應第三句的「妳應打給搬家公司才對」。

21. Henry：What's the matter?

（你是怎麼了？）

Jill：＿＿＿＿＿＿＿

Henry：How many times do I have to tell you to be more organized!

（我要告訴妳多少次文件要存放好不要隨便放。）

(A) I think I am sick. 我大概是病了。 (B) I'm so happy for you. 我真為你高興。 (C) I think I've lost my report. 我的報告弄丟了。 (D) I've found a new job. 我已找到新工作。

解析

(1)答題關鍵在第三句。

(2)在四個選項中，第二句只有選 (C) 項的「我的報告弄丟了」，第三句才會接著說「我要告訴妳多少次……」。

22. Customer：Do you take credit card?

（你們收信用卡嗎？）

Cashier： Sorry, cash only.

（抱歉，只收現金）

Customer：＿＿＿＿＿＿＿

Cashier： Yes, there is an ATM right around the corner.

（有，街角就有一臺提款機）

(A) Is there another store around here? 這附近還有商店嗎？ (B) Is this on sale? 這個是促銷品嗎？ (C) Is there any place I can get some money? 有什麼地方我可以領些錢？ (D) Is there a restroom? 有洗手間嗎？

解析

(1)答題關鍵在第四句。

(2)在四個選項中，第三句只有選 (C) 項的「有什麼地方我可以領些錢？」，第四句才會接著說「街角就有一臺提款機」。

23. John：Have you ever tried diving?

（你有試過潛水嗎？）

Lisa：No, I haven't. ＿＿＿＿＿＿＿ 。

（沒，沒有試過 ＿＿＿＿＿＿＿ 。）

John：Really? Why?

（真的？為什麼？）

Lisa：Because I'm afraid of water.

（因為我怕水。）

(A) Diving seems fun. 潛水很好玩　(B) How about you? 那你呢？　(C) And I don't think I want to. 我也不想試。　(D) You can say that again. 你說對了。

解析

(1)答題關鍵在第三句。

(2)在四個選項中，第二句只有選 (C) 項的「沒試過，我也不想試」，第三句才會驚奇的問「真的？為什麼？」。

24. Man：　Excuse me. Could you tell me how to get to the Metropolitan Museum of Art?

（不好意思，你可以告訴我怎麼去大都會藝術博物館嗎？）

Woman：Walk along this street and you'll see it on your right. ＿＿＿＿＿＿＿

（沿這條街直走，它會在你的右手邊。 ＿＿＿＿＿＿＿ ）

Man：　Thanks. 謝謝。

(A) It's a pity.那很遺憾　(B) What for? 幹什麼用？　(C) How about that? 那個可以嗎？

(D) You can't miss it. 你不會錯過的。

解析

(1)答題關鍵在第二句的「它會在你的右手邊」。

(2)在四個選項中，第二句後段只有選 (D) 項的「你不會錯過的」，才可整句連成「它會在你的右手邊，你不會錯過的（你不會看不到之意）」。

25. Elisa：Wow! That's a cool ringtone!

（哇！那個答鈴聲很酷！）

Jerry：Thanks, I downloaded it from a website.

（謝謝，我從網站下載的）

Elisa：Really? ＿＿＿＿＿＿＿

（真的嗎？ ＿＿＿＿＿＿＿ ）

Jerry：Not much, and it's worth every penny.

（不多，但非常值得）

(A) What's the name of the song? 那首歌是什麼歌名？　(B) Which website? 哪個網站　(C) How much did you pay? 妳付了多少錢？　(D) How did you do it? 妳怎麼辦到的？

解析

(1)答題關鍵在第四句。

(2)在四個選項中，第三句只有選 (C) 項的「妳付了多少錢」，第四句才會接著説「不多，但值得」。

III. 綜合測驗

下面兩篇短文共有 15 個空格，為 26-40 題，請依各篇短文文意，選出一個最適合該空格的答案。

題型説明：「綜合測驗」就是以前所稱的「克漏字測驗」。其題型特色如下：

1. 克漏字測驗的試題格式是，在一篇文章裡，分隔成若干個「＿＿＿＿＿＿」填空格，每一空格上，標有阿拉伯數字的題號。

2. 接著，把每個標有題號（＿＿＿31＿＿＿）的句子單獨列出來，把它當做一般的填空題看，答題會更容易。

3. 句子單獨列出的方法是：從「題號空格」往前或往後，找出逗點或句點，此範圍內的字句就是該題號的題句。

4. 以本文第 26 題號爲例：該句單獨列出，只有「Wang started playing baseball in his ＿＿26＿＿ grade,」八個字。

5. 單獨列出的有題號的題句格式，跟一般的填空題的題句格式沒有兩樣，只要在空格左、右兩邊各三個字之內，絕大部分都可找到答題關鍵，即可快速作答得分。

　　　At 26, Chien-Ming Wang is a national hero in his home country. Wang started playing baseball in his ＿＿26＿＿ grade, as a pitcher, first baseman and outfielder in elementary school. He ＿＿27＿＿ high school in Taipei, on the north side of Taiwan; his hometown, Tainan, is in the south. Then he went to a sports college and was signed ＿＿28＿＿ the Yankees in 2000. Wang pitched for the Taiwan national baseball team in the 2002 Asian Games, and he also ＿＿29＿＿ the Taiwan team to the 2004 Olympic Games in Athens. He has come to be ＿＿30＿＿ as the Yankees ace pitcher over the 2006 and 2007 seasons. Wang has been idolized in his native country ＿＿31＿＿ all of his games are televised nationwide. Wang, a 19-game winner in each of the past two seasons, got a ＿＿32＿＿ from nearly half a million U.S. dollars to $ 4 million. Because of his popularity, he was named one of the *Time 100* for 2007.

　　　（二十六歲的王建民在其國內被視爲英雄人物。王建民在國小 ＿＿26＿＿ 年級時開始打棒球，擔任捕手、一壘手及外野手。他在臺北 ＿＿27＿＿ 高中。他的故鄉臺南，在臺灣南部。之後他讀體專於 2000 年時 ＿＿28＿＿ 洋基隊簽爲球員。2002年的亞洲棒球賽，王建民擔任國家隊的投手並且 ＿＿29＿＿ 臺灣隊前往雅典參加2004 年的奧運會。在 2006 與 2007 兩年他 ＿＿30＿＿ 洋基隊的王牌投手。他成爲母國人民的偶像，＿＿31＿＿ 他的每一場球賽都做全國電視轉播。王建民在過去兩季

都贏得十九勝，並獲得 _____32_____ 從近 50 萬美金調高到 400 萬美金。由於他的知名度，2007 年時，登上《時代雜誌》的百人排行榜。）

**26. 題句：Wang started playing baseball in his _____26_____ grade,
　　　　（王建民在國小 _____26_____ 年級時開始打棒球，）

　　選項：(A) fourth 第四　(B) four 四個　(C) fourteen 十四　(D) forty 四十

解析

(1)答題關鍵在空格右邊的「年級」。

(2)四個選項中，只有選(A)項的「第四」放入空格，才符合「年級之前要放序數而非基數」文法規定的正確選項。

27. 題句：He _____27_____ high school in Taipei
　　　　（他在臺北 _____27_____ 高中）

　　選項：(A) contended 爭奪　(B) intended 有意　(C) pretended 假裝　(D) attended 參加

解析

(1)答題關鍵在題目空格左、右方的「高中」。

(2)四個選項中，只有選(D)項的「參加」放入空格，才可有意義地連成「他在臺北參加高中（讀高中）」，才是正確選項。

**28. 題句：Then he went to a sports college and was signed _____28_____ the Yankees in 2000.
　　　　（之後他讀體專於 2000 年時 _____28_____ 洋基隊簽為球員。）

　　選項：(A) by 被……　(B) over 在上方　(C) out 外面　(D) at 在……

解析

(1)答題關鍵在空格左邊的被動語態「was signed」二字。

(2)被動語態的固定結構是 be + pp。像是合約被簽 was signed、書信被寫 was written……等。

(3)四個選項中，只有選(A)項的「by」才是被動語態的正確介係詞。

**29. 題句：and he also _____29_____ the Taiwan team to the 2004 Olympic Games in Athens.
　　　　（並且 _____29_____ 臺灣隊前往雅典參加 2004 年的奧運會。）

　　選項：(A) lead 現在式動詞（帶領）　(B) led 過去式動詞　(C) was led 被動語態過去式
　　　　　(D) is leading 現在進行式

解析

(1)答題關鍵「2004 Olympic Games」是「表示過去的時間副詞」，所以要用過去式動詞。

(2)四個選項中，只有選(B)項的 led 是過去式動詞，才是合文法的正確選項。

**30.題句：He has come to be _____30_____ as the Yankees ace pitcher over the 2006 and 2007 seasons.

（在 2006 與 2007 兩年他_____30_____洋基隊的王牌投手。）

選項：(A) know 原形動詞　(B) known 過去分詞　(C) knew 過去式　(D) knowing 動名詞

解析

(1)答題關鍵在空格左邊的「to be...as」。

(2)本題是考片語「be known as」被認知爲～之意。

(3)四個選項中，只有選 (B) 項的過去分詞「known」才能連成「to be known as the Yankees ace pitcher...」才是正確選項。

**31.題句：Wang has been idolized in his native country _____31_____ all of his games are televised nationwide.

（他成爲母國人民的偶像，_____31_____他的每一場球賽都做全國電視轉播。）

選項：(A) whichever 無論哪個　(B) whatever 任何……的　(C) whether 是否　(D) where 在那裡

解析

(1)答題關鍵在空格左邊的前述詞也是地方副詞的 country 一字。

(2)四個選項中，只有選 (D) 項、同時也是表示地方的關係副詞，才是符合文法的正確選項。

32. 題句：got a _____32_____ from nearly half a million U.S. dollars to $ 4 million.

（並獲得_____32_____從近 50 萬美金調高到 400 萬美金。）

選項：(A) raise 加薪　(B) risen 過去分詞　(C) rose 過去式　(D) raised 升高的

解析

(1)答題關鍵在空格左邊的「獲得一次」。

(2)四個選項中，只有選 (A) 項的「加薪」才符合文法，才是正確選項。

　　Can everyone be an astronomer? It certainly seems that way, especially with some of the _____33_____ tools at our fingertips, like Google Sky, which allows Internet users to navigate through a digitized map of space.

　　Bob Park, a professor of physics at the University of Maryland, believes that virtual space _____34_____ using telerobots, which humans control from the ground, is a better solution than _____35_____ astronauts, which he calls a waste of _____36_____ . "We've gone about as far as we can with manned space _____37_____ ," Park says. "We could go to Mars at _____38_____ expense, but what would a human do when he got there? We can't do much locked in a _____39_____ . There isn't much to hear except a very low rumble from the Martian wind. The only sense that would be available to us is our eyes, and we can build robots with _____40_____ better eyes than humans. Already, the little rovers on Mars right now can focus in on a distant mountain or a grain of sand. We can build telescopes on our robots with any sort of visual capability that we want.

（每一個人都可成為天文學家嗎？好像是的，特別是有了很方便 _____33_____ 的工具，像是的，特別是有了很方便 _____33_____ 的工具，像是 Google Sky 就是。它讓上網的人可以在太空數據地圖上瀏覽。馬里蘭大學物理學教授鮑伯帕克相信，由人類在地面上操控，由電傳機器人在太空 _____34_____ ，比 _____35_____ 真人上太空的方法更好。後者而言他認為是一種 _____36_____ 浪費。我們已盡力做好有載人的太空 _____37_____ ，鮑伯說。我們也可花 _____38_____ 的費用上火星。但把人送上火星後他能做什麼呢？在封閉的 _____39_____ 裡做不了什麼事，除了火星的隆隆風聲之外，什麼也聽不到。我們有感覺的只有我們的雙眼，而我們卻可造出比人類視覺功能更好 _____40_____ 的機器人。在火星上的小漫遊者現在已經可以聚焦遠處的山景或一粒細沙。我們也可在機器人上裝置附有各種功能的望遠鏡。）

33. 題句：especially with some of the _____33_____ tools at our fingertips, like Google Sky,
（特別是有了很方便 _____33_____ 的工具，像是 Google Sky 就是。）
選項：(A) old-fashion 過時的　(B) latest 最新事物　(C) out-of-date 不流行的　(D) least 最少的

解析
(1)答題關鍵在題目空格右邊的「tools...like Google Sky」。
(2)四個選項中，只有選(B)項的「latest」放入空格，才是有意義連成整題句的正確選項。

34. 題句：Bob Park, ... believes that virtual space _____34_____ using telerobots, ...
（由電傳機器人在太空 _____34_____ ……）
選項：(A) exploration 瀏覽　(B) explanation 解釋　(C) expectation 期待　(D) exception 例外

解析
(1)答題關鍵在題目空格左邊的「virtual space」。
(2)四個選項中，只有選(A)項的「exploration」放入空格，才是有意義連成整題句的正確選項。

**35.題句：... is a better solution than _____35_____ astronauts,
（比 _____35_____ 真人上太空的方法更好。）
選項：(A) send 現在式　(B) sent 過去式　(C) sending 動名詞　(D) to send 不定詞

解析
(1)答題關鍵在空格左、右邊的 better solution than、astronauts。
(2)四個選項中，只有選 (C) 項的「sending」才符合「連接詞 than 之後須放子句或動名詞片語」的文法規定，才是正確選項。

36. 題句：which he calls a waste of _____36_____ .
（後者而言他認為是一種 _____36_____ 浪費。）

選項：(A) relations 關係　(B) sausages 香腸　(C) resources 資源　(D) sauces 醬汁

解析

(1)答題關鍵在題目空格左邊的「一種浪費」。

(2)四個選項中，只有選(C)項的「資源」放入空格，才是有意義連成整句的正確選項。

37. 題句："We've gone about as far as we can with manned space ＿＿＿37＿＿＿," Park says.

（我們已盡力做好有載人的太空＿＿＿37＿＿＿，鮑伯說。）

選項：(A) miles 英哩　(B) mistakes 錯誤　(C) memories 記憶　(D) missions 飛行任務

解析

(1)答題關鍵在題目空格左邊的「manned space」。

(2)四個選項中，只有選(D)項的「mission」放入空格，才是有意義連成整句的正確選項。

38. 題句：「We could go to Mars at ＿＿＿38＿＿＿ expense

（我們也可花＿＿＿38＿＿＿的費用上火星。）

選項：(A) sloppy 懶散的　(B) enormous 巨大的　(C) slippery 易滑的　(D) economics 經濟的

解析

(1)答題關鍵在題目空格右邊的「expenses」。

(2)依本篇短文內容，四個選項中只有選(B)項的「enormous」放入空格，才是有意義連成整句的正確選項。

39. 題句：We can't do much locked in a ＿＿＿39＿＿＿

（在封閉的＿＿＿39＿＿＿裡做不了什麼事，）

選項：(A) ski suit 滑雪裝　(B) swim suit 泳裝　(C) space suit 太空裝　(D) black suit 黑色禮服

解析

本篇短文敘述的是一些有關太空之事，所以(C)項的「太空裝」才是正確選項。

**40.題句：and we can build robots with ＿＿＿40＿＿＿ better eyes than humans.

（而我們卻可造出比人類視覺功能更好＿＿＿40＿＿＿的機器人）

選項：(A) much 量多　(B) many 數多　(C) very 非常　(D) well 好

解析

(1)形容詞的比較級用 better than～、larger than……等就可以，但如果兩者相差太懸殊時，則在比較級前加much即可。如 much better than～、much larger than……等。

(2)四個選項中，只有選(A)項的「much」放於比較級 better 之前，才是符合文法的正確選項。

IV. 閱讀測驗

下面兩篇短文共有 10 題，每篇有 5 題，為第 41-50 題，請閱讀短文後，選出最適當的答案。

TW University
Mark T. School of Education
Associate Professorship for Foreign Literature

This is a full-time position for four years, beginning September 1, 2008. Candidates for the position should have a proven track record in teaching and professional experience in Foreign Literature, as well as Educational Policy. Expertise in other areas of education is highly favorable. The main language of instruction will be English; however, candidates must also conduct some courses in Chinese. The successful applicant who does not have adequate Chinese skills must undergo Chinese training during the first year of employment.

Applicants must reach the Dean of Mark T. School of Education, 66 TW Rd.Taipei, by March 1, 2008.

Documents for application should include: a letter of interest, a resume, the names of three references, a list of publications, and copies of all academic certification.

For further information, please contact Professor Jean Liu by e-mail at lc@twu.edu.

（這是為期四年的全職工作，從 2008 年 9 月 1 日起。應徵者須有教學與外語文學的專業經驗，以及教育策略。有其他教育經驗更受歡迎。主要是用英文教學；然而應徵者也同時會有中文的教學課程。如果沒有足夠的華語能力，必須在上班後一年內接受中文訓練課程。

請於 2008 年 3 月 1 日前與教育學院的馬克院長連絡。

應徵的必備文件有：工作意願函、履歷表、三份推薦函、出書清單及學歷證件影本。另外，請致 lc@twu.edu 電郵與 Jean Liu 教授連絡。）

41. What is the purpose of this notice?

（這份通知的目的何在？）

(A) Job opportunity. 工作機會。　(B) Telephone message. 電話訊息。　(C) E-mail message. 電郵訊息。　(D) Complaint letter. 抱怨函。

解析

從答題關鍵「This is a full-time position for four years, 這是為期四年的全職工作……」可看出(A)項的「工作機會」才是正確選項。

42. According to this passage, what is required of a successful applicant?

（根據本文，成功的應徵者要求為何？）

(A) Five references. 五封推薦函。　(B) Experience in teaching Chinese. 具中文教學的經驗。

(C) Ability to teach courses using English and Chinese. 能用中英文做教學。

(D) Experience in teaching French. 有教法文的經驗。

解析

從答題關鍵「The main language of instruction will be English; however, candidates must also conduct some courses in Chinese. 主要是用英文教學；然而應徵者也同時會有中文的教學課程。」可看出 (C) 項的「Ability to teach courses using English and Chinese.」才是正確選項。

43. What is required of an applicant who is not able to conduct courses using Chinese?

（對無法用中文教學的應徵者有何要求？）

(A) The applicant must be able to do so by the time he or she starts working.

應徵者開始上班時必須要有此能力。

(B) The applicant must accept lower pay until he or she is able to do so.

應徵者在有此能力前，必須接受較低薪水。

(C) The applicant must teach courses in French instead.

應徵者必須用法語教學以資取代。

(D) The applicant must be trained in Chinese for the first year of employment.

應徵者必須在上班後一年內接受中文訓練課程。

解析

從答題關鍵「The successful applicant who does not have adequate Chinese skills must undergo Chinese training during the first year of employment.」可看出 (D) 項的 The applicant must be trained in Chinese for the first year of employment. 才是正確選項。

44. If one is unclear about how to apply for this position, what should he or she do?

（如果某人對應徵事項不清楚，應該怎麼辦？）

(A) Visit the university. 去造訪該大學。　(B) Contact Professor Liu. 與劉教授聯絡。

(C) E-mail a friend. 寄電郵給朋友。　(D) Write a letter to the publisher. 給出版商寫信。

解析

(1)從答題關鍵「For further information, please contact Professor Jean Liu by e-mail at lc@twu.edu.」可看出 (B) 項的「Contact Professor Liu」才是正確選項。

45. What is NOT a requirement for the position?

沒有要求的項目有什麼？

(A) Expertise in all areas of politics. 政治專長。

(B) A resume. 履歷表。

(C) Teaching and working experience in Educational Policy. 教育策略的教學與經驗。

(D) A letter of interest. 工作意願函。

解析

整段文章都沒要求政治專長之事，所以 (A) 項的「Expertise in all areas of politics.」才是沒被要求的正確選項。

　　The host city for the Games of the XXX Olympiad will be the city of London, and the 2012 Summer Olympic Games are to be held from July 27 to August 12, 2012. London hosted Olympic Games in the 1908 Summer Olympics and the 1948 Summer Olympics. On May 18, 2004, the International Olympic Committee (IOC) reduced the number of candidate cities to five: London, Madrid, Moscow, New York, and Paris. By November 19, 2004, all five candidate cities had submitted their candidate files to the IOC. The IOC inspection team visited the five candidate cities during February and March of 2005. On June 6, 2005, the IOC released its evaluation reports for the five candidate cities. Throughout the process, Paris was widely seen as the favorite to win the nomination. On July 6, 2005, the final selection was announced in Singapore. Surprisingly, at the end of the fourth round of voting, London won the right to host the 2012 Games. The voting results of the four rounds are shown in the following table:

　　（倫敦將是舉辦第 30 屆奧運會的地主城市，而 2012 年夏季奧運會從 7 月 27 日到 8 月 12 日舉行。倫敦主辦過 1908 與 1948 的夏季奧運。2004 年的 5 月 18 日國際奧委會將主辦城市減至五個：倫敦、馬德里、莫斯科、紐約與巴黎。到了 2004 年的 11 月 19 日，都向奧委會，評審小組在 2005 年的 2 月與 3 月造訪了這五個城市。在 2005 年的 6 月 6 日，國際奧委會向這五個城市寄出它的評估函，在整個過程裡，巴黎被認為是最有機會獲提名主辦。在 2005 年的 7 月 6 日，在新加坡公布了最後名單。出乎意料的，在第四輪投票結束後，倫敦贏得 2012 的奧會主辦權。四個回合的投票結果如下表：）

2012 Summer Olympics Voting Results					
City	Country	Round 1	Round 2	Round 3	Round 4
London	United Kingdom	22	27	39	54
Paris	France	21	25	33	50
Madrid	Spain	20	32	31	-
New York City	United States	19	16	-	-
Moscow	Russia	15	-	-	-

　　The 2012 Summer Olympic program features 26 sports and a total of 39 disciplines. London's bid featured 28 sports, but the IOC voted to drop baseball and softball from the 2012 Games two days after it selected London as the host city. They will be Olympic sports for the last time at Beijing in 2008.

（2012 年夏季奧運的特色有 26 種運動及總數 39 個罰則。倫敦推出 28 種運動，但在倫敦獲主辦權的兩天後，國際奧會投票在 2012 的奧運會放棄棒球與壘球。這兩種比賽在 2008 年的北京奧運會被視為最後一場的奧會項目。）

46. Which city polled the most votes in the second round?

（在第二輪時哪個城市獲最多票？）

(A) Paris　(B) Moscow　(C) New York　(D) Madrid

解析

從統計表可以看出，(D) 項 Madrid 的32票才是第二輪的最多票。

47. Which of the following statements is true?

（下列哪項為真？）

(A) London is the city to host the Olympic Games three times. 倫敦主辦了三次奧運。

(B) Madrid was the first city to be eliminated. 馬德里是第一個被排除的城市。

(C) Moscow is a city in Spain. 莫斯科是西班牙的城市。

(D) London was ahead in every round of voting. 倫敦每一輪都獲高票。

解析

從答題關鍵的「The host city for the Games of the XXX Olympiad will be the city of London, and the 2012 Summer Olympic Games are to be held from July 27 to August 12, 2012. London hosted Olympic Games in the 1908 Summer Olympics and the 1948 Summer Olympics」可看出 (A) 項的「London is the city to host the Olympic Games three times.」才是正確選項。

48. According to this article, what happened in June 2005?

（根據本文 2005 年六月發生什麼事？）

(A) The IOC reduced the number of candidate cities to five. 國際奧委會把提名城市減至五個。

(B) The IOC visited all five candidate cities. 國際奧委會造訪了所有五個提名城市。

(C) All five candidate cities had submitted their candidate files. 所有五個提名城市提出提名案。

(D) The IOC released its evaluation reports. 國際奧委會釋出它的評估報告。

解析

從答題關鍵的「On June 6, 2005, the IOC released its evaluation reports for the five candidate cities」可看出 (D) 項的「The IOC released its evaluation reports.」才是正確選項。＊注意此題

49. When did the IOC decide to drop baseball and softball from the 2012 Games?

（國際奧委會何時決定取消 2012 年以後的棒球與壘球？）

(A) May 2004　(B) November 2004　(C) March 2005　(D) July 2005

解析

從答題關鍵的「but the IOC voted to drop baseball and softball from the 2012 Games two days after it selected London as the host city. They will be Olympic sports for the last time at Beijing in 2008.」可看出 (D) 項的「July 2005」才是正確選項。

50. Which of the following is <u>NOT</u> true about the 2012 Olympic Games?

（有關 2012 奧運，下列哪項爲非？）

(A) It will be held in London. 將會在倫敦舉行。

(B) It will be held from July to August. 會在七到八月舉行。

(C) There will be 26 sports. 會有 26 種比賽。

(D) Baseball and softball will be played for the last time. 將是最後一次舉辦棒球與壘球賽。

解析

從答題關鍵的「but the IOC voted to drop baseball and softball from the 2012 Games two days after it selected London as the host city. They will be Olympic sports for the last time at Beijing in 2008.」可看出 (D) 項的「Baseball and softball will be played for the last time」才是正確選項。

98 年統測（二技考試）

I. 字彙測驗

共有 15 題，第 1-7 題，每題均有一個劃底線的字，請在四個備選字中，選擇一個與劃底線的字意義最接近的答案。第 8-15 題，請選擇一個最適合的答案，以完成該句。

1. You can't imagine how beautiful the garden is. It is amazing .
   （你無法想像那花園有多漂亮。實在太驚奇了。）
   (A) normal 正常的　(B) unbelievable 無法相信的　(C) scary 害怕的　(D) perfect 完美的
   解析
   (1)先看底線字的中文意思為「驚奇的」。
   (2)在四個選項中，只有(B)項的「無法相信的」才是與底線字意思最接近的正確選項。

2. I think Michael is an avid swimmer, because you will always see him at the swimming pool.
   （我認為麥可是一位有幹勁的泳者，因為你都會在泳池看到他。）
   (A) outspoken 坦率的　(B) irresponsible 不負責任的　(C) enthusiastic 熱誠　(D) aging 老化
   解析
   (1)先看底線字的中文意思為「有幹勁的」。
   (2)在四個選項中，只有(C)項的「熱誠」才是與底線字意思最接近的正確選項。

3. You should definitely see the Great Wall when you go to China.
   （當你去了中國，一定要去看看長城。）
   (A) effectively 有效率地　(B) carefully 小心地　(C) patiently 耐心地　(D) certainly 無疑地
   解析
   (1)先看底線字的中文意思為「明確地」。
   (2)在四個選項中，只有(D)項的「無疑地」才是與底線字意思最接近的正確選項。

4. The saleswoman tried to convince the customer to buy the products.
   （銷售員試著說服顧客買產品。）
   (A) contact 接觸的　(B) persuade 說服　(C) disturb 打擾　(D) correct 正確的
   解析
   (1)先看底線字的中文意思為「使信服」。

(2)在四個選項中，只有(B)項的「說服」才是與底線字意思最接近的正確選項。

5. This medicine can <u>reduce</u> your pain.

（這個藥可以減少你的疼痛。）

　(A) decrease　(B) trouble　(C) affect　(D) promote

解析

(1)先看底線字的中文意思為「減少」。

(2)在四個選項中，只有(A)項的「減小」才是與底線字意思最接近的正確選項。

6. I <u>value</u> my teacher because he, unlike several people these days, is a very honest person.

（我尊重我的老師，他不像近來有些人，是一位很誠實的人。）

　(A) tend to avoid 有意避免　(B) depend a lot on 十分信賴　(C) report others to 檢舉他人

　(D) have appreciation for 為某事感激

解析

(1)先看底線字的中文意思為「尊重、價值」。

(2)在四個選項中，只有(D)項的「為某事感激」才是與底線字意思最接近的正確選項。

7. Most people in Taiwan <u>admit</u> that Chien-Ming Wang is an excellent baseball pitcher.

（臺灣的大多數人都承認王建民是一位很優秀的棒球投手。）

　(A) insist 堅持　(B) reveal 揭露　(C) accept 接受　(D) predict 預測

解析

(1)先看底線字的中文意思為「承認」。

(2)在四個選項中，只有(C)項的「接受」才是與底線字意思最接近的正確選項。

8. Joe could not find a job that he really wanted. Therefore, he felt very ＿＿＿＿＿＿.

（喬找不到他想要的工作。因此他感到很 ＿＿＿＿＿ 。）

　(A) disappointed 失望　(B) satisfied 滿意　(C) cheerful 高興　(D) capable 有能力

解析

(1)答題關鍵在題起題句前段的「找不到工作」。

(2)四個選項中，只有選(A)項的「失望」，才可有意義連成「找不到工作……很失望」。

9. I need someone to help me solve this ＿＿＿＿＿＿ math problem. It is not easy for me to understand.

（我需要有人幫我解答這個 ＿＿＿＿＿ 數學問題。這個問題對我而言太難了。）

　(A) complicated 複雜　(B) energetic 有精力的　(C) extravagant 奢侈、浪費的　(D) intelligent 聰明的

解析
(1)答題關鍵在題目空格左、右方的「解答這個」與「數學問題」。
(2)四個選項中，只有選 (A) 項的「複雜的」，才可有意義連成「幫我解答這個複雜的數學問題」。

10. When you are depressed, try to replace all your ＿＿＿＿＿ thoughts with positive ones.
（當你感到沮喪時，試著改變你的 ＿＿＿＿＿ 想法為正面想法。）
(A) cherished 珍惜　(B) easygoing 容易相處　(C) flexible 有彈性　(D) negative 負面的
解析
(1)答題關鍵在題目空格左、右方的「　」與「　」。
(2)四個選項中，只有選 (D) 項的「負面的」，才可有意義連成「改變你的負面想法為正面想法」。

11. The letter ＿＿＿＿＿ , so you should reply to it as soon as possible.
（這封信 ＿＿＿＿＿ ，所以你應該儘快回信。）
(A) is lacking an address 沒有寫地址　(B) is lost among my papers 遺失在資料堆裡　(C) requires your urgent comment 需要你的緊急評論　(D) has been posted as you requested 依你要求貼出去了
解析
(1)答題關鍵在題目空格右方的「你應該儘快回信」。
(2)四個選項中，只有選 (C) 項的「需要你的緊急評論」，才可有意義連成「這封信需要你的緊急評論，所以你應該儘快回信」。

12. The old building has been discovered to be ＿＿＿＿＿ It is vacant precisely for this reason.
（這棟舊房子被發現有 ＿＿＿＿＿ 的現象。這正是它仍是空屋的原因）
(A) rented out lately 最近租出去了　(B) seriously deteriorating 情況（屋況）嚴重惡化　(C) well-cared by its tenants 被房客照顧得很好　(D) unfortunately occupied 遺憾地被占用
解析
(1)答題關鍵在題目空格右方的「它仍是空屋的原因」。
(2)四個選項中，只有選 (B) 項的「情況嚴重惡化」，才可有意義連成「房子被發現有情況嚴重惡化的現象。這正是它仍是空屋的原因」。

13. Scientists have ＿＿＿＿＿ that the greenhouse effect caused global warming.
（科學家已經 ＿＿＿＿＿ ，溫室效應導致地球暖化。）
(A) debated 辯論　(B) alternated 代替的　(C) founded 發現　(D) inherited 繼承

解析

(1)答題關鍵在題目空格右方的「that the greenhouse ... warming」

(2)四個選項中，只有(A)選項的「辯論」，才可有意義連成「已經辯論過……地球暖化」。

14. I am sincere about completing this project. Let me _____ that I will.

（我很誠意想完成這個企劃案。讓我 _____ 我會的。）

(A) introduce 引見　(B) demonstrate 示範、證明　(C) pretend 假裝　(D) disprove 反駁

解析

(1) 答題關鍵在題目空格左、右方的「讓我」與「我會的」。

(2)四個選項中，只有選(B)項的「證明」，才可有意義連成「讓我證明我會辦到的。」。

15. Software _____ is the illegal copying of copyrighted software.

（軟體盜拷是指合法軟體的非法拷貝。）

(A) contribution 貢獻　(B) development 發展　(C) purchase 購買　(D) piracy 海盜行為

解析

(1)答題關鍵在題目空格左方的「軟體盜拷」。

(2)四個選項中，只有選 (D) 項的「海盜行為」，才可有意義連成「軟體盜拷是指……的非法拷貝」。

II. 對話測驗

共有 10 題，為第 16-25 題，請依對話內容選出一個最適當的答案，使其成為有意義的對話。

16. Paul： How do you usually get to school?

（你平常怎麼去學校？）

Daniel：_____ , so you can guess how I get to school.

（ _____ ，因此你可猜出我是怎麼去的。）

Paul： Really? I'm a cyclist myself, too.

（真的嗎？我自己也是單車族。）

(A) think driving a car is convenient 開車很方便　(B) tend to enjoy walking a lot 很喜歡走路

(C) love riding my bicycle 很喜歡騎單車　(D) take the train on most days 多半搭火車

解析

(1)答題關鍵第三句。

(2)在四個選項中，只有選 (C) 項的「很喜歡騎單車」第三句才會接著說「真的嗎？我自己也是單車族」。

17. Max：Hurry! The lecture starts exactly at six.

（趕快，課程整點六點鐘開始。）

Lucy：What time do you have?

（你的手錶現在幾點？）

Max：My watch says a quarter to six.

（現在是 5 點 45 分。）

Lucy：＿＿＿＿＿＿＿

(A) It begins in fifteen minutes then? 那就還有 15 分鐘囉？　(B) So ... the lecture starts in just four minutes. 還有四分鐘就開始了。　(C) Oh, it started fifteen minutes ago! 15 分鐘前就開始了！　(D) We're only four minutes late for the lecture. 我們僅遲到 4 分鐘。

解析

(1)答題關鍵第一、三兩句的「六點鐘開始」「現在是 5 點 45 分」。

(2)在四個選項中，只有選(A)項的「那就還有 15 分鐘囉？」才可回應第一、三句兩句。

18. Scott：Come over to my house after school. I have a new computer game.

（放學後來我家一下，我買了新的電玩。）

Eric：　I can't. ＿＿＿＿＿＿＿

（不行。）

Scott：Well, come to my house after that.

（好吧，事情辦完再來。）

(A) I'm addicted to computer games. 我沉迷於電玩。　(B) I like to stay at home. 我要待在家裡。　(C) I have to walk the dog. 我必須去遛狗。　(D) It's a long distance from here. 離這裡很遠。

解析

(1)答題關鍵在第三句。

(2)在四個選項中，只有選(C)項的「我必須去遛狗」第三句才會接著「好吧事情辦完再來」。

19. Ellen：　Hello. Can I speak to David?

（我可以和大衛講話嗎？）

Richard：Sorry. He's not in right now.

（抱歉。他現在不在。）

Ellen：　Oh, well, this is Ellen. ＿＿＿＿＿＿＿

（那好，我是艾倫 ＿＿＿＿＿＿＿ ）

Richard：Okay.

（好的。）

(A) Couldn't he wait for me to call? 他不能等我打給他嗎？ (B) What time do you expect him back? 他什麼時候會回來 (C) Has he been out for a long time? 他出去很久了嗎 (D) Could you ask him to return my call? 可以請他回我電話嗎？

解析

(1)答題關鍵第四句。

(2)在四個選項中，只有選(D)項的「可以請他回我電話嗎？」第四句才會接著說「好的」。

20. Mr. Benson：We're in class now. Please switch off your cell phone or turn it to the silent mode.
（我們在上課，請把手機關機或轉成靜音模式。）

Jimmy：_____

Mr. Benson：Okay, Jimmy. But please be more vigilant about your forgetfulness.
（好吧，吉米。但要更注意你的健忘。）

(A) I'm sorry, but it's Lisa's cell phone that's ringing. 抱歉，那是麗莎的手機在響。

(B) I'm sorry that I didn't realize the volume. 抱歉我沒注意到音量。

(C) Sorry, my feeling is that it's not disturbing anyone. 抱歉我感覺並沒有吵到人。

(D) Sorry to keep you waiting for your order, sir. 抱歉讓你久等。

解析

(1)答題關鍵在第三句。

(2)在四個選項中，只有選 (B) 項的「抱歉我沒注意到音量」第三句才會接著說「好吧，吉米。但要更注意你的健忘。」。

21. Becky：Have you thought of how to begin your writing assignment?
（有沒想到怎麼開始你的寫作功課？）

Terry：_____

Becky：But the website is currently under construction. They're adding works by other authors.
（但是該網站正在維修。它們在加些其他作者的作品。）

(A) I'll need a room with an Internet connection. 我需要留一些網路部分的空間。

(B) I thought of surfing the online library. 我想到過要瀏覽線上圖書館。

(C) We can chat about it later on the MSN messenger. 我們晚一點在 MSN 線上再聊。

(D) I'll probably type it out using a writing software. 我可能會用寫作軟體打出來。

解析

(1)答題關鍵在第三句。

(2)在四個選項中，只有選 (B) 項的「我想到過要瀏覽線上圖書館」第三句才會接著說「但是該網站正在維修。」。

22. Sharon：We are going to a karaoke club. Would you care to join us?

（我們要去卡拉 OK 俱樂部。你要一起去嗎？）

Bonnie：Sorry, I can't. I have to prepare the upcoming exams.

（抱歉，我不能去。我必須準備即將到來的考試。）

Sharon：＿＿＿＿＿＿＿＿

Bonnie：At least you realize your weakness.

（至少你還知道自己的弱點。）

(A) You know it isn't as difficult as you imagine it to be. 它沒有你想像中那麼困難。

(B) We'll have to reschedule the whole thing then. 那麼我們就必須重新安排一下。

(C) In my opinion, you shouldn't get all so stressed up. 依我看，你不應太緊張。

(D) Well ... I guess I shouldn't keep delaying my studies. 我不應常常延誤功課。

解析

(1)答題關鍵在第四句。

(2)在四個選項中，只有選 (D) 項的「我不應常常延誤功課」第四句才會接著說「至少你還還知道自己的弱點」。

23. James：What kind of movies did you rent?

（你租的是什麼樣的片子？）

Mike： Let me see. Well, I have science fiction and action movies.

（我看看。是科幻功夫片。）

James：＿＿＿＿＿＿＿＿

Mike： I'm afraid that the latest ones were rented out.

（新的喜劇片都被租走了。）

(A) Are they from the campus video store? 是從校園影片中心租來的嗎？

(B) I don't like the recent ones. 我不喜歡最近的片子。

(C) Where are the new comedies? 新的喜劇片在哪裡有？

(D) Seems you've made good choices. 似乎你選對了。

解析

(1)答題關鍵第四句。

(2)在四個選項中，只有選 (C) 項的「新的喜劇片在哪裡有？」第四句才會接著說「新的喜劇片都被租走了」。

24. Rick：How are you going to use your voucher?

（你的優惠券要怎麼用？）

Lisa：I haven't decided yet. ＿＿＿＿＿＿＿＿

（還沒有決定 ＿＿＿＿＿＿＿＿ 。）

Rick：Sure. My mom promised me that I can use it to buy a new MP4.

（我媽答應我可用來買 MP4。）

Lisa：That's cool.

（那太棒了。）

(A) Well, why don't you tell me about your voucher? 告訴我一些有關消費券的事

(B) I've heard you've already bought something, right? 聽說你已經買了一些東西了

(C) When will you be shopping with your mom? 你什麼時候會跟你媽媽去購物？

(D) Is that new gadget hanging from your neck an MP4? 你脖子上掛的小東西就是 MP4 嗎？

解析

(1)答題關鍵在第一句。

(2)在四個選項中，只有選 (A) 項的「告訴我一些有關消費券的事」才可回應第一句的「你的優惠券要怎麼用？」。

25. Joy： How's your new job going, Sara?

（妳的新工作還作得習慣嗎？）

Sara：It's great. ＿＿＿＿＿＿＿＿

（很棒。＿＿＿＿＿＿＿＿）

Joy： What exactly do you do at your company?

（在公司你到底擔任什麼工作？）

Sara：Well, I work as a tour guide.

（我擔任導遊工作。）

(A) At least I don't have to deal with people. 我不必跟人打交道。

(B) It's going to be an exciting opportunity. 那會是一個很好的機會。

(C) I couldn't have gotten a better job. 再也找不到比這個更好的工作了。

(D) It's the best trip our company went on. 那是我們公司去過的最佳之旅。

解析

(1)答題關鍵在第一句。

(2)在四個選項中，只有選 (C) 項的「也找不到比這個更好的工作了」才可回應第一句的「妳的新工作還作得習慣嗎」。

III. 綜合測驗

下面三篇短文共有 15 個空格，為 26-40 題，請依各篇短文文意，選出一個最適合該空格的答案。

(1)

　　Contrary to what some people think, there are several extravagant hotels in the Middle East. ＿＿＿26＿＿＿, the Arabian Towers is believed by a large percentage of hotel reviewers to express this quality the most. Built on a man-made island, the Arabian Towers, which is shaped like the sail of a boat, is one of the tallest hotels in the world. It is often described in newspaper advertisements and ＿＿＿27＿＿＿ as the only 7-star hotel in the world. It might be difficult to decide what a 7-star hotel is in the first place, ＿＿＿28＿＿＿ the Arabian Towers is certainly a luxurious hotel. From the expensive cars the guests arrive and leave in, to the butlers who are on call 24 hours, everything is done to make the guests feel ＿＿＿29＿＿＿. All this pampering, however, comes at a shocking rate. The cheapest rate for staying in the Arabian Towers is US$13,000 per night— breakfast ＿＿＿30＿＿＿! It is not surprising then that all of its guests are strapped with cash.

　　（有別於一般人的想法，在中東卻有幾家極盡奢侈的旅館，＿＿＿26＿＿＿，阿拉伯塔酒店被多數的旅遊業觀察家相信，是最好的等級。建造在人工島上，外形像船帆的阿拉伯塔酒店，是世界上最高的旅館之一，報紙廣告與＿＿＿27＿＿＿上常形容它是世上唯一的七星級旅館。首先要定義何謂七星級酒店可能有些困難，＿＿＿28＿＿＿阿拉伯塔酒店絕對是一家豪華酒店。從客人抵達所停放在酒店的昂貴車子，到服務人員提供的 24 小時服務，都是爲了要讓客人感到＿＿＿29＿＿＿。如此的嬌寵，來自於嚇人的高房價，住宿阿拉伯塔酒店每晚房價從美金一萬三千元起跳，早餐＿＿＿30＿＿＿。另人不會感到意外，因爲它的房客都是用大批現金交易的。）

26. 題句：there are several extravagant hotels in the Middle East. ＿＿＿26＿＿＿, the Arabian Towers is believed ... to express this quality the most

　　　　（在中東卻有幾家極盡奢侈的酒店，＿＿＿26＿＿＿，阿拉伯塔酒店被多數的旅遊業觀察家相信，是最高的等級。）

　　選項：(A) According to them 根據　(B) As a result of this 後果是　(C) In addition to this 另外地　(D) Of these hotels 這些酒店中

解析

(1)答題關鍵在題目空格左邊的整句。

(2)四個選項中，只有選(D)項的「這些酒店中」放入空格，才是有意義連成整句的正確選項。

27. 題句：It is often described in newspaper advertisements and ＿＿＿27＿＿＿ as the only 7-star hotel in the world.

　　　　（報紙廣告與＿＿＿27＿＿＿上常形容它是世上唯一的七星級旅館。）

　　選項：(A) personal recipes 個人食譜　(B) complaint forms 投訴表格　(C) travel brochures 旅遊小冊　(D) class registers 課程註冊

解析

(1)答題關鍵在題目空格左邊的「in newspaper advertisements and」。

(2)四個選項中，只有選(C)項的「旅遊小冊」放入空格，才是有意義連成整句的正確選項。

**28.題句：It might be difficult to decide what a 7-star hotel is in the first place, _____28_____ the Arabian Towers is certainly a luxurious hotel.

（首先要定義何謂七星級酒店可能有些困難，_____28_____ 阿拉伯塔酒店絕對是一家豪華酒店。）

選項：(A) but 但是　(B) and 並且　(C) because 因為　(D) so 如此

解析

(1)答題關鍵在空格左、右方 It might be ...與 the Arabian Towers is.... 的兩個子句。

(2)依題意，在這兩子句間只能選(A)項的對等連接詞「but」，才符合題意與文法。請看本題的中譯文就更清楚。

29. 題句：everything is done to make the guests feel _____29_____ .

（都是為了要讓客人感到 _____29_____ 。）

選項：(A) trusted 信任　(B) neglected 疏忽　(C) secured 保障　(D) royal 皇室、皇族

解析

(1)答題關鍵在題目空格左邊的「to make the guests feel」。

(2)四個選項中，只有選(D)項的「royal」放入空格，意指讓客人感覺到接近皇族的接待規格才是有意義連成整句的正確選項。

30. 題句：The cheapest rate for staying in the Arabian Towers is US$13,000 per night— breakfast _____30_____ !

（住宿阿拉伯塔酒店每晚房價從美金一萬三千元起跳，早餐_____30_____ 。）

選項：(A) for two, sir 給兩位的　(B) not included 不包括在內　(C) in the morning 早上

(D) receipt provided 提供收據

解析

(1)答題關鍵在題目空格左邊的「住宿阿拉伯塔酒店每晚房價從美金一萬三千元起跳」。

(2)四個選項中，只有選(B)項的「不包括在內」放入空格，才是有意義連成整句的正確選項。

(2)

　　Almost all ATM machines in Taiwan offer services in English and Chinese. Though these frequently used cash dispensers have become more _____31_____ , many of these machines suffer from an important translation error related to the "cancel your transaction" option. _____32_____ a withdrawal situation. Once you have told the bank machine how much money you would like to withdraw, it will respond by saying, "Processing ... Please wait." This means that the machine is _____33_____ completing the service you requested. If the process has been successful, the machine will ask you, "Do you want to cancel this transaction?", instead of "Do you want to continue with another transaction?", before ＿＿＿34＿＿＿ your cash. Canceling this transaction would mean that you've realized you have made ＿＿＿35＿＿＿ , and would like the machine to return your bank account to its original status. The problem is that the machine interprets "canceling your transaction" as meaning that you would not like to continue using it and would now like to take your card back.

　　（幾乎臺灣所有的自動提款機都提供中英文服務。雖然這些經常被使用到的自動提款機已更＿＿＿31＿＿＿使用，有許多卻受到取消交易選項譯錯的麻煩，＿＿＿32＿＿＿在你領款時。一旦你告訴銀行機器你要領多少錢時，它就回應說：「資料處理中、請稍候」，這表示機器正＿＿＿33＿＿＿完成你要求的服務。如果交易成功，在鈔票＿＿＿34＿＿＿之前，機器會先問你「你要取消本筆交易嗎？」而不是問你「你要繼續另一筆交易嗎？」取消本筆交易原意是指：你已了解你有操作上的＿＿＿35＿＿＿，而要機器恢復原先的狀況。問題是，機器把「取消你的交易」解讀為「你不要繼續操作而要收回你的金融卡。」）

31. 題句：Though these frequently used cash dispensers have become more ＿＿＿31＿＿＿ ,

　　　　（雖然這些經常被使用到的自動提款機已更＿＿＿31＿＿＿使用，）

　　選項：(A) accessible 容易使用　(B) casual 非正式的　(C) well-placed 置於適當地點　(D) focused 專心於

解析

(1)答題關鍵在題目空格左邊的「have become」。

(2)四個選項中，只有選(A)項的「accessible」放入空格，才是有意義連成整句的正確選項。

32. 題句：＿＿＿32＿＿＿ a withdrawal situation. Once you have told the bank machine how much money you would like to withdraw,

　　　　（＿＿＿32＿＿＿領款情況之時。一旦你告訴銀行機器你要領多少錢時，它就回應說：「……」）

　　選項：(A) The other solution is 其他解決方於是　(B) Have you ever tried 你有試過嗎　(C) Take an example of 舉例來說　(D) Fortunately, there is 還好有

解析

(1)答題關鍵在題目空格右邊的「a withdrawl situation」。

(2)四個選項中，只有選(C)項的「Take an example」放入空格，才是有意義連成整句的正確選項。

33. 題句：This means that the machine is ＿＿＿33＿＿＿ completing the service you requested

　　　　（這表示機器正＿＿＿33＿＿＿完成你要求的服務。）

　　選項：(A) finished 完成　(B) busy 忙於　(C) refusing 拒絕　(D) interrupted 干擾

解析

(1)答題關鍵在題目空格右邊的「completing the service you requested」。

(2)四個選項中，只有選(B)項的「busy」放入空格，才是有意義連成整句的正確選項。

34. 題句：If the process has been successful, the machine will ask you, "Do you want to cancel this transaction?", instead of "Do you want to continue with another transaction?", before _____34_____ your cash.

（如果交易成功，在鈔票 _____34_____ 之前，機器會先問你「你要取消本筆交易嗎？」而不是問你「你要繼續另一筆交易嗎？」）

選項：(A) handing you 交給你　(B) exchanging 交換　(C) distributing 分配　(D) repaying you 還錢給你

解析

(1)答題關鍵在題目空格左邊的「before」。

(2)四個選項中，只有選(A)項的「handing you」放入空格，才是有意義連成整句的正確選項。

35. 題句：Canceling this transaction would mean that you've realized you have made _____35_____ ,

（取消本筆交易原意是指：你知道你在操作上有 _____35_____ ，）

選項：(A) an arrangement 一個安排　(B) a decision 一個決定　(C) a confirmation 一個確認　(D) an error 一個錯誤

解析

(1)答題關鍵在題目空格左邊的「you've realized you have made」。

(2)四個選項中，只有選(D)項的「an error」放入空格，才是有意義連成整句的正確選項。

(3)

　　Teenagers and old people are similar to each other in several respects. Teenagers, for example, are _____36_____ in schools, and many old people in retirement communities, assisted-living facilities and nursing homes. Also, both groups tend to be poorer than young adults or middle-aged people: teenagers because they do not yet have the education or experience to _____37_____ high salaries, and old people because they are retired and living on their savings and social security. Third, independence is important for both groups— they are conscious of _____38_____ , whereas young adults and middle-aged people _____39_____ . Teenagers want to become independent of their parents; old people want to keep their independence instead of relying on their children or on social institutions. Fourth, both tend to have a relatively large amount of leisure time or, at least, time that they can choose or not choose to fill with study or work. _____40_____ , young and middle-aged adults typically spend most of their time in their jobs or taking care of home duties such as child-rearing.

　　（少年與老年在許多方面是相似的。舉例來說，少年被 _____36_____ 在學校，而多數老年人則在退休機構、有人協助場所與看護之家等。同時，這兩組人比青壯年人有更可憐的傾向：少年人因還沒有相關的教育與經驗 _____37_____ 高薪，老年人則因已退休且倚賴自己儲蓄及社會福利金而活。第三，能否獨立生活對這兩組人都是很重要的——他們意識到 _____38_____ ，而青壯年人士卻 _____39_____ 。少年人想離開雙

親獨立，老年人不想倚賴子女或福利機構生活。第四，少、老年人似乎都有過多的閒暇時間，或者至少選擇或不選擇念書或工作。____40____，青年人的大部分時間是花在工作或教育小孩方面。）

36. 題句：for example, are ____36____ in schools,
　　　　（舉例來說，少年被 ____36____ 在學校，）
　　選項：(A) located 位於　(B) bestowed 給予　(C) isolated　(D) charged 緊張的

　解析
　(1)答題關鍵在題目空格右邊的「in school」。
　(2)四個選項中，只有選(C)項的「隔離」放入空格，才是有意義連成整句的正確選項。

37. 題句：because they do not yet have the education or experience to ____37____ high salaries,
　　　　（少年人因還沒有相關的教育與經驗 ____37____ 高薪，）
　　選項：(A) demand 要求　(B) give up 放棄　(C) donate 捐款 (D) misuse 誤用

　解析
　(1)答題關鍵在題目空格右邊的「higher salaries」。
　(2)四個選項中，只有選(A)項的「demand」放入空格，才是有意義連成整句的正確選項。

38. 題句：independence is important for both groups — they are conscious of ____38____,
　　　　（能否獨立生活對這兩組人都是很重要的——他們意識到 ____38____，）
　　選項：(A) wanting it 缺少　(B) programming 編製程序　(C) the agenda 議程　(D) uniting them 聯合他們

　解析
　(1)答題關鍵在題目空格左邊的「they are conscious of」。
　(2)四個選項中只有選(A)項的「缺少」放入空格，才是有意義連成整句的正確選項。

39. 題句：whereas young adults and middle-aged people ____39____。
　　　　（而青壯年人士卻 ____39____ 。）
　　選項：(A) are pulled together 通力合作　(B) take it for granted 視為理所當然　(C) are naturally awaken 自然甦醒　(D) keep it safe for sure 存放安全處

　解析
　(1)答題關鍵在題目空格左邊的「whereas young adults and middle-aged people」。
　(2)四個選項中，只有選(B)項的「take it for granted」放入空格，才是有意義連成整句的正確選項。

40. 題句：that they can choose or not choose to fill with study or work. _____40_____ , young and middle-aged adults typically spend most of their time in their jobs

（少、老年人似乎都有過多的閒暇時間，或者至少選擇或不選擇唸書或工作。_____40_____，）

選項：(A) In the years that followed 隨後幾年　(B) Less than pleased 不情願　(C) Mysteriously 神祕地　(D) In contrast 相反地

解析

(1)答題關鍵在題目空格左、右兩邊的子句。

(2)四個選項中，只有選(D)項的「」放入空格，才是有意義連成兩個整句的正確選項。

IV. 閱讀測驗

下面兩篇短文共有 10 題，每篇有 5 題，為 41-50 題，請閱讀短文後，選出最適當的答案。

⑴

The Chinese government promised to offer two pandas to Taiwan as a gift in 2005. The rare animals, named Tuan Tuan and Yuan Yuan, were delivered to Taiwan on Dec. 24, 2008. The combined name of the two pandas - Tuan Yuan - means reunion in Chinese. They have been housed at the Taipei Zoo since their arrival. But they were not shown in public until Jan. 26, 2009, because they had to be kept separate from others to be examined for at least one month. The reason for this was to prevent the spread of diseases such as canine distemper and rabies—the two most likely to infect pandas. Finally, they proved to be healthy, so the Taipei Zoo's new panda house was opened in time for the first day of the Chinese New Year, and attracted thousands of children and parents to see the chubby bamboo-eating animals.

（中國政府許諾在 2005 年給臺灣提供兩隻貓熊作為一個禮物。該稀有動物，命名團團和圓圓，在 2008 年 12 月 24 日運到臺灣。這一組名字的二隻貓熊——團圓中文意思為重聚。牠們來臺後就一直棲息在臺北市立動物園。直到 2009 年的 1 月 26 日牠們才公開露面。因為牠們隔離一個月做檢驗。以防止傳播像是犬熱病和狂犬病——這兩種貓熊最可能感染的疾病。最後，他們被證明很健康，因此臺北市立動物園的新貓熊房子趕上春節的第一天啟用，並且吸引數千個孩子和父母看圓嘟嘟的吃竹子動物。）

The Giant Panda is an endangered species and highly threatened. There might be only 2,000 giant pandas in the wild. It once lived in lowland areas, but farming, forest clearing, and other developments now restrict the Giant Panda to mountains in central-western and southwestern China. The Giant Panda has a diet which is 99% bamboo. However, only a few bamboo species are widespread at the high altitudes pandas now inhabit. Bamboo leaves contain some protein; the stems have even less. The Giant Panda may eat other foods such as honey, eggs, fish, yams, shrubs leaves, oranges and bananas, when these are available. Because this diet is low in nutrition, it affects the panda's behavior. Most of the pandas sleep at least 10 hours a day, and tend to avoid activities which will use up too much energy.

（大貓熊是瀕危物種並且非常受威脅。在野生貓熊可能只有 2,000 隻。牠們曾經居住在低地地區，但是在農作，森林整理及其他開發，迫使貓熊只能在中國的中西、

西南方的山區活動。大貓熊的食物 99% 是竹子。不過，只有少數品種的貓熊散布在高緯度地區。竹子葉子含有一些蛋白質；梗部的蛋白質就更少。大貓熊也可能吃其他食品像是蜂蜜、蛋、魚、山芋、灌木葉、橙和香蕉。因為這種飲食營養低，會影響貓熊的行為。大多數貓熊一天最少睡 10 小時，並且傾向於避免將用掉太多能量的活動。）

41. When did the two pandas come to Taiwan?

（該兩隻貓熊何時來臺灣？）

(A) In the year 2005. 於 2005 年。　(B) On Dec. 24, 2008. 於 2008 年 12 月 24 日。

(C) On Jan. 26, 2009. 於 2009 年 1 月 26 日。　(D) In the year 2000. 於 2000 年。

解析

從答題關鍵的「The rare animals, named Tuan Tuan and Yuan Yuan, were delivered to Taiwan on Dec. 24, 2008.」可看出 (B) 項的「On Dec. 24, 2008.」才是正確選項。

42. What happened to the pandas right after they came?

（剛來時，這兩隻貓熊有何狀況？）

(A) They got sick and needed treatment. 牠們生病需要治療。　(B) They got tired and rested for a month. 牠們太累休息了一個月。　(C) They were threatened by visitors. 牠們受到遊客的威脅。　(D) They were examined to see if they carried diseases. 牠們受檢查看有無病菌。

解析

從答題關鍵的「They were examined to see if they carried diseases.」可看出 (D) 項的「They were examined to see if they carried diseases」才是正確選項。

43. What are canine distemper and rabies?

（犬瘟及狂犬病是什麼？）

(A) Animals. 動物。　(B) Medicines. 醫藥。　(C) Diseases. 疾病。　(D) Panda food. 貓熊食物。

解析

從答題關鍵的「to prevent the spread of diseases such as canine distemper and rabies」可看出 (C) 項的「Diseases.」才是正確選項。

44. Which statement about the Giant Panda is correct?

（有關大貓熊，以下哪一項為真？）

(A) The Giant Panda does not experience any threats. 大貓熊並未受到任何威脅。

(B) Bamboo is the only thing eaten by the Giant Panda. 竹子是大貓熊所吃唯一食物。

(C) Wild pandas are living in the lowland areas of China. 野生貓熊生長在中國的低地區。

(D) Farming and other developments made the Giant Panda change his place to live. 農業及其他開發促使大貓熊改變牠的棲息地。

解析

從答題關鍵的「but farming, forest clearing, and other developments now restrict the Giant Panda to mountains in central-western and southwestern China.」可看出 (D) 項的「Farming and other developments made the Giant Panda change his place to live.」才是正確選項。

45. Which section of the newspaper will the passage most likely appear in?

（報紙的哪一版比較會出現本段文章？）

(A) Local News. 本地新聞。　(B) Editorial. 社論。　(C) Business News. 商業新聞。

(D) Sports Illustrated. 運動插圖。

解析

只有(A)項的「Local News.」才是正確選項。因本文內容不屬社論、商業新聞或運動插圖。

(2)

　　For most of us, the holidays are a great time to gather family, but your holiday experiences can be quickly forgotten with time because of the limitations of memory. You might therefore want to think of ways of recording those experiences. One very useful way of recording those experiences is by keeping a holiday journal.

　　An important advantage of keeping a holiday journal is that it allows you to record changes that have happened to you and your family members. As you go through your journal, you'll see how everybody has grown, the directions they have taken in life, friends who might have joined your family on the holidays and so on. These changes can be recorded by photographs as well. However, writing about your holiday experiences allows you to record several details about them which a photograph can not. This does not mean that photographs are not important. The best, of course, is for your journal to include both photographs and writing in order for it to be rich in detail.

　　Another important benefit of a holiday journal is that it can give you an opportunity to appreciate your family members. Perhaps, you have made the mistake that most of us do, namely forgetting how important family members are and taking them for granted. As you read your holiday journal, however, you might feel like you want to reconnect with your loved ones and re-establish your relationship with them.

　　（對我們多數人而言，假期是家庭聚集的時間，但是你的假期經驗可能被迅速隨著時間忘記，因為記憶量的限制。你可能因此想找可記錄那些經驗的方法。記錄那些經驗的有用方法是寫下度假日記。

　　保持度假日記可使你記錄假期中發生在你與家庭成員的一些變化。當你閱讀你的日記時，你將看出每人如何成長，他們在生命中所走的方向，以及與你們同行出遊的朋友等等。這些變化也可以用照片作記錄。不過，用寫的度假經驗可寫下更多細節，而這是拍照所辦不到的。這並非說拍照不重要。最好的，當然用書寫與拍照兩方式來記錄你的日記，使內容更豐富。

　　度假日記的另一重要好處是，它可使你有機會欣賞你的家人。或許，你已經做了

大家都會犯的錯誤，就是忘記家庭成員的重要性，並且認為那是理所當然的。在你閱讀你的渡假日記時，不管怎樣，你可能想要再與你的親人聯絡，並且重建你們之間的關係。）

46. What can be quickly forgotten with time?

（時間的消逝會讓如很快忘記什麼？）

(A) Training one's memory to be good. 訓練一個人有好記性。

(B) The holiday journal you are making. 你所參加的假日之旅。

(C) The holiday experiences you have had. 你已有過的度假經驗。

(D) Having celebrations on holidays. 在假日舉行慶祝。

解析

從答題關鍵的「your holiday experiences can be quickly forgotten with time because of the limitations of memory.」可看出 (C) 項的「The holiday experiences you have had.」才是正確選項。

47. How can one record one's holiday experiences?

（一個人如何留下他的旅遊經驗？）

(A) By keeping a diary of them. 用日記寫下來。

(B) By writing to an academic journal. 寫給學術期刊。

(C) By thinking carefully about them. 小心地回想一下。

(D) By regularly discussing them. 定期的討論它。

解析

從答題關鍵的「One very useful way of recording those experiences is by keeping a holiday journal.」可看出 (A) 項的「By keeping a diary of them」才是正確選項。

48. Why do family members become less close to each other? Because they ＿＿＿＿＿＿ .

（為何家人的關係越來越疏遠？因為他們＿＿＿＿＿＿。）

(A) don't write to or call each other often 他們之間不常寫信或打電話

(B) immigrate to different countries 移民去不同國家

(C) forget to be thankful for each other 忘記互相感謝對方

(D) have poorly managed schedules 日程表安排得不好

解析

從答題關鍵的「Perhaps, you have made the mistake that most of us do, namely forgetting how important family members are and taking them for granted.」可看出 (C) 項的「forget to be thankful for each other」才是正確選項。

49. Which advantage of a holiday journal is NOT mentioned by the author?

（未被作者提到的旅遊好處是哪一項？）

(A) It helps us to understand better how we've developed over time.

它有助我們更瞭解我們如何隨時間有所進步。

(B) It gives us a chance to be grateful to our family members.

它給我們機會感激我們的家人。

(C) It helps us to relive our experiences in a more detailed way.

它有助我們更徹底地再體驗我們的經驗。

(D) It can become a family treasure for the next generation to read.

它會成為下一代可讀的傳家之寶。

解析

看完文章內容，就是沒提到 (D) 項「It can become a family treasure for the next generation to read.」所以 (D) 項才是正確選項。

50. What is most likely the tone of the writer?

（作者的語氣是什麼？）

(A) Pessimistic and insensitive. 悲觀與遲鈍。

(B) Thoughtful and positive. 設想周到與正面。

(C) Serious and demanding. 嚴肅與高要求。

(D) Humorous and entertaining. 幽默與愉快。

解析

看完文章內容只有 (B) 項的「Thoughtful and positive.」才是正確選項。

99 年統測（二技考試）

I. 字彙測驗

共有 15 題，第 1-7 題，每題均有一個劃底線的字，請在四個備選字中，選擇一個與劃底線的字意義最接近的答案。第 8-15 題，請選擇一個最適合的答案，以完成該句。

1. The highways are usually <u>crowded</u> before and after long holidays.

　（長期假日前後的公路交通，通常較為擁擠。）

　　(A) packed 塞滿　(B) parked 停泊　(C) passed 通過　(D) polluted 受污染

解析

(1)先看底線字 crowded，其中文意思為「擁擠」。

(2)在四個選項中，只有(A)項的「塞滿」才是與底線字意思最接近的正確選項。

2. Many people's <u>fantasy</u> is to win the lottery and never need to work anymore.

　（許多人的幻想是：中了樂透獎就不必再工作了。）

　　(A) decision 決定　(B) recommendation 推薦　(C) imagination 想像力　(D) immigration 外來移民

解析

(1)先看底線字 fantasy，其中文意思為「幻想」。

(2)在四個選項中，只有(C)項的「想像力」，才是與底線字意思最接近的正確選項。

3. In the winter time, it is very common to see people killed by <u>invisible</u> gases due to the mishandling of their heater.

　（在冬天，常看到人們使用瓦斯不當而喪生。）

　　(A) invalid 殘疾者　(B) jointly 共同地　(C) hidden 隱藏的　(D) dangerous 危險的

解析

(1)先看底線字 invisible，其中文意思為「看不見的」。

(2)在四個選項中，只有(C)項的「隱藏的」才是與底線字意思最接近的正確選項。

4. Many sounds are not <u>sensed</u> by human ears because, unlike other animals, our ears are not as sensitive.

　（許多聲音人耳感應不到，因為不像其他動物人耳無法那麼敏銳。）

　　(A) detected 偵測　(B) destroyed 毀滅　(C) developed 發展　(D) delivered 傳送

解析

(1)底線字 sensed 之中文意思為「感覺到」。

(2)在四個答項中，只有(A)項的「偵測到」，才是與底線字意思最接近的正確選項。

5. Many new cell phones are equipped with software that is <u>flexible</u> enough for several functions.

（許多行動電話具有多變化性的多種功能。）

　(A) adjustable 可調整　(B) adequate 足夠的　(C) advanced 在前面　(D) additional 附加的

解析

(1)底線字 flexible 之中文意思為「易彎曲的、有彈性的」。

(2)在四個答項中，只有(A)項的「可調整的」，才是與底線字意思最接近的正確選項。

6. Although koalas seem quiet, they should not be considered <u>handicapped</u> in racing because they can run as fast as rabbits.

（無尾熊似乎很安靜，但當跑步時牠們並非弱勢，牠們可跑得和兔子一樣快。）

　(A) promoted 推廣　(B) divided 分離的　(C) disadvantaged 弱勢團體　(D) benefited 受惠

解析

(1)底線字 handicapped 之中文意思為「殘障的、有生理缺陷者」。

(2)在四個答項中，只有(C)項的「弱勢的」，才是與底線字意思最接近的正確選項。

7. By buying your high-speed rail tickets online, you can avoid <u>hassles</u> at the station.

（在網路上購買高鐵車票，可避免去車站的麻煩。）

　(A) payments 付款　(B) customers 顧客　(C) pedestrians 行人　(D) troubles 麻煩

解析

(1)底線字 hassles 之中文意思為「爭論、找麻煩」。

(2)在四個答項中，只有(D)項的「麻煩」，才是與底線字意思最接近的正確選項。

8. Many studies ＿＿＿＿＿＿ that elderly people who have pets live longer than those who do not.

（許多研究 ＿＿＿＿＿＿ 有寵物的老人比無寵物的老人長壽。）

　(A) invade 侵略　(B) indicate 指出　(C) include 包括　(D) insert 插入、放入

解析

(1)答題關鍵在題目空格右方的 that 子句（that+其後的整個子句 elderly people who have pets live longer than those who do not.）

(2)四個選項中，只有(B)項的「指出」放入空格，才可有意義地連成「許多研究指出有寵物的老人比無寵物的老人長壽」，才是正確選項。

(3)that 子句是「連接詞 that+從屬子句」之謂。同理，連接詞 who+子句稱為「who 子句」連接詞 what+子句稱為 what 子句……以此類推。

(4)主要子句要敘述的句子太長時，通常用從屬子句的方式寫出來。

9. Concert tickets are usually cheaper if you buy them two weeks ＿＿＿＿＿＿ .

（音樂會的票如果兩週前買會便宜些。）

(A) in vain 枉然　(B) in between 兩者間　(C) in advance 預先　(D) in principle 原則上

解析

(1)答題關鍵在題目空格左方的「購買兩週」。

(2)四個選項中，只有選 (C) 項的「預先」，才可有意義地連成「……兩週前預先購買會便宜些」。

10. To many people, verbal ＿＿＿＿＿＿ can be more hurtful and damaging than non-verbal or physical ones.

（對許多人來說，口語的 ＿＿＿＿＿＿ 可能會比非口語的或軀體侮辱更傷害。）

(A) knocks 撞擊　(B) insults 羞辱　(C) shifts 轉移　(D) concepts 觀念

解析

(1)答題關鍵在題目空格左方的「口語的」。

(2)四個選項中，只有選 (B) 項的「羞辱」，才可有意義地連成「口語的羞辱可能會比非口語的更……」

11. Mr. Wang drove through a red light, and ＿＿＿＿＿＿ got a ticket.

（王先生開車闖紅燈，而 ＿＿＿＿＿＿ 是收到了罰單。）

(A) friendly 友善　(B) partly 部分的　(C) mentally 心理上　(D) consequently 結果

解析

(1)答題關鍵在題目空格左方的「開車闖紅燈」。

(2)四個選項中，只有選 (D) 項的「結果」，才可有意義地連成「開車闖紅燈，而結果是收到了罰單」。

12. If there is a sign "no ＿＿＿＿＿＿ " on the door of every hotel, this means we are in the busy season.

（如果每個旅館門口都掛有「無＿＿＿＿＿＿」的牌子，這表示這是我們的旺季到了。）

(A) alcohol 酒精　(B) smoking 冒煙　(C) policies 政策　(D) vacancies 空房

解析

(1)答題關鍵在題目空格左方的「無」。

(2)四個選項中，只有選 (D) 項的「空房」，才可有意義地連成「無空房」，才是正確選項，也才符合句後「表示這是我們的旺季到了」的說法。

13. For many college students, financial burden can be the single biggest ＿＿＿＿＿＿ in the way of finishing their degrees.

（對許多大學生而言，在完成學業之路財力負擔可能是唯一最大的 ＿＿＿＿＿＿。）

(A) moment 瞬間　(B) wealth 財富　(C) obstacle 障礙　(D) channel 水道

解析

(1)答題關鍵在題目空格左方的「財力負擔可能是最大大」與空格右方的「完成學業之路」

(2)四個選項中，只有選 (C) 項的「障礙」，才可有意義地連成「……在完成學業之路上，財力負擔可能是唯一最大的障礙」。

14. On a rainy day, fast-moving motorcycles or automobiles may ＿＿＿＿＿＿ mud and dirt all over you.

（雨天時，快速的摩托車或汽車可能濺得你滿身髒泥。）

(A) jingle 叮噹聲　(B) splash 濺起（水花）　(C) irritate 激怒　(D) terminate 結束

解析

(1)答題關鍵在題目空格右方的「濺起（水花）」。

(2)四個選項中，只有選 (B) 項的「濺起」，才可有意義地連成「摩托車或汽車可能濺得你滿身髒泥」

15. Plastic has become extraordinarily important in our daily life, but the process of burning or recycling it often creates ＿＿＿＿＿＿ chemicals.

（在我們日常生活中塑膠已是非常重要，但將之燃燒或回收過程常產生 ＿＿＿＿＿＿ 化學物質。）

(A) toxic 有毒的　(B) interior 內部的　(C) prestigious 有名望　(D) radical 基本的

解析

(1)答題關鍵在題目空格右方的「化學物質」。

(2)四個選項中，只有選(A) 項的「有毒的」，才可有意義地連成「……常產生有毒的化學物質」。

II. 對話測驗

共有 10 題，為第 16-25 題，請依對話內容選出一個最適當的答案，使其成為有意義的對話。

16. Vicky：Hi, Stacy. What do you do to keep fit?

（嗨，斯代西，妳怎樣保持好身材？）

Stacy：＿＿＿＿＿＿ Right here at the beach.

（就在這個海邊。）

Vicky：It sounds like a great idea!

（這個點子不錯！）

(A) The food makes me really weak. 食物使我虛弱　(B) I swim. 我游泳　(C) It's a size 14 jacket. 那是 14 號的夾克　(D) It's happening today. 今天發生了

解析

(1)答題關鍵在第一句。

(2)在四個選項中，只有選(B)項的「我游泳」，才可回應第一句的「你怎樣保持好身材」。

17. Betsy：I noticed that you've received lots of packages recently.

（我注意到你最近收到很多包裹。）

Cindy：Yes. ＿＿＿＿＿＿ I shop online for everything I need now.

（是的。＿＿＿＿＿＿ 我都上網買東西。）

Betsy：Take my advice. Watch out for your budget!

（聽我勸，還是要小心妳的預算。）

(A) Like what? 是什麼呢？　(B) What for? 幹麼用？　(C) How can it be? 怎可這樣？　(D) Guess what? 妳知道嗎？

解析

(1)答題關鍵在第一句。

(2)在四個選項中，第二句句前，只有選(D)項的「妳知道嗎？」，才可有意義的連成「妳知道嗎，我都上網買東西」，這才是回答第一句的選項。

(3)英語口語 Guess what？字譯爲「妳猜怎麼著？」等於中文的：「妳知道嗎？」之意。

18. Hannah：　Let's do some sports outdoors.

（我們去做戶外運動。）

Jonathan：I'm not good at sports at all.

（我一點都不懂運動。）

Hannah：　＿＿＿＿＿＿

Jonathan：That sounds OK.

（那很好。）

(A) How long will it take? 要多久？

(B) What's your problem? 你有什麼問題？

(C) How about taking a walk? 去散步好嗎？

(D) When can you get outdoors? 你何時可去室外？

解析

(1)答題關鍵在第二句。

(2)在四個選項中，第三句只有選(C)項的「去散步好嗎？」這才是回應第二句「我一點都不懂運動」的正確選項。

19. Jenny： What did you do last weekend?

（你上週末做些什麼？）

Yvonne： _____

Jenny： Did you buy anything?

（妳買了些什麼？）

Yvonne：Yes, I got myself a nice laptop.

（我買了一臺筆電。）

(A) I went to the electronic fair downtown. 我去了鬧區的電子展。

(B) I studied in the library all day. 我整天在博物館看書。

(C) I wasn't capable then. 我當時做不到。

(D) I spent time with my family. 我與家人度過。

解析

(1)答題關鍵第三句。

(2)在四個選項中，第二句只有選 (A) 項的「我去了鬧區的電子展」第三句才會接著問「妳買了些什麼？」。

20. Julie： I got to go now to meet a friend at the station.

（我現在要趕去車站見個朋友。）

Amanda： _____

Julie： I think riding a motorbike is more convenient.

（我想騎機車方便些。）

Amanda：Be careful then.

（那就小心啦。）

(A) Why don't you take the subway? 你為什麼不搭地鐵？　　(B) Who is he? 他是誰？

(C) Where is it? 在哪裡？　　(D) How long will it take? 要多久時間？

解析

(1)答題關鍵在第三句。

(2)在四個選項中，第二句只有選 (A) 項的「你為什麼不搭地鐵」，第三句才會說「我想騎機車方便些」。

21. Josh： Can I borrow your suit?

（我可以跟你借西裝嗎？）

Parker：Sure. I thought you only wear jeans.

（當然可以。我以為你只穿牛仔褲。）

Josh： _____

Parker：Good luck.

（祝你好運。）

(A) I have a job interview tomorrow. 我明天要去應徵工作。

(B) I have to study tomorrow. 我明天要準備功課。

(C) I'll buy you a tie. 我買一條領帶送給你。

(D) I like them very much. 我很喜歡。

解析

(1)答題關鍵在第二句。

(2)在四個選項中，第三句只有選 (A) 項的「我明天要去應徵工作（所以才會向你借西裝）」，才是回應第二句的「我以為你只穿牛仔褲」。

22. Wade：　You've been studying for three straight hours. _____

（你已連續作了三小時的功課。_____ ）

Morgan：I'm not tired at all.

（我一點都不累。）

Wade：　Ten minutes' rest will give you another fresh start.

（休息個十分鐘會使你精神煥發。）

Morgan：O.K.

（好罷。）

(A) You'd better hurry. 你最好快一點。　　(B) You need a break. 你需要休息。　　(C) Keep going. 繼續保持。　　(D) You should work harder. 你應該更用功。

解析

(1)答題關鍵在第二句的「我一點都不累」。

(2)在四個選項中，第一句只有選 (B) 項的「你需要休息」，第二句才會說「我一點都不累」。

23. Teresa：What did you have for dinner?

（妳晚餐吃了什麼？）

Volta：　I only had a piece of bread.

（只吃一個麵包。）

Teresa：_____

Volta：　I'm trying to control my weight.

（我想減重。）

(A) I had vegetables, too. 我也吃了蔬菜。　　(B) Broccoli is the best kind of vegetable. 球花甘藍是最好的青菜。　　(C) It sounds like a lot. 好像太多了。　　(D) Why? I thought you were hungry. 為什麼？我以為你餓了。

24. Tony： It's getting warmer this weekend. Let's go bicycling.
（這個週末不那麼冷。我們去騎單車。）

　　Mona：I'd love to, but _____
　　（我很願意，但是 _____ ）

　　Tony： It's four days away. I'll help you with it.
　　（還有四天，我可以幫你做。）

　　Mona：Thank you.
　　（謝謝你。）

　　(A) I have to turn in a report next Monday. 我下週一要交報告。　　(B) I feel excited. 我感到很興奮。　　(C) I am not available. 我沒空。　　(D) my parents are sick. 我的雙親病了。

25. Mother：Maria, would you take out the garbage now?
（瑪麗亞，妳拿垃圾去倒好嗎？）

　　Maria： _____

　　Mother：If you don't do it now, you'll miss the garbage truck.
　　（如妳現在不拿，妳會錯過垃圾車。）

　　Maria： Alright! Alright!
　　（好啦！）

　　(A) Which is the best? 哪一個最好？　　(B) But I'm on the phone. 但我正在講電話。
　　(C) Can I get you anything? 妳要點什麼嗎？　　(D) It's coming. 來了。

III. 綜合測驗

下面三篇短文共有 15 個空格，為 26-40 題，請依各篇短文文意，選出一個最適合該空格的答案。

▲下篇短文共有 5 個空格，為第 26-30 題，請依短文文意，選出一個最適合該空格的答案。

　　Some teenagers ask for cosmetic surgery to get a better look, but often the real reason to change themselves is skin deep. _____26_____ to psychologist Dorothy Ratusny, these teenagers are trying to overcome a low belief and confidence in themselves. She goes on to explain that teenagers worry a lot about _____27_____ others, especially their friends and classmates, think about them. Adolescence is also a time when other events are more likely _____28_____ in their family and these can also negatively affect the self-belief and confidence of teenagers. These events include divorce, a decline in the financial situation of the family, child abuse, and _____29_____ . As a result of these deeper issues, Dr. Ratusny believes that it is _____30_____ important to provide these teenagers with psychological help and support than to conduct cosmetic surgery. She believes that cosmetic surgery is not a long lasting solution.

　　（一些青少年要求整容手術得到美貌，但是經常換自己的真正的原因是表面的。_____26_____ 心理學家桃樂斯 Ratusny 所言，這些青少年試圖克服對本身的低信仰與信任。她接著解釋青少年很擔心其他人、特別是他們的朋友和同班同學對自己的想法 _____27_____ 。青春期也是其很多事情會在家裡 _____28_____ 的時期，這些事情對青少年的自我信任可能有負面影響。這些事件包括離婚、家庭財務惡化、虐待孩子 _____29_____ 。由於這些更深的問題，Ratusny 博士相信在家提供少年人心理協助與支持比少年人去做美容 _____30_____ 重要。她相信做美容手術不是長久的解決辦法。

26. 題句：_____26_____ to psychologist Dorothy Ratusny, these teenagers ...

　　（心理學家桃樂斯 Ratusny，這些青少年……。）

　　選項：(A) Next 下一個　(B) According 根據　(C) In addition 另外　(D) By agreeing 同意

解析

(1)四個選項中，只有選 (B) 項的「根據……」，才能有意義連成「根據心理學家桃樂斯 Ratusny（的研究、的調查、的報告……等），這些青少年試圖」……，才是正確選項。

(2)本題是考片語 according to。

**27.題句：She goes on to explain that teenagers worry a lot about _____27_____ others, especially their friends and classmates, think about them.

　　（她接著解釋青少年很擔心其他人、特別是他們的朋友和同班同學對自己的想法 _____27_____ 。）

　　選項：(A) when 何時　(B) what 什麼　(C) who 誰　(D) why 為什麼

解析

(1)本題是考「what others think about them」（他人對他們的想法／看法是什麼）的句構，但本題

卻在 others 之後加入 especially their friends and classmates 多字來補充説明 others 的範圍，這樣就會使有些考生弄不清楚。

(2)依題意，只能選 (B) 項的 what，才能有意義連成「teenagers worry a lot about whatothers think about them」，才是正確選項。

**28.題句：Adolescence is also a time when other events are more likely _____28_____ in their family,

（青春期也是其很多事情會在家裡 _____28_____ ）

選項：(A) happened 過去式　(B) been happening 過去進行被動式　(C) not to have happened 否定現在完程式　(D) to happen 不定詞

解析

(1)「be likely」是「有可能」之意，它之後只能接不定詞。

(2)四個選項中，只有選 (D) 選項的「to happen」，才是符合文法的正確選項。

**29.題句：These events include divorce, a decline in the financial situation of the family, child abuse, and _____29_____ .

（這些事件包括離婚、家庭財務惡化、虐待孩子 _____29_____ ）

選項：(A) so on 等等　(B) etc 等等　(C) another 另一　(D) the others 其他各種

解析

(1)……這些事件包括離婚、家庭財務惡化、虐待孩子 _____29_____ 。

(2)依題意，(A) 項的「等等」放入空格才是正確選項。etc 是陷阱，它也是等等之意，但少了句點。

**30.題句：Dr. Ratusny believes that it is _____30_____ important to provide these teenagers with psychological help and support than to conduct cosmetic surgery.

（Ratusny 博士相信在家提供少年人心理協助與支持比少年人去做美容 _____30_____ 重要）

選項：(A) most 大多數　(B) as 當　(C) more 更　(D) so 如此的

解析

(1)important 是多音節的形容詞，依文法，多音節形容詞前的比較級要放「more」。

(2)四個選項中，只有選 (C) 項的 more 才是符合文法的正確選項。

▲下篇短文共有 5 個空格，為第 31-35 題，請依短文文意，選出一個最適合該空格的答案。

"Dangerous Minds" is a touching movie about a teacher who tries to change a class of "rude" and "violent" students who have no interest in education. Lou Ann Johnson is hired on the spot to teach English and is told that her students are _____31_____ but that they are special kids. Another teacher describes them as "bright kids, with _____32_____ education, and what we politely refer to as social problems." When Johnson enters the classroom, her mainly non-white students call her "white bread" and boo her down in other ways. _____33_____ , Johnson does not let the difference between her and their _____34_____ stop her. She hands out candy bars to them and takes them on free trips to the amusement park. However, the real _____35_____ happens when she involves them in some very powerful words: I will not carry myself to die. When I go to my grave my head will be high.

（「危險的想法」是一部動人的電影，是敘述一位老師要改變一班對功課不感興趣的「粗魯」且「激烈」的學生。盧‧安‧江森是當場被聘僱來教英語的老師，也被告知她的學生是 _____31_____ 然而他們是特別的孩子。另一名教師把他們描述為「聰明的孩子，只受 _____32_____ 教育，我們禮貌地說法稱之為社會問題。「當江森進入教室，被她多數的非白人學生稱為「白色麵包」並對她噓聲糗她。_____33_____ ,江森不讓她和他們 _____34_____ 的差別所阻。她把糖果發給他們並帶他們免費去遊樂園。不過，當她使他們專注在某些強有力的字句：「我不會把自己帶往死亡、當我要步入墳墓時，我還是抬頭挺胸」，真正的 _____35_____ 發生了。）

31. 題句：Lou Ann Johnson is hired on the spot to teach English and is told that her students are _____31_____ but that they are special kids.

　　選項：(A) passionately 熱情地　(B) passion 熱情　(C) passionate 熱情的
　　　　　(D) passionless 不熱情

解析

(1)答題關鍵在題目空格左、右邊的「her students are」與「but」。

(2)四個選項中，只有選 (C) 項的「passionate」放入空格，才是有意義連成整句的正確選項。

(3)連接詞 but 前、後的兩個子句內容，通常是互為反向的。所以 (C) 項的「熱情」是正面的，而 special kids（有缺陷小孩）代表負面意思。

32. 題句：Another teacher describes them as "bright kids, with _____32_____ education,

　　選項：(A) up and down 到處　(B) little or no 幾乎沒有　(C) few and far between 罕見稀少的　(D) developed or growing

解析

(1)答題關鍵在題目空格左、右邊的「with」與「education」。

(2)四個選項中，只有選 (B) 項的「little or no」放入空格，才是有意義連成整句的正確選項。

33. 題句：her mainly non-white students call her "white bread" and boo her down in other ways. _____33_____ Johnson does not let the difference between her and their race stop her.

　　選項：(A) On the other hand 相反地　(B) Similarly 相似地　(C) Otherwise 否則　(D) Nonetheless 但是、仍然

解析

(1)答題關鍵在題目空格左、右邊的兩個子句。

(2)四個選項中，只有選(D)項的「nonetheless」放入空格，才是有意義連成整句的正確選項。

(3)本題是考兩子句間連接詞的應用。

34. 題句：Johnson does not let the difference between her and their _____34_____ stop her

選項：(A) religion 宗教　(B) nationality 國籍　(C) race 種族　(D) gender 性別

解析

(1)答題關鍵在題目空格左邊的「the difference between her and their」。

(2)四個選項中，只有選(C)項的「race」放入空格，才是有意義連成整句的正確選項。

35. 題句：However, the real _____35_____ happens when she involves them in some very powerful words: ...

選項：(A) turning point 轉變　(B) let down 使失望　(C) conflict 衝突　(D) reunion 再聯合

解析

(1)答題關鍵在題目空格左、右邊的「the real」與「happens」。

(2)四個選項中，只有選(A)項的「turning point」放入空格，才是有意義連成整句的正確選項。

▲下篇短文共有 5 個空格，為第 36-40 題，請依短文文意，選出一個最適合該空格的答案。

　　An e-book, known as a digital book, is an electronic version of a printed book. It can be _____36_____ on a personal computer or hand-held device designed specifically for this purpose. E-books have numerous advantages _____37_____ printed books. There are over 2 million free books available for download, _____38_____ we can save a great deal of money. Another advantage is the portability: an e-reader with thousands of books can be carried easily to everywhere. However, one of the drawbacks is the advances in technology or the introduction of new formats. _____39_____ printed books remain readable for many years, e-books may need to be copied to a new carrier over time. In addition, paper books can provide visual appeal, yet the digital nature of e-books makes _____40_____ non-visible and intangible. E-books cannot provide the physical feel of the cover, paper, and binding of the original printed work.

　　（一本電子書就是大家熟知的數據書，是一個印刷書的電子版本。它可以在個人電腦上 _____36_____ 被讀出，或為這目的特別設計的掌中型配備。電子書 _____37_____ 印刷書許多優勢。有超過可供下載的 200 萬本免費書，_____38_____ 我們能節省很多錢。另一個優勢是輕便性：內含數千本書的電子閱讀機可以帶著到處走。不過，缺點之一是在技術或新形式的引進方面。_____39_____ 印刷書多年後仍然可讀，而電子書過些時候可能要複製到另一個新型的閱讀載具。另外，印刷書能提供視覺的要求，而以數據本質的電子書是看不見及觸摸不到的。電子書不能提供印刷書封面、紙張及裝訂等的實質感覺。）

**36.題句：It can be _____36_____ on a personal computer or hand-held device...

選項：(A) reading 現在分詞　(B) read 過去分詞　(C) being read 正在被閱讀　(D) to read 不定詞

解析

(1)答題關鍵在空格左方的「It can be ...」。依文法，be 動詞後接過去分詞才構成被動語態，而文章只能被讀，所以要用被動語態。

(2)只有(B)選項的過去分詞 read 放入空格，才可連成被動語態的 can be read，才是正確選項。

(3)read 的現在式、過去式與過去分詞字型皆相同，只是發音不同。

**37.題句：E-books have numerous advantages ____37____ printed books.

　　選項：(A) at 在　(B) above 在……上　(C) in 在……內　(D) over 在……上

解析

(1)本題是考「A has advantage over B」是「A 比 B 有優勢」的用法，over 是 advantage 後的固定搭配介係詞。

(2)因此，四個選項中只有選(D)項的 over 才是符合文語法的正確選項。

**38.題句：There are over 2 million free books available for download, ____38____ we can save a great deal of money.

　　選項：(A) so that 因此　(B) even though 即使　(C) as if 好像　(D) despite of 不管

解析

(1)本題關鍵字是空格左、右方的兩個子句。

(2)依題意，四個選項中只有選(A)項的片語連接詞 so that（因此），才是符合文法的正確選項。

**39.題句：____38____ printed books remain readable for many years, e-books may need to be copied to a new carrier over time.

　　選項：(A) Then 當時　(B) Whatever 任何的　(C) While 當　(D) Unless 除外

解析

(1)本題是考「當某事、物如何如何，另一事、物卻是如何如何」的用法。

　　例句：We are singing while they are dancing. 或 While they are dancing, we are singing.

(2)依題意，四個選項中只有選(C)項的 while 才是符合文法的正確選項。

**40.題句：yet the digital nature of e-books makes ____38____ non-visible and intangible.

　　選項：(A) it 它　(B) its 它的　(C) it's 它是　(D) itself 它自己

解析

(1)本題是考 make it ...的句型。常用的有 make it possible、make it worse、make my dream come true……等。

(2)make 之後如果受詞不明確，可用虛受詞 it 代替，因此，選(A)項的 it 才是符合文法的正確選項

IV. 閱讀測驗

下面兩篇短文共有 10 題，每篇有 5 題，為 41-50 題，請閱讀短文後，選出最適當的答案。

▲閱讀下文，回答第 41-45 題

For the most part, I was excited to begin college life. All through the summer vacation, I kept thinking of this fresh, new period of my life. Some of my thoughts were centered on what to take with me. Eventually, I left home with very little.

Looking back, I am glad I left several things behind. I did not take every DVD, computer game, and comic book with me, or any closet groceries such as crackers, peanut butter, jam, dried fruits, or coffee. If I had, I would have been tied up in my room most of the time. I also did not take any furniture, appliances, or any decorations for my room. Basically, I just got there with very little and planned with my roommates how we were going to make our room look. It was only after I had gotten their input that I made a trip back home to get some items. Not having taken so many things already sounds like it was a major achievement, but there were other things that I left behind too.

These other things were not objects. They were things like my high school friends. I left all of them behind. By this, I do not mean that I cut them out of my life. What I mean is that I was not held back by my friendship with them. I was able to reach out and make new friends at college. I also left behind any fears, worries, and doubts concerning what college life might or might not turn out to be. I found calm in the belief that I should begin my college life with a fresh view.In the end, I arrived at my college dorm with nothing but a sleeping bag, some clothes, and a willingness to experience and learn.

（我很興奮來開始我的大學生活整個暑假，我一直在想這個我一生當中新階段。我的一些想法是集中在我要帶走什麼。最終，幾乎不帶東西就離開家裡。

回顧一下，我高興我留下幾件東西沒帶走。我沒帶走每片 DVD，電腦遊戲和漫畫書，或櫥櫃食品雜貨（像是餅乾、花生醬、乾果或者咖啡）。如果我帶了這些東西，我大部分時間就會在我的房間。我也沒帶走任何家具，家電或房內裝飾品。基本上，我剛到時幾乎不帶東西，並與我室友計劃要怎麼裝璜我們的房間。在弄到一些電腦的輸入資料後，我回家拿了些東西。沒有帶走那麼多東西聽起來好像是了不起的成就，但我還是有留下一些沒帶走。

這些其他事情不是物件。他們是我的高中朋友。我離開他們所有的人。 關於這一點，並不是說我一輩子要離開他們。我的意思是我們的友誼不變。我能伸出雙手並且在學校結交新朋友。我也沒帶走我的恐懼，憂慮，和關於學校生活的懷疑。我發現信仰裡的平靜，我應該以開闊的視野來開始我的學校生活。最後，我只帶睡袋、一些衣服與極願體會與學習的心到學校宿舍。）

41. What did the author do during the summer vacation?
（暑假期間作者做了些什麼？）

(A) He exercised to keep fit. 他作運動保持身材。　(B) He thought about college life. 他想到校園生活。　(C) He had a part-time job. 他有兼差。　(D) He left home for a long vacation.

他離家度長假。

解析

從答題關鍵的「All through the summer vacation, I kept thinking of this fresh, new period of my life」可看出，(B)項的「He thought about college life」才是正確選項。

42. What did the author and his roommates do first?

（作者與他的室友先做了什麼？）

(A) They made a plan. 他們做了一個計畫。　(B) They went out for some drinks. 他們出外喝一杯。　(C) They played online games. 他們玩線上遊戲。　(D) They cooked a meal together. 他們共同做菜。

解析

從答題關鍵的「and planned with my roommates how we were going to make our room look.」可看出，(A)項的「They made a plan」才是正確選項。

43. According to the third and fourth paragraphs, which of the following did the author NOT leavebehind?

（根據第三、四段文章，哪一項作者沒有留在家鄉的？）

(A) His high school friends. 他的高中朋友。　(B) Uncertainty about college life. 有關大學生涯的不確定性。　(C) A fear of being alone at college. 擔心在大學會孤單。　(D) A heart to learn new things. 一顆想學習的心。

解析

從答題關鍵的「I arrived at my college dorm with nothing but a sleeping bag, some clothes, and a willingness to experience and learn.」可看出，(D)項的「A heart to learn new things.」才是正確選項。

44. Which of the following best describes the author's attitude?

（下列哪一項最能描述作者的態度？）

(A) shocked 震驚　(B) unreasonable 不合理　(C) open-minded 很開朗　(D) disagreeable 不同意

解析

從答題關鍵的「I found calm in the belief that I should begin my college life with a fresh view.」可看出，(C)項的「open-minded」才是正確選項。

45. What is the best title for this passage?

（本文的最佳標題是什麼？）

(A) Controlling Your Finances 控制你的財務　(B) Adjusting to College Life 調整至校園生活

(C) Campus Safety 校園安全　　(D) Time Management 時間管理

解析

看完本文內容可看出，(B) 項的「Adjusting to College Life」才是正確選項。

▲閱讀下文，回答第 46-50 題

　　People are making lifestyle choices to reduce greenhouse gas emissions globally. Among greenhouse gases, carbon dioxide is the main reason for climate change and natural disasters, such as flooding and droughts. There are many things that we can do about our food, travel, and electricity to reduce the speed of global warming.

　　It is well known that the food system is responsible for at least 20 percent of greenhouse gases. A low carbon diet reduces emissions released from the production, packing, processing, transport, and preparation of food. It is recommended for one to buy organic food instead of eating imported, processed, and frozen foods. Eat only food which is in season or from your region. Avoid eating red meat and dairy products, which are the most emission-intensive foods. Other actions include eating a vegetarian diet and proper portion to reduce the waste of food.

　　The burning of gasoline to power vehicles that transport food over long distances by air, ship, truck, and rail releases a great amount of carbon dioxide. Walk, bike, carpool, or take mass transportation whenever possible. As a driver, prevent unnecessary idling of engines, avoid aggressive driving, rapid acceleration or sudden stops, and keep vehicles in good running condition.

　　Unlike incandescent bulbs, compact fluorescent lamps use 70-80 percent less energy and last at least 8-13 times longer. Other tips include turning off lights and appliances when they are not in use. Unplug cellular phone chargers when the battery is fully charged, and reduce the use of the dryer by hanging up your laundry on a clothesline.

　　We can slow down the climate change by making personal commitment to protect our planet, thereby avoiding the dangerous consequences of global warming.

　　（人們建立生活模式的選擇以降低全球溫室氣體的擴散。在溫室氣體中，二氧化碳是氣候變化和自然災害的主要原因，像是水災和乾旱。在食品、旅行，及電力方面，我們可做很多事來減緩全球暖化的速度。

　　眾所周知食品系統對形成溫室氣體有百分之 20 的責任。低碳飲食可降低從生產、包裝、處理、運輸及食品準備過程所散發的有害氣體。我們建議人們購買有機食品而不是吃進口的、加工過的、與冷凍食品。只吃當令季節或你們地區的食品。避免吃紅肉和乳製品，這是散發最多有害氣體的食品。其他行動包括吃素食和適當的降低食品的浪費。

　　汽油的燃燒提供車輛動力，利用空運陸路和鐵路的長距離運送食品會釋放大量二氧化碳。只要可行的話，儘量步行、單車、車輛共乘或大眾運輸。作為一個司機，防止不必要的引擎怠速，避免好鬥式駕駛、瞬間加速或緊急煞車，以保持車輛的良好狀況。

　　與白熱燈泡不同，小型螢光燈能省去 70-80%的能源，而壽命卻至少多出 8 到 13 倍。其他的竅門是關掉不使用時的燈光和家電。行動電話充完電後要拔下插頭，並且

減少風乾機的使用而將衣服掛起來風乾。

我們就能減緩氣候變化，因此避免全球暖化的危險結果。）

46. What is the best title for this passage?

（這段文章的最好的標題是什麼？）

(A) Natural Disaster 自然災害

(B) Low Carbon Living 低碳生活方式

(C) The Importance of Transportation 運輸的重要性

(D) The Effects of Global Warming 全球暖化的影響

解析

依據本文內容，只有 (B) 項的「Low Carbon Living」才是最佳標題。請注意，(D) 選項是陷阱，因本文雖有提到「我們可做很多事來減緩全球暖化的速度」。不是全球暖化後的影響。

47. Which action can be taken at home to help reduce carbon dioxide?

（在家裡，有哪種行動可用來幫助減少二氧化碳？）

(A) Carpool with friends or co-workers. 與朋友或同事的汽車共乘。

(B) Ride your bike to school. 騎車到學校。

(C) Avoid sudden stops while driving. 開車時避免緊急煞車。

(D) Use compact fluorescent. 使用小型螢光燈。

解析

請注意題目裡有「at home」二字，所以 (D) 項的 " Use compact fluorescent. " 才是正確選項。

48. According to the passage, which of the following is the main cause of global warming?

（根據本文，下列哪一項是全球暖化的主因？）

(A) Carbon dioxide. 二氧化碳。　　(B) Organic food. 有機食品。

(C) Red meat. 紅肉。　　(D) Cellular phone charger. 行動電話充電器。

解析

從答題關鍵的「carbon dioxide is the main reason for climate change and natural disasters,」可看出，(A) 項的「Carbon dioxide.」才是正確選項。

49. To live on low carbon diet, which of the following is recommended?

（爲了以低碳飲食爲食物，如下哪一項可被推薦？）

(A) Drinking bottled water. 喝瓶裝水。

(B) Eating imported food. 吃進口食品。

(C) Growing food in your garden. 在你的花園種菜。

(D) Taking a large portion of food. 吃大量食物。

解析

從答題關鍵的「Eat only food which is in season or from your region.,」可看出，(C) 項的「Growing food in your garden」才是正確選項。

50. According to the passage, which of the following statements is true?

（根據短文如下哪一項為真？）

(A) Compact fluorescent lamps relatively use more energy than incandescent bulbs.

與白熾的燈泡相比較，小型螢光燈相對使用更多的能量。

(B) Incandescent bulbs last longer than compact fluorescent lamps.

白熱燈泡比小型螢光燈壽命長。

(C) Compact fluorescent lamps use 20 - 30 percent of the energy incandescent bulbs consume.

小型螢光燈使僅用了白熱燈泡耗電能的 20-30%。

(D) People using compact fluorescent lamps pay a higher electricity bill.

使用小型螢光燈的人們支付較高電費。

解析

(1)文內答題關鍵是：「compact fluorescent lamps use 70-80 percent less energy ....（小型螢光燈能省下 70-80%的能源）」。

(2)(C) 項的「Compact fluorescent lamps use 20-30 percent of the energy incandescent bulbsconsume.」。（小型螢光燈使僅用了白熱燈泡耗電能的 20-30%）

(3)這樣就可明顯看出，本題正確選項為 (C) 項內容。

100年統測 (二技考試)

I. 字彙測驗

共有 15 題，第 1-7 題，每題均有一個劃底線的字，請在四個備選字中，選擇一個與劃底線的字意義最接近的答案。第 8-15 題，請選擇一個最適合的答案，以完成該句。

1. Nowadays, dogs and cats are popular pets in people's homes in many countries.
   （目前，很多國家飼養貓狗當寵物的情行很普遍。）
   (A) common 普通　(B) useless 沒用的　(C) free 免費　(D) strange 奇怪

   解析
   (1)先看底線字的中譯為「普通的、流行的」。
   (2)只有(A)選項的「普通」，才是與底線字意思最接近的正確選項。

2. Most coffee shops create a comfortable and casual atmosphere for their customers.
   （大多數咖啡館為他們的顧客創造舒適和不拘束的氣氛。）
   (A) informal 非正規的　(B) serious 嚴肅的　(C) professional 專業　(D) cautious 謹慎

   解析
   (1)先看底線字的中譯為「非正式的」。
   (2)只有(A)選項的「非正規的」，才是與底線字意思最接近的正確選項。

3. Keeping our homes clean and tidy is essential for our health and comfort.
   （保持家裡乾淨和整潔對我們的健康與舒適是必要的。）
   (A) chaotic 混亂的　(B) plastic 塑膠　(C) orderly 整齊的　(D) jointly 共同

   解析
   (1)先看底線字的中譯為「整潔」。
   (2)只有(C)選項的「整齊的」，才是與底線字意思最接近的正確選項。

4. Most people believe that scientific advancement such as new medicine can help us live longer and healthier.
   （大多數人相信像新藥物那樣的進步科技能使人類長壽與健康。）
   (A) protection 保護　(B) program 計畫　(C) promise 許諾　(D) progress 發展

解析
(1)先看底線字的中譯爲「進展的」。
(2)只有(D)選項的「發展」，才是與底線字意思最接近的正確選項。

5. The human brain is such a <u>complex</u> system that scientists are still trying to figure out how it functions.
　（人腦是一個很複雜的系統，科學家仍然努力想出它如何運作？）
　(A) confirmed 確認　(B) composed 組成　(C) complicated 錯綜複雜　(D) concentrated 集中

解析
(1)先看底線字的中譯爲「複雜的」。
(2)只有(C)選項的「錯綜複雜」，才是與底線字意思最接近的正確選項。

6. After having studied for twelve hours, I could <u>hardly</u> keep my eyes open.
　（研習了 12 個小時之後，我幾乎張不開眼睛。）
　(A) nicely 很好　(B) barely 勉強　(C) often 經常　(D) finally 最後

解析
(1)先看底線字的中譯爲「幾乎不」。
(2)只有(B)選項的「勉強」，才是與底線字意思最接近的正確選項。

7. Growing up in this area, I saw this place <u>change</u> from a small town into a big city. 7.
　（在這個地區發展，我看見這個地方從一個小的鎮改變成一座大的城市。）
　(A) transport 運輸　(B) transplant 移植　(C) transmit 傳送　(D) transform 改變

解析
(1)先看底線字的中譯爲「改變、變化」。
(2)只有(D)選項的「改變」，才是與底線字意思最接近的正確選項。

8. Comfort food gives us a warm feeling and helps us ＿＿＿＿＿ and feel better.
　（方便的食物給我們我們溫暖的感覺，並幫我們 ＿＿＿＿＿ 並且感覺好點。）
　(A) increase 增加　(B) tighten 收緊　(C) alert 警惕的　(D) relax 放鬆

解析
(1)答題關鍵在「給我們我們溫暖的感覺，並幫我們 ＿＿＿＿＿」。
(2)只有(D)選項的「放鬆」放入空格，才是符合題意的正確選項。

9. Most young people now cannot ＿＿＿＿＿ to buy a house with their current salaries.
　（多數年輕人現在都不能 ＿＿＿＿＿ 用他們目前薪水買一棟房子。）
　(A) afford 付擔得起　(B) applaud 鼓掌　(C) appoint 任命　(D) affect 影響

解析

⑴答題關鍵在「多數年輕人現在都不能 ＿＿＿＿＿＿ 用薪水買房子」。

⑵只有(A)選項的「付擔得起」放入空格，才是符合題意的正確選項。

10. Passengers are ＿＿＿＿＿＿ to leave the priority seat for elderly people on public transportation.

　　（乘客是 ＿＿＿＿＿＿ 在公車上禮讓博愛座給老人。）

　　(A) supplied 提供　(B) suspected 懷疑　(C) succeeded 成功　(D) supposed 假定

解析

⑴答題關鍵在「乘客是＿＿＿＿在公車上禮讓博愛座」。

⑵只有(D)選項的「supposed」放入空格，才符合片語「be supposed to（應該）」說法。

11. Surfing the Internet and playing online games in one's room are common ＿＿＿＿＿＿ activities among young people in Taiwan.

　　（在台灣，年輕人在自己房間上網瀏覽與玩線上遊戲是普遍的 ＿＿＿＿＿＿ 活動。）

　　(A) outdoor 戶外　(B) leisure 休閒　(C) diving 潛水　(D) medical 醫學

解析

⑴答題關鍵在「玩線上遊戲是普遍的 ＿＿＿＿＿＿ 活動」。

⑵只有(B)選項的「休閒」放入空格，才是符合題意的正確選項。

12. For many marathon runners, the sport is not about winning; finishing a long distance race itself gives them a sense of ＿＿＿＿＿＿ .

　　（對很多馬拉松運動員來說，運動不在輸贏；跑完全程會給他們一種 ＿＿＿＿＿＿ 感覺。）

　　(A) achievement 成就　(B) confusion 混亂　(C) guilt 有罪　(D) humor 幽默

解析

⑴答題關鍵在「跑完全程會給他們一種 ＿＿＿＿＿＿ 感覺」。

⑵只有(A)選項的「成就」放入空格，才是符合題意的正確選項。

13. The series of Twilight movies are ＿＿＿＿＿＿ and have made the leading actor and actress rich and famous.

　　（一系列的電影舊片 ＿＿＿＿＿＿ 並且已使男主角和女演員名利雙收富有和著名。）

　　(A) beliefs 信仰　(B) blockbusters 暢銷電影　(C) batteries 電池　(D) bookmarks 書籤

解析

⑴答題關鍵在「一系列的電影舊片 ＿＿＿＿＿＿ 並且已使男主角和女演員名利雙收」。

(2)只有(B)選項的「暢銷電影」放入空格，才是符合題意的正確選項。

14. Most criminals leave something of themselves at the place of the crime, such as a hair or a fingerprint, and are caught with the ＿＿＿＿＿＿ of science and computers.

（多數罪犯在犯罪現場留下他們自己的東西，像是一根頭髮或指紋，最後利用科學與電腦 ＿＿＿＿＿＿ 逮捕罪犯。）

(A) romance 浪漫　(B) distance 距離　(C) ignorance 無知　(D) assistance 協助

解析
(1)答題關鍵在「最後利用科學與電腦 ＿＿＿＿＿＿ 逮捕罪犯。」
(2)只有(D)選項的「協助」放入空格，才是符合題意的正確選項。

15. Every year since 1901, the Nobel Peace Prize has been ＿＿＿＿＿＿ to persons or organizations for their effort in creating peace.

（從 1901 年起每年的諾貝爾和平獎 ＿＿＿＿＿＿ 給對人類和平有貢獻的個人或組織）

(A) admired 欣賞　(B) analyzed 分析　(C) accused 指責　(D) awarded 授予

解析
(1)答題關鍵在「諾貝爾和平獎 ＿＿＿＿＿＿ 給對人類和平有貢獻的人……」。
(2)只有(D)選項的「授予」放入空格，才是符合題意的正確選項。

II. 對話測驗

共有 10 題，為第 16-25 題，請依對話內容選出一個最適當的答案，使其成為有意義的對話。

16. Adam: Excuse me. I'd like to return this MP3 player I bought here yesterday.
（亞當：對不起。我想退貨這台我昨天在這裡買的 MP3 播放器。）

Clerk: ＿＿＿＿＿＿
（辦事員：＿＿＿＿＿＿）

Adam: Then, can I exchange it for a new one?
（亞當：那麼，可以換一台新的嗎？）

(A) Yes, you can download music to it. 是的，你可以下載音樂。
(B) Why did you borrow it so long? 你為什麼借那麼久？
(C) Sorry, we have a no-refund policy. 抱歉，我們有一項不退貨條款。
(D) It's in the third row actually. 它實際上在第 3 排。

解析
(1)答題關鍵在第 2 句的「我們有一項不退貨條款。」。

(2)只有 (C) 選項的「那麼，可以換一台新的嗎？」放入空格，才是有意義回應店員講的第 2 句。

17. Nurse: Good morning. Dr. Shaw's Office.

（護士：早安。邵醫師辦公室。）

Bill: Hello, ＿＿＿＿＿＿＿

（比爾：你好，＿＿＿＿＿＿＿）

Nurse: Okay, your name please? And would you like to reschedule it?

（護士：好，你名字是？你要重新預約嗎？）

(A) I'd like to make an appointment at 3 o'clock. 我想預約 3 點鐘的。

(B) I'm calling to cancel my 3 o'clock appointment. 我是打來取消我的 3 點鐘預約。

(C) I have a terrible headache. I need to see a doctor. 我頭很痛。我要看醫生。

(D) I'm in great pain. Can I get some pain killers now? 我現在很痛，可以給我一些止痛藥嗎？

解析

(1)答題關鍵在第 2 句的「你要重新預約嗎」？

(2)只有 (B) 選項的「我是打來取消我的 3 點鐘預約」放入空格，護士才會接著問「你要重新預約嗎？」

18. Waiter: Excuse me, sir. You cannot smoke in here.

（服務生：先生，對不起。你不能在這裡吸煙。）

Bob: Why? I didn't see any "No Smoking" sign.

（鮑伯：為什麼？我沒看見「禁止吸菸」的牌子。）

Waiter: ＿＿＿＿＿＿＿

（服務生：＿＿＿＿＿＿＿）

Bob: Oh, I didn't know that. I'll step out to smoke.

（鮑伯：噢，我不知道。我走到外面抽好了。）

(A) Who said anything about smoking? 誰提到吸菸的事？

(B) Sorry, the last guest was probably smoking. 抱歉，可能是最後客人當時有抽菸。

(C) Would you like smoking or non-smoking? 你要吸菸區還是非吸菸區？

(D) Smoking is not allowed inside all public buildings. 所有公共大樓裡都不能抽菸。

解析

(1)答題關鍵在第 2 句的「為什麼不能抽？沒看到『禁止吸菸』的牌子。」

(2)只有 (D) 選項的「所有公共大樓裡都不能抽菸」放入空格，才是有意義回應第 2 句的正確選項。

19. Lily: Why are you wearing a face mask?

（麗莉：你為什麼戴口罩？）

Phoebe: _____

（菲碧：_____ ）

Lily: Don't forget to put on a helmet as well.

（麗莉：不忘記也要戴上安全帽。）

(A) Ok, I'll wear it if you insist. Ok，如果你堅持，我就穿。

(B) I'm going to ride a motorcycle. 我要騎機車。

(C) I think I dropped it somewhere. 我大概掉在某個地方

(D) It's easy. Let me show you. 那很容易。讓我做給你看。

解析

(1)答題關鍵在第 1 句的「你為什麼戴口罩？」。

(2)只有(B) 選項的「我要騎機車。」放入空格，才是有意義回應第 1 句的正確選項。

20. Carl: May I speak to Lisa, please?

（凱爾：請問我可以跟麗莎講話嗎？）

Becky: _____

（貝基：_____ ）

Carl: Isn't this 522-6171?

（凱爾：這不是 522-6171 嗎？）

Becky: I'm sorry. You've dialed the wrong number.

（貝基：對不起。你已經撥錯號。）

(A) May I ask who's calling, please? 請問你是那位？

(B) Just a moment, please. I'll get her. 請等一會兒。我去叫她來聽。

(C) I'm sorry, but there's no one named Lisa here. 對不起，但這裡沒有叫做麗莎的人。

(D) She's not in. Would you like to leave a message? 她不在。你要留言嗎？

解析

(1)答題關鍵在第 3 句的「你們不是 522-6171 嗎？」。

(2)只有 (C) 選項的「對不起，但這裡沒有叫做麗莎的人」放入空格，才是引起對方說出第 3 句對話的正確選項。

21. Denise: I don't feel like staying home.

（丹尼斯：我不想要待在家裡。）

Jane: _____ Why don't we go to the art museum?

（簡：_____ 我們為什麼不去藝術博物館？）

Denise: Great. There is a special exhibit this week.

（丹尼斯：太好了。這星期有特展。）

(A) That's a good question. 那問題很好。

(B) Sorry, I won't be able to. 抱歉，做不到。

(C) To be honest, neither do I. 老實說，我也不想。

(D) When did it happen? 它什麼時候發生？

解析

(1)答題關鍵在第 1 句的「我不想要待在家裡。」。

(2)只有(C)選項的「老實說，我也不想」放入空格，才是有意義回應第 1 句的正確選項。

22. Peter: Congratulations, Jolin.

（彼得：恭喜你，裘琳 Jolin。＿＿＿＿＿＿＿＿）

Jolin: Absolutely fabulous.

（Jolin：太棒了。）

Peter: Everybody loved your performance.

（彼得：每人都很欣賞你的表現。）

Jolin: Thank you.

（Jolin：謝謝。）

(A) How did you do it? 你怎樣辦到的？

(B) You did it terribly. 你做的很糟。

(C) You forgot your lines. 你忘記你的界線。

(D) How does it feel to win? 贏的感覺怎樣？

解析

(1)答題關鍵在第 2 句的「太棒了」。

(2)只有(D)選項的「贏的感覺怎樣？」放入空格，才是引起對方說出第 2 句的正確選項。

23. Caleb: Mom, can you lend me your laptop?

（凱萊布：媽媽，妳的筆電可以借我嗎？）

Mom: Why? Doesn't your computer run faster?

（媽媽：為什麼要借？你的電腦不是跑得比較快嗎？）

Caleb: Well, I need to do a project with my classmates at school.

（凱萊布：是這樣的，我要和同學在學校做專案課程。）

Mom: Ok.

（媽媽：可以＿＿＿＿＿＿＿＿）

(A) But, why are you blaming me? 但是，你為什麼責備我？

(B) Just don't break it, please. 不要弄壞了就好。

(C) They should run faster. 他們應該跑得更快。

(D) I appreciate your help. 我感激你的幫助。

解析

(1)依題意，只有(B)選項的「不要弄壞了就好。」放入空格，才是符合題意的正確選項。

24. Teacher: Mary, what do you want to do after high school?

（教師：瑪莉，中學畢業後你想做什麼？）

Mary: _____ I might go to college.

（瑪莉：_____ 我可能上大學。）

Teacher: If so, you need to prepare in advance.

（教師：如果這樣，你要早做準備。）

(A) I'm not sure. 還不一定。

(B) I don't think so. 我不這樣想。

(C) That's perfectly true. 那是真的。

(D) I won't be doing that. 我不會那麼做。

解析

(1)答題關鍵在第 1 句後半的「我可能上大學」。

(2)只有(A)選項的「還不一定」放入空格，才是連接後半句「我可能上大學」的正確選項。

25. Julie: How do you feel now with your leg?

（朱莉：你的腿現在感覺怎樣？）

Karen: After resting for two months, _____

（凱倫：休息了兩個月之後，_____ ）

Julie: Then, I suggest you get more medicine for it.

（朱莉：然後，我建議繼續用藥。）

(A) I still feel the pain unfortunately. 很糟糕還是會痛。

(B) I weigh three kilograms more. 我重了 3 公斤。

(C) I'm perfectly fine now. 我現在很好。

(D) I'm behind my school work. 我的功課落後了。

解析

(1)答題關鍵在第 2 句前半句的「休息了兩個月之後」。

(2)只有(B)選項的「我重了 3 公斤」放入空格，才是有意義連接前半句的正確選項。

III. 綜合測驗

下面三篇短文共有 15 個空格，為 26-40 題，請依各篇短文文意，選出一個最適合該空格的答案。

▲閱讀下文，回答第 26-30 題

　　The article "Principal Suspended over Bullying" is about the suspension of a principal at a junior high school in Taiwan. Apparently, sixty teachers from the school signed a petition against the principal for ＿＿＿ 26 ＿＿＿ ignoring students' bullying behavior. Addressing the problem, the Minister of Education said that, ＿＿＿ 27 ＿＿＿ getting into a good high school or university is important, it is ＿＿＿ 28 ＿＿＿ to teach students how to get along with others. The Minister emphasized that students learn to respect ＿＿＿ 29 ＿＿＿ protect others. Surprisingly, the school had won an award last year for being a model school in the area. Now, because of the bullying event, the award might be ＿＿＿ 30 ＿＿＿ away from the school. The school will be informed of the decision soon.

　　（「因霸凌遭停職的校長」這篇文章是有關台灣的一所國中校長的故事。顯然，該校的 60 名教師聯署抗議校長 ＿＿＿ 26 ＿＿＿ 忽視學生的霸凌行為。對此問題，教育部長說，＿＿＿ 27 ＿＿＿ 要進入好高中或大學就讀很重要，＿＿＿ 28 ＿＿＿ 要教學生怎樣與他人相處。部長強調學生學習尊重 ＿＿＿ 29 ＿＿＿ 保護他人。令人吃驚的是，該校去年在當地才贏得一項模範學校獎。現在，由於霸凌事件，該獎項可能會 ＿＿＿ 30 ＿＿＿，相關的決定不久就會通知學校。）

26. 題句：抗議校長 ＿＿＿ 26 ＿＿＿ 忽視學生的霸凌行為
　　選項：(A) repeat 重複　(B) repeatedly 一再地　(C) repetition 反覆　(D) repetitive 反覆的
　　解析
　　四選項中只有(B)選項的「一再地」放入空格，才是符合題意的正確選項。

27. 題句：教育部長說，＿＿＿ 27 ＿＿＿ 要進入好高中或大學就讀很重要
　　選項：(A) however 然而　(B) indeed 的確　(C) nonetheless 仍然　(D) although 雖然
　　解析
　　(1)四選項中只有(D)選項的「雖然」放入空格，才是符合題意的正確選項。

28. 題句：＿＿＿ 28 ＿＿＿ 要教學生怎樣與他人相處。
　　選項：(A) important 重要的　(B) more important 更重要的　(C) as importantly 也很重要
　　　　　(D) most importantly 最重要地
　　解析
　　(1)四選項中只有(B)選項的「更重要的」放入空格，才是符合題意的正確選項。

29. 題句：部長強調學生要學習尊重 ＿＿＿ 29 ＿＿＿ 保護他人
　　選項：(A) and 以及　(B) for 為了　(C) in 之內　(D) nor 也不

解析

(1)四選項中只有(A)選項的「以及」放入空格，才是符合題意的正確選項。

30. 題句：because of the bullying event, the award might be _____30_____ away from the school.

　　　　由於霸凌事件，該獎項可能會 _____30_____

　　選項：(A) take 現在式　(B) took 過去式　(C) taken 過去分詞　(D) taking 動名詞

解析

(1)本題是考文法的被動語態 be taken away。

(2)四選項中只有(C)選項的「taken」放入空格，才是符合「be taken away」的文法規定。

▲ 閱讀下文，回答第 31-35 題

　　It is not easy to decide what job to do, but you should find something you love. Try to find a job that you enjoy and get satisfaction _____31_____ , instead of one you do just for money. _____32_____ you have graduated from college, you will be spending a great amount of your time working, so it is quite important to think of what you can enjoy in a job whether it is the lifestyle、job duties or work relationships, _____33_____ are many parts of a job that you can enjoy. Of course, you most likely will not find the perfect job _____34_____ . Nonetheless, stay calm and give yourself a chance to _____35_____ parts of the job you think you like and even parts you are still not sure about. Finding a job you enjoy will definitely help you develop your career.

　　（要決定做什麼工作不是那麼容易，你應該找到你愛做的事。想辦法找一份你喜歡也會 _____31_____ 滿意的工作而不是只有薪水的考量。_____32_____ 從學校畢業後，你的大部份時間是在工作，因此找一份妳會有樂趣的工作相當重要，不論它是生活模式、工作職責、或者工作關係，工作 _____33_____ 許多你會喜歡的部份。當然，很可能你無法 _____34_____ 找到好工作。不過，保持冷靜並給自己一個機會 _____35_____ 工作裡你認為你喜歡的部份、甚至是你不確定是否喜歡的部份。找到你喜愛的工作絕對有助於發展你的專業。）

31. 題句：Try to find a job that you enjoy and get satisfaction _____31_____

　　　　想辦法找一份你喜歡也會 _____31_____ 滿意的工作

　　選項：(A) to 對　(B) with 有了……　(C) at 在　(D) from 從

解析

(1)答題關鍵在「you enjoy and get satisfaction _____31_____ 」。

(2)四選項中只有(D)選項的「from」放入空格，才符合「get satisfaction from」的文法規定。

32. 題句：_____32_____ you have graduated from college, you will be spending a great amount of your time working

　　　　_____32_____ 從學校畢業後，你的大部份時間會是在工作

選項：(A) Once 一旦　(B) Would 決心　(C) Either 兩者任一　(D) Likewise 同樣

解析

(1)答題關鍵在「_____32_____ you have graduated from college」。

(2)四選項中只有(A)選項的「Once」放入空格，才是符合題意的文法規定。

33. 題句：_____33_____ are many parts of a job that you can enjoy.

　　　工作_____33_____許多你會喜歡的部份，

　　選項：(A) any 任何　(B) here 這裡　(C) there 那裡　(D) none 無一

解析

(1)答題關鍵在「are many parts of a job...」。

(2)四選項中只有(C)選項的「there」放入空格，才符合「there are」的文法規定。

34. 題句：很可能你無法_____34_____找到好工作

　　選項：(A) right on 就在　(B) right away 立刻　(C) right down 沿著　(D) right out 坦白

解析

(1)答題關鍵在「很可能你無法_____34_____找到好工作」。

(2)四選項中只有(B)選項的「right away」放入空格，才是符合題意的片語說法。

35. 題句：保持冷靜並給自己一個機會_____35_____工作裡你認為你喜歡的部份、

　　選項：(A) experience 體驗（原形動詞）　(B) experienced（過去式）　(C) experiencing（動名詞）　(D) experiential（形容詞）

解析

(1)答題關鍵在空格左邊的「to」一字。

(2)四選項中只有(A)選項的「experience」放入空格，才符合「to＋原形動詞」的文法規定。

▲閱讀下文，回答第 36-40 題

　　The Taipei International Flora Expo is the first international flower show in history held in the heart of a city. For such an international event, the ideal place would have been the Guandu Plain, _____36_____ is suitable for a show built around wetlands and paddy fields. Yet, it was impossible to acquire the massive lands Therefore, another option was to _____37_____ the public land and facilities around Yuan Shan Now, the expo has been created within parks that _____38_____ by urban areas. Although a _____39_____ urban area may not be an ideal location for a flower show, the "peaceful existence" of architecture and environment in Taipei has shown the way to an alternative model for such an event. It is the _____40_____ of parks and urban structures that forms a unique character for the expo. Some experts say that the Taipei show has created a model for flora expos in the future.

　　（台北花博使史上第一個在市中心舉辦的國際花展。對這樣的國際活動來說，理想的地方本會是關渡平原，_____36_____在那裡適合在濕地與稻田周遭建造花展場。然而，因無法獲得大塊土地。因此，另一選擇是在圓山附近_____37_____公

共土地和設備。現在，已在被都會區 ____38____ 的公園內闢建花博展覽區。雖然 ____39____ 都會區可能不是花展的理想位置，台北建築物的「和平共存」已經表現出這類活動的替代模式。它是由多個公園與都市結構的 ____39____ 。形成花博獨有的特色。）

36. 題句：____36____ is suitable for a show built around wetlands and paddy fields.

____36____ 在那裡適合在濕地與稻田周遭建造花展場。

選項：(A) what 什麼 (B) why 為什麼 (C) which 哪個 (D) when 什麼時候

解析

(1)答題關鍵在「____36____ is suitable for...」（適合～用途）。

(2)四選項中只有選(A)選項的「what」放入空格，才是符合「What is suitable for」的正確選項。

37. 題句：另一選擇是在圓山附近 ____37____ 公共土地和設備。

選項：(A) make off 逃走 (B) make over with 改造 (C) make use of 利用 (D) make out 看清楚

解析

(1)答題關鍵在「____37____ 公共土地和設備」。

(2)四選項中只有c選項的「利用」放入空格，才是符合「make use of」的片語說法。

38. 題句：已在被都會區 ____38____ 的公園內闢建花博展覽區。

選項：(A) surrounded 圍繞 (B) are surrounded 被圍繞 (C) are surrounding 正圍繞 (D) has surrounded 已經圍繞

解析

(1)答題關鍵在「被都會區 ____38____ 的公園內……」。

(2)四選項中只有(B)選項的「are surrounded」放入空格，才符合題意是被動語態的文法規定。

39. 題句：雖然 ____39____ 都會區可能不是花展的理想位置，

選項：(A) develop 開發 (B) developed 已開發 (C) development 名詞 (D) developer 開發者

解析

(1)答題關鍵在「____39____ 都會區可能不是」。

(2)四選項中只有(B)選項的「已開發」放入空格，才是符合題意的文法規定。

40. 題句：It is the ____40____ of parks and urban structures

它是由多個公園與都市結構的 ____40____

選項：(A) memorization 記憶 (B) education 教育 (C) destination 目的地 (D) combination 組合

解析

(1)答題關鍵在「多個公園與都市結構的＿＿＿＿40＿＿＿＿」。

(2)四選項中只有(D)選項的「combination」放入空格，才是符合題意的正確選項。

IV. 閱讀測驗

下面兩篇短文共有10題，每篇有5題，為41-50題，請閱讀短文後，選出最適當的答案。

▲閱讀下文，回答第 41-45 題

April 03, 2011　2011 年 4 月 03 日

Dear Sir / Madam, 親愛的先生／夫人，

　　Over the past 6 months, the service from the garbage collection truck has been very disappointing. We have complained to the truck driver, but he has done very little to solve the problems. Therefore, I am writing directly to your department to request your help.

　　在過去的 6 個月，垃圾車的服務非常令人失望。我們已經向卡車司機抱怨，但是幾乎毫無作為。因此，我直接寫信向貴部門請求協助。

　　Basically, there are two problems. The first is that the truck never follows the correct time schedule. Your notice says that garbage will be collected in our area from Monday to Friday at 6 p.m., but the truck always either arrives too early or too late. It has been as much as 15 minutes early and 25 minutes late. The second problem, which is more serious, is that the truck moves off too quickly. I have seen people running after the moving vehicle almost every time, making a disaster very likely. What if the person running were pregnant, disabled, or elderly?

　　基本上，有兩個問題。第 1 是卡車從未依時刻表準時清運垃圾。你們的通知單是說，我們這一區的垃圾運送時間是週一到週五的下午 6 點，但垃圾車不是太早或太晚到來。早到有時多達 15 分鐘，遲到更多達 25 分鐘。第 2 個問題更嚴重，是垃圾車只停一下下就開走，我幾乎每次都會看到有人跑著追行駛中的垃圾車。這樣很可能會造成傷害。如果跑的人是孕婦，殘障人士或年長者，怎麼辦？

　　As I mentioned at the beginning, we did express our concerns to the driver. The first time we spoke to him, he was very kind. He explained very patiently that the department was trying to make a better time schedule. Thereafter, he just started ignoring us. Honestly speaking, I felt this was very rude of him and unprofessional.

　　就像我一開始就提到的，我們向司機表示過我們的關心。我們第一次告訴他時，他很客氣。他耐心地解釋說，貴單位有意做一份較好的垃圾清運時刻表。但之後，他又開始不理會我們。老實說，我感到他這樣做很粗魯且不符專業。

　　If these problems continue, I am worried that residents will start dropping their trash on the corner of the street. Therefore, for both the safety and health of everybody, I hope that you will look into this matter as soon as possible.

　　如果這些問題繼續發生，我擔心居民會開始到處亂丟垃圾。因此，為每人的安全

和健康，我希望你將看儘快處理此事。

您忠誠的，

蔡佳文

tsai.ch@pmail.com tsai.ch@pmail.com

41. What is the purpose of this letter?

（這封信的目的是什麼？）

(A) To find out about recycling garbage. 查明回收垃圾。

(B) To complain about a service problem. 有關服務問題的客訴。

(C) To apologize for a late delivery. 為延遲交貨道歉。

(D) To thank a government department. 感謝政府部門。

解析

根據整封信函內容的敘述，(B) 選項的「有關服務問題的客訴。」才是正確選項。

42. When does the garbage truck arrive?

（垃圾車什麼時候抵達？）

(A) Almost half an hour late sometimes. 有時幾乎會晚到半小時。

(B) On time, as per schedule. 按時間表準時到。

(C) Always on the weekend. 總是在週末才到。

(D) Monday to Friday, early in the morning. 星期一到星期五一大早。

解析

從答題關鍵的「早到有時多達 15 分鐘，遲到更多達 25 分鐘」可看出，(A) 選項的「有時幾乎會晚到半小時。」才是正確選項。

43. According to Ms. Tsai, how did the driver treat them later on?

（根據蔡女士說法，司機後來的態度如何？）

(A) Reasonably. 講理。

(B) Impolitely. 粗魯

(C) Gently. 溫柔。

(D) Professionally. 專業。

解析

從答題關鍵的「老實說，我感到他這樣做很粗魯且不符專業。」可看出，(B) 選項的「粗魯」才是正確選項。

44. What does Ms. Tsai hope the department would do?

（蔡女士希望有關單位怎麼做？）

(A) Compliment the driver. 恭維司機。

(B) Ignore Ms. Tsai's previous letter. 忽視蔡女士的前封信。

(C) Investigate the issue. 調查問題。

(D) Buy a new garbage disposal truck. 買一輛新的垃圾車。

解析

從答題關鍵的「為每人的安全和健康，我希望你將看儘快處理此事。」可看出，(C) 選項的「調查問題」才是正確選項。

45. Which problem is NOT mentioned in the letter?

（下列哪一項沒在信中提及？）

(A) The garbage truck leaves too soon. 垃圾車太快離開。

(B) Accidents could easily happen. 事故容易發生。

(C) Trash will be dumped on the street corner. 垃圾會被到處亂倒。

(D) Residents are already dying of poor health. 居民因健康不好快死了。

解析

根據整篇文章內容，(D) 選項的「居民因健康不好快死了。」才是正確選項。

▲閱讀下文，回答第 46-50 題

Time magazine has honored a Taiwanese vegetable vendor Chen Shu-chu as one of the 100 most influential people of 2010. Chen was also selected by Forbes magazine as one of the 48 heroes of philanthropy _ from Asia. Out of her modest income, she has donated NT$10 million to charity over the years, including a children's fund, construction of a library at a school, and construction of the local orphanage, where she also gives financial support to three children.

「時代」雜誌賦予榮譽給一位在台灣菜販陳淑珠，成為 2010 年前 100 位最有影響力的人。陳女士也被富比士雜誌選為亞洲前 48 位最仁慈的人。從她不算多的收入裡，多年來她已經捐贈了一千萬新台幣給慈善機構，包括一個兒童基金會，學校圖書館的建設和本地育幼院的興建。她也財力支助三位育幼院童。

Everyday around 3 a.m., Chen shows up at the wholesale market to pick fresh produce. At4 a.m., her stall opens for business, and customers are already waiting. She came from a poor family and was forced to drop out of school at the age of 13 to support her six brothers and sisters following the death of her mother. Her mother died in labor and her brother died of illness because her family could not afford medical care. She took over her mother's vegetable stand and has been selling vegetables at Central Market in Taitung since 1963.

每天清晨 3 點左右，陳女就會去批發市場批貨。她的攤位在上午 4 點始叫賣，顧客早已等候多時。她來自窮苦家庭，13 歲母親過世後，被迫輟學工作來幫助 6 個兄弟姊妹。她的母親過勞而死，她的兄弟由於付不起醫藥費而病死。她接手母親的蔬菜攤

位，且從 1963 年起就一直在台東的中央市場賣菜。

She makes a small profit of five to ten NT dollars on each sale. The nickels and dimes she earns are the basis for her charitable giving. Many poor students and families whom she has never met have had their lives changed by her generosity. Chen Shu-chu is merely a common grocery vendor. She is not famous. The 61-year-old once told a newspaper that money is not useful unless it is given to those in need. Her story encourages many people that even though they may not be rich, their small donations may come as a great help to some less fortunate people.

她每賣一次青菜只賺 5 到 10 元台幣。所賺的蠅頭小利就是捐款的基礎。許多從未謀面但受她資助的人，生活有了改善。陳女士只是一名平凡的菜販，她並不出名。這位 61 歲的好人有一次告訴記者說，錢不實用除非它給了需要的人。她故事鼓勵很多人，即使本身並不富有，但他們的小額捐款對不幸的人幫助很大。

46. What is the best title for this passage?
（本文的最佳標題是什麼？）
(A) The Poor Family 不幸的家庭
(B) How to Save Money 怎樣省錢
(C) The Remarkable Woman 卓越的婦女
(D) A Famous Market 一個著名的市場

解析

根據本文內容，(C) 選項的「卓越的婦女」才是正確選項。

47. Chen has donated for various causes over the years, except _____ .
（陳以多種原因捐贈多年，除了 _____ 。）
(A) construction of a library 一座圖書館的建設
(B) a medical center 一個醫療中心
(C) a children's fund 一項孩子的專款
(D) support of children 孩子的支援

解析

根據文章「捐贈了一千萬新台幣給慈善機構，包括一個兒童基金會，學校圖書館的建設和本地育幼院的興建。她也財力支助三位育幼院童」。(B) 選項的「一個醫療中心」才是文章沒提到之事的正確選項。

48. How long has Chen been selling vegetables at the market?
（陳女士在市場賣菜多少年了？）
(A) For nearly fifty years. 差不多 50 年。
(B) From 2010. 從 2010。

(C) Since the age of forty-eight. 從 48 歲起。

(D) Between five to ten. 5 到 10 年之間。

解析

從答題關鍵的「她接手母親的蔬菜攤位，且從 1963 年起就一直在台東的中央市場賣菜。」可看出，(A) 選項的「差不多 50 年」才是正確選項。

49. According to the passage, which of the following is true?

　（根據本文，如下內容哪項為真？）

(A) Time magazine selected Chen as one of the 48 heroes from Asia.

　《時代》雜誌選擇陳為來自亞洲的 48 名英雄之一。

(B) Her stall opens for business at 3 a.m., when there are lots of customers waiting.

　她的攤位在上午 3 點開始做生意，而那時已有多人排隊等候了。

(C) She has changed many poor people's lives by her generosity.

　透過她的慷慨改變很多窮人的生活。

(D) Forbes magazine honored Chen as one of the 100 most influential people of 2010.

　富比士雜誌尊敬陳女士為 2010 年最有影響力的百人名單之一。

解析

根據文章內容，(C) 選項的「透過她的慷慨改變很多窮人的生活。」才是正確選項。

50. Her story tells us that ＿＿＿＿＿＿ .

　（她的故事告訴我們 ＿＿＿＿＿＿ 。）

(A) we can devote our time to professional works

　我們能專心致力於專業的工作

(B) people can sell a variety of fresh produce in the market

　人們在市場能出售多種新鮮的農產品

(C) if a vegetable vendor can be so selfless, so can we

　如果一個賣菜的人能夠如此無私，我們也能。

(D) people from a poor family will be poor for the rest of their lives

　出生於貧窮家庭的人會一輩子貧窮

解析

根據文章內容，(C) 選項的「如果一個賣菜的人能夠如此無私，我們也能。」才是正確選項。

統測（四技二專）

（97～100年統測）

97 年統測（四技二專考試）

I. 字彙測驗

第 1-10 題，每題均有一個劃底線的字，請在四個選項中，選出一個與劃底線的字意義最接近的答案。第 11-15 題，請選擇一個最適當的答案，以完成該句。

1. If you want to buy some food, you'd better <u>hurry</u>. The store will be closed in ten minutes.
   （你要買東西的話要趕快。再 10 分鐘商店就要打烊了。）
   (A) tremble 顫抖　(B) hurt 傷痛　(C) vanish 消失　(D) rush 快速

   解析

   (1)先看底線字的中文意思為「趕快」。
   (2)在四個選項中，只有(D)項的「快速」才是與底線字意思最接近的正確選項。

2. Overweight, we are <u>advised</u> to pay close attention to our daily diet.
   （過重了，我們建議更要注意飲食。）
   (A) liked 喜歡　(B) related 相關的　(C) suggested 建議　(D) treated 對待

   解析

   (1)先看底線字的中文意思為「勸告」。
   (2)在四個選項中，只有(C)項的「建議」才是與底線字意思最接近的正確選項。

3. Research has shown that loneliness is <u>harmful</u> to health.
   （研究顯示寂寞有害健康。）
   (A) bad 不好的　(B) deep 深的　(C) free 自由　(D) heavy 重的

   解析

   (1)先看底線字的中文意思為「有害的」。
   (2)在四個選項中，只有(A)項的「不好的」才是與底線字意思最接近的正確選項。

4. The coach was <u>proud</u> because his basketball team won the championship.
   （球隊贏得冠軍，教練引以為傲。）
   (A) absent 缺席　(B) famous 著名　(C) pleased 愉快　(D) worried 擔心

解析

(1)先看底線字的中文意思為「為傲」。

(2)在四個選項中，只有(C)項的「愉快」才是與底線字意思最接近的正確選項。

5. The tropical weather in Taiwan makes it possible to grow <u>various</u> types of fruits such as watermelons, bananas, and pineapples.

（臺灣的熱帶型氣候可生長西瓜香蕉及鳳梨等水果。）

　　(A) different 不同的　(B) whole 全部　(C) general 一般的　(D) special 特別的

解析

(1)先看底線字的中文意思為「各種各樣的」。

(2)在四個選項中，只有(A)項的「不同的」才是與底線字意思最接近的正確選項。

6. Because of the heavy rain, Mr. Johnson drove down the hill very slowly and <u>cautiously</u>.

（由於大雨，江森先生開車下山時很慢很小心。）

　　(A) carefully 小心地　(B) naturally 自然地　(C) quickly 快速地　(D) entirely 全部的

解析

(1)先看底線字的中文意思為「小心地」。

(2)在四個選項中，只有(A)項的「小心地」才是與底線字意思最接近的正確選項。

7. The most <u>frequently</u> used service on the Internet is electronic mail (e-mail), which is fast and convenient.

（網路上最常用的服務是電子郵件，又快又方便。）

　　(A) easily 容易　(B) recently 最近　(C) commonly 一般的　(D) possibly 可能的

解析

(1)先看底線字的中文意思為「常常地」。

(2)在四個選項中，只有(C)項的「通常地」才是與底線字意思最接近的正確選項。

8. Some people prefer to follow a predictable <u>pattern</u> in their life: school, then marriage and children.

（有些人一生中較喜歡用可預知的模式做事：求學、結婚、生小孩。）

　　(A) design 設計　(B) turn 轉動　(C) rate 比率　(D) review 再檢查

解析

(1)先看底線字的中文意思為「模式」。

(2)在四個選項中，只有(A)項的「設計」才是與底線字意思最接近的正確選項。

9. Greenpeace, which aims to protect the environment, is an international <u>institution</u>.

（綠色和平，目的在保護環境，是一個國際組織。）

(A) alternative 選擇　(B) organization 組織　(C) expansion 擴展　(D) invention 發明

解析

(1)先看底線字的中文意思為「機構」。

(2)在四個選項中，只有(B)項的「組織」才是與底線字意思最接近的正確選項。

10. The player's <u>outstanding</u> performance won him a gold medal in the Olympic Games.

（運動員傑出的表現贏得一面奧運金牌。）

　(A) excellent 優秀的　(B) proper 適當的　(C) accidental 意外的　(D) allergic 過敏

解析

(1)先看底線字的中文意思為「傑出的」。

(2)在四個選項中，只有(A)項的「優秀的」才是與底線字意思最接近的正確選項。

11. With the population _____ day by day, more and more space is needed for public activities.

　（人口一天一天 _____ ，更多的空間需要用來做公共活動。）

　(A) observing 觀察　(B) attracting 吸引　(C) examining 檢驗　(D) increasing 增加

解析

(1)答題關鍵在題目空格左方的「一天一天」。

(2)四個選項中，只有選(D)項的「增加」，才可有意義連成「人口一天一天增加，更多的空間……」。

12. Many Allied airmen _____ in World War II escaped from German prison camps successfully.

　（二次大戰有許多被捕的盟軍空軍人員成功的逃出德國的戰俘營。）

　(A) captured 被捕　(B) murdered 謀殺　(C) realized 體會　(D) compared 比較

解析

(1)答題關鍵在題目空格左、右方的「與」

(2)四個選項中，只有選(A)項的「被捕」，才可有意義連成「許多被捕的盟軍空軍人員……」。

13. Crime is growing at a rapid rate, _____ in urban areas.

　（犯罪率快速增加 _____ 都會區。）

　(A) cheerfully 愉快地　(B) appropriately 適當地　(C) reasonably 合理的　(D) especially 尤其是

解析

(1)答題關鍵在題目空格右方的「都會區」。

(2)四個選項中，只有選(D)項的「尤其是」，才可有意義連成「……快速增加尤其是都會區」。

14. Jane ＿＿＿＿＿＿＿＿ to the waiter that her meal was cold.

（珍向服務員 ＿＿＿＿＿＿＿＿ 她的食物是冷的。）

(A) happened 發生　(B) celebrated 慶祝　(C) complained 抱怨　(D) admired 欽佩

解析

(1)答題關鍵在題目空格左、右方的「珍」與「向服務員」。

(2)四個選項中，只有選(C)項的「抱怨」，才可有意義連成「珍向服務員……」。

15. The famous singer's wonderful voice made a deep ＿＿＿＿＿＿＿＿ on the audience.

（著名歌者的美妙聲音使觀眾留下很深的 ＿＿＿＿＿＿＿＿ 。）

(A) progress 進步　(B) impression 印象　(C) promise 承諾　(D) introduction 介紹

解析

(1)答題關鍵在題目空格左、右方的「與」

(2)四個選項中，只有選 (B) 項的「印象」，才可有意義連成「美妙聲音使觀眾留下很深的印象」。

II. 對話測驗

第 16-25 題，請依照對話內容選出一個最適當的答案，使其成為有意義的對話。

16. Jenny：　　I'll take a pair of jeans in this style.

（這款式我買兩件。）

Salesclerk：Great! Will that be all?

（很好，就買這些嗎？）

Jenny：　　Yes, that's all.

（是，就這些。）

Salesclerk：＿＿＿＿＿＿＿＿

Jenny：　　Cash, please.

（付現金。）

(A) I'll think it over and let you know. 我考慮後再告訴你　(B) I am very busy. Maybe tomorrow. 我很忙 也許明天吧　(C) Would you like to pay by cash or credit card? 妳付現或刷卡？　(D) To be honest, I am not very good at it. 坦白說，我不太懂這些

解析

(1)答題關鍵在第 句。

(2)在四個選項中，第四句只有選(C)項的「妳付現或刷卡？」，第五句才會接著說「付現金」。

17. Tony：　Would you like to get together tomorrow?

（妳明天想見個面嗎？）

Sandy：OK. What would you like to do?

（好。你想做些什麼？）

Tony：＿＿＿＿＿＿＿

Sandy：That sounds good. Let's go!

（太好了。我們走吧！）

(A) Are you with me so far? 你還在聽嗎？　(B) How about seeing a movie? 去看場電影如何？　(C) How would you like it? 你喜歡嗎？　(D) What did you do next? 那你後來怎麼做？

解析

(1)答題關鍵在第四句。

(2)在四個選項中，第三句只有選 (B) 項的「去看場電影如何」，第四句才會接著說「太好了。我們走吧」。

18. Teresa：　Could you give me an extra blanket?

（可以再給我一條毯子嗎？）

Attendant：＿＿＿＿＿＿＿

Teresa：　Thank you very much.

（非常謝謝。）

Attendant：You're welcome.

（不客氣。）

(A) See you tomorrow. 明天見。　(B) Sure, here you are. 好的，在這兒。　(C) I beg your pardon. 請再說一遍。　(D) I don't think so. 我不這麼想。

解析

(1)答題關鍵在第一句。

(2)在四個選項中，第二句只有選 (B) 項的「好的，在這兒」，這才是回應第一句的「可以再給我一條毯子嗎」。

19. Judy：　I hear you have a new girl friend.

（聽說你有新女友？）

Mike：Yes. Her name is Amy, and she is gorgeous!

（有。她名叫艾咪，她太可愛了！）

Judy：　Really? ＿＿＿＿＿＿＿

Mike：She's tall with red hair.

（她個子高還有一頭紅髮。）

Judy：　And how old is she?

（她多大年紀？）

Mike：I don't know. She won't tell me.

（不知道。她不告訴我。）

(A) Is she outgoing? 她外向嗎？　(B) Is she intelligent? 她聰明嗎？　(C) What does she look like? 她長得如何？　(D) It looks good on her. 她穿起來很好看。

解析

(1)答題關鍵在第四句。

(2)在四個選項中，第三句只有選 (C) 項的「她長得如何」，第四句才會接著說「她個子高還有一頭紅髮」。

20. Andrew：You look pale. Are you all right?

（妳臉色蒼白，不舒服嗎？）

Candy：　I don't feel well. I'm not sure what's wrong with me.

（我不舒服。也不曉得怎麼了。）

Andrew：＿＿＿＿＿＿＿

Candy：　You're right. Thanks for your advice.

（妳說對了。謝謝妳的忠告。）

(A) That's a wonderful idea! 那主意很棒！　(B) You should take a rest. 妳應該多休息。

(C) Is there anything I can do for you? 我幫得上忙嗎？　(D) I think I'm going to be sick. 我快生病了。

解析

(1)答題關鍵在第四句。

(2)在四個選項中，第三句只有選 (B) 項的「妳應該多休息」，第四句才會接著說「妳說對了……」。

21. Patient：I feel very dizzy and sick. And my stomach hurts.

（我又暈又病，我的肚子也痛。）

Doctor：I see. How long have you felt like this?

（妳這樣的感覺多久了？）

Patient：＿＿＿＿＿＿＿

Doctor：When did you eat last night?

（妳昨晚幾點吃飯？）

Patient：Around ten.

（十點左右。）

(A) It hurts a lot. 很痛。　(B) It is a dull pain. 隱隱作痛。　(C) For two days. 已兩天了。

(D) I am ahead of the times. 我提前了。

解析

(1)答題關鍵在第二句。

(2)在四個選項中，第三句只有選 (C) 項的「已兩天了」，才是回應第二句的「妳這樣的感覺多久了」。

22. Ann： I see you're washing the windows.
（你在洗窗子呀。）

Joan：Yes. They have not been washed for a long time.
（好久沒洗了。）

Ann：_____

Joan：Sure, if you don't mind.
（好呀，如你不介意的話。）

Ann：No, not at all.
（不會的。）

(A) I don't know yet. 還不知道。　(B) I appreciate that. 很感謝。　(C) For what date? 哪一天？　(D) Need any help? 需要幫忙嗎？

解析

(1)答題關鍵在第四句。

(2)在四個選項中，第三 句只有選 (D) 項的「需要幫忙嗎」，第四句才會接著說「好呀，如你不介意的話」。

23. Helen：I'd like to return this hat.
（我來退這頂帽子。）

Clerk：_____

Helen：It's too old-fashioned.
（樣子太老式了。）

Clerk：Would you like to exchange it for a more stylish one?
（要不要換一頂新一點款式？）

Helen：No, I'd like a refund, please.
（不，我要退錢。）

(A) We'll be happy to see you again. 很高興以後再見到你。　(B) What seems to be the problem with it? 有什麼不妥嗎？　(C) Which one do you like? 妳喜歡哪一個？　(D) I'd like to expand the company. 我想擴大營業。

解析

(1)答題關鍵在第三句。

(2)在四個選項中，第二句只有選 (B) 項的「有什麼不妥嗎」，第三句才會接著說「樣子太老式了」。

24. Mary：What's the matter, Joe? You look upset.

（喬，發生了什麼事？你看來不愉快。）

Joe：　I lost my job today.

（我今天失業了。）

Mary：＿＿＿＿＿＿＿

(A) You are missing the point. 妳會錯意了。　(B) I am just kidding. 我開玩笑的。　(C) I am sorry to hear that. 很遺憾聽到這件事。　(D) It's very nice of you to say so. 謝謝你這麼說。

解析

(1)答題關鍵在第二句。

(2)在四個選項中，第三句只有選 (C) 項的「很遺憾聽到這件事」，這才是回應第二句的「我今天失業了」。

25. Woman：　　　I'd like to order breakfast, please.

（我要點早餐了。）

Room Service：May I have your name and room number?

（請告訴我妳的名字與房號？）

Woman：　　　Helen Brown. Room 12.

（海倫・布朗。12 號房。）

Room Service：Ms. Brown, ＿＿＿＿＿＿＿

（布朗太太，＿＿＿＿＿＿＿）

Woman：　　　Some toast and a tomato juice.

（幾片土司與一杯番茄汁。）

(A) what would you like today? 妳今天要點什麼？　(B) is everything OK? 一切沒事吧？

(C) when do you want that? 妳什麼時候要？　(D) I wonder if I could have some of that. 我可要一點那個嗎？

解析

(1)答題關鍵在第五句。

(2)在四個選項中，第四句只有選 (A) 項的「妳今天要點什麼」，第五句才會接著說「幾片土司與一杯番茄汁」。

III. 綜合測驗

下面三篇短文共有十五個空格，為第 26-40 題，每題有四個選項，請依各篇短文文意，選出一個最適合該空格的答案。

It is becoming increasingly urgent for us to know our family's medical history, as more and more diseases are found to have genetic ____26____ . Researchers are working to isolate all of the body's 50,000 to 100,000 genes and ____27____ them to specific diseases. It may be only a matter of time before scientists ____28____ the genes that cause such common illnesses as diabetes and high blood pressure. ____29____ unfortunately, time is not on our side. Hereditary diseases are a ____30____ potentially affecting many people in the world.

（知道我們的家庭病歷正變得越來越急迫，越來越多的疾病被發現有遺傳學的 ____26____ 。研究人員研究要分離人體的 5 萬到 10 萬個基因並且與特定的疾病做 ____27____ 。科學家要 ____28____ 由基因所引起像糖尿病和高血壓這麼普遍的疾病，應該只是時間問題。____29____ 令人遺憾，時間不在我們這邊。遺傳的疾病是在世界上侵襲很多人的一種潛在 ____30____ 。）

26. 題句：as more and more diseases are found to have genetic ____26____ .
    選項：(A) genes 基因　(B) links 連結　(C) bacteria 細菌　(D) pains 疼痛

    解析
    (1)答題關鍵在題目空格左邊的「to have genetic」。
    (2)四個選項中，只有選 (B) 項的「links」放入空格，意指與基因有關，才是有意義連成整句的正確選項。

27. 題句：Researchers are working to isolate all of the body's 50,000 to 100,000 genes and ____27____ them to specific diseases.
    選項：(A) deal 交易　(B) experiment 實驗　(C) conduct 引導　(D) match 作比對

    解析
    (1)答題關鍵在題目空格右邊的「them to specific diseases」。
    (2)四個選項中，只有選(D)項的「match」放入空格，才是有意義連成整句的正確選項。

28. 題句：It may be only a matter of time before scientists ____28____ the genes that cause such common illnesses as diabetes and high blood pressure
    選項：(A) favor 認同　(B) locate 找出　(C) fasten 綁緊　(D) depend 依賴

    解析
    (1)答題關鍵在題目空格右邊的「the genes that cause such common illnesses」。
    (2)四個選項中，只有選(B)項的「locate」放入空格，才是有意義連成整句的正確選項。

**29.題句：the genes that cause such common illnesses as diabetes and high blood pressure. ____29____ unfortunately, time is not on our side.

選項：(A) But 但是　(B) Although 雖然　(C) Even if 即使　(D) Now that 既然

解析

(1)本題是考連接詞，所以答題關鍵在空格左右邊的兩個子句。

(2)依題意，四個選項中只有選(A)項的「but」當連接詞才符合文法，才是正確選項。

30. 題句：Hereditary diseases are a ＿＿＿30＿＿＿ potentially affecting many people in the world.

選項：(A) number 數字　(B) piece 一片　(C) duty 職責　(D) crisis 危機

解析

(1)答題關鍵在題目空格左邊的「Hereditary diseases are a」。

(2)四個選項中，只有選(D)項的「crisis」放入空格，才是有意義連成整句的正確選項。

In Taiwan, setting off sky lanterns is now considered a custom at Lantern Festival. The custom came from the Han people ＿＿＿31＿＿＿ wanted to send a peaceful message to their families and friends. ＿＿＿32＿＿＿ the first Han people came to Taiwan, they didn't get along with the aborigines. They had many ＿＿＿33＿＿＿ over the land. The aborigines accused the Han people ＿＿＿34＿＿＿ stealing their land. So, they fought with each other and some people died. Later some Han people began to learn to live with the aborigines. They even moved up to the mountains and ＿＿＿35＿＿＿ a village there. Every year when those Han people living in the mountains wanted to send messages to their families and friends living on the plains, they set off sky lanterns.

（在臺灣，放天燈已經是元宵節的習俗。該習俗來自漢人，＿＿＿31＿＿＿ 他們想把平安的訊息傳遞給他們的家人和朋友。＿＿＿32＿＿＿ 第一批漢人來臺灣時，他們與原住民相處不好。他們為土地發生了多次 ＿＿＿33＿＿＿。原住民 ＿＿＿34＿＿＿ 漢人偷他們的土地。因此，他們彼此戰鬥，也有些傷亡。之後有些漢人開始學習與原住民相處。他們甚至遷往山上也 ＿＿＿35＿＿＿ 村落。每年，那些住山上的漢人想要傳遞訊息給居住平地的親友，他們就放天燈。）

**31.題句：The custom came from the Han people ＿＿＿31＿＿＿ wanted to send a peaceful message to their families and friends

選項：(A) who 誰　(B) while 當　(C) what 什麼　(D) where 哪裡

解析

(1)答題關鍵在空格右邊的「wanted」一字，因它是動詞，其前須放主格的關係代名詞。

(2)四個選項中，只有選(A)項的「who」才是主格關係代名詞，才是正確選項。

**32.題句：＿＿＿32＿＿＿ the first Han people came to Taiwan, they didn't get along with the aborigines.

選項：(A) When 當……　(B) Although 雖然　(C) So 如此　(D) If 假設

解析

依題意，只有選(A)項的連接詞 when 才是正確選項。看了題句的中譯就更清楚。

(1)答題關鍵在題目空格右邊的「the first Han people came to Taiwan」。

(2)四個選項中，只有選(A)項的「When」放入空格，才是有意義連成整句的正確選項。

33. 題句：They had many _____33_____ over the land.

選項：(A) agreements 同意　(B) ancestors 祖先　(C) robots 機器人　(D) quarrels 爭吵

解析

(1)答題關鍵在題目空格左、右邊的「many」。

(2)四個選項中，只有選(D)項的「quarrels」放入空格，才是有意義連成整句的正確選項。

**34.題句：The aborigines accused the Han people _____34_____ stealing their land.

選項：(A) in 在……之內　(B) at 在……地點　(C) of ……的　(D) by 被

解析

(1)答題關鍵在 accused 一字，本題是考片語 accused ~of~ （＝accused someone of something 指控某人做某事）。

(2)四個選項中，只有(C)項的「of」才是符合上述片語用法的正確選項。

**35.題句：They even moved up to the mountains and _____34_____ a village there.

選項：(A) forms 現在式　(B) to form 不定詞　(C) forming 動名詞　(D) formed 過去式

解析

答題關鍵在過去式動詞「moved」一字，其後要選(D)項的過去式動詞 formed，才是符合對等連接詞「and」前後兩子句動詞時態一致的文法規定，才是正確選項。

Many great colonists made an impact on American history. _____36_____ them was Benjamin Franklin, who left his mark as a writer, inventor, scientist and statesman.

Franklin was born in Boston in 1706, in a very religious household. _____37_____ he had less than two years of formal education, he enjoyed learning and read a lot of books. At age 12, he began writing articles for a newspaper, and that made _____38_____ famous as a young writer.

In 1723, Franklin ran away to Philadelphia, _____39_____ he started his own newspaper. He was very active in the Philadelphia community. He operated a bookstore and _____40_____ postmaster. He also helped to establish a library, a fire company, a college, an insurance company and a hospital.

（很多偉大的殖民地居民對美國歷史產生了影響。他們_____36_____就有身為作家，發明家，科學家和政治家的班哲明·法蘭克林。

法蘭克林 1706 年出生於波士頓一個篤信宗教的家庭。_____37_____他只有不到兩年的正式教育，他喜愛學習並且閱讀很多書。在 12 歲的時候，他開始替報社寫文章，而使_____38_____以年輕作家成名。

在 1723 年，法蘭克林離家到費城，_____39_____他開始辦報紙。他在費城社區

非常活躍。他經營一家書店，＿＿＿40＿＿＿為郵政局長。他也幫助成立一家圖書館、一個消防隊、一所學院、一家保險公司和一所醫院。）

**36.題句：Many great colonists made an impact on American history. ＿＿＿36＿＿＿ them was Benjamin Franklin,

　　　選項：(A) Inside 內部　(B) Among 在……之中　(C) Within……之內　(D) Beside 在……旁

解析

(1)答題關鍵在空格右邊的「them」。

(2)四個選項中，只有選(B)項的「among」才是符合文法的正確選項。

**37.題句：＿＿＿37＿＿＿ he had less than two years of formal education, he enjoyed learning and read a lot of books.

　　　選項：(A) For 為了　(B) If 假如　(C) Perhaps 也許　(D) Although 雖然

解析

(1)答題關鍵在題句的兩個子句：he had less than... 與 he enjoyed learning...。

(2)四個選項中，只有選(D)項的的連接詞「although」才是符合題意與文法規定的正確選項。

**38.題句：he began writing articles for a newspaper, and that made ＿＿＿38＿＿＿ famous as a young writer.

　　　選項：(A) it 它　(B) him 他　(C) them 他們　(D) her 她

解析

(1)答題關鍵在空格左右方的「made ...famous」。

(2)題句一開頭就看出主詞是「he」因此在四個選項中，只有選(B)項的「him」才符「he 的受格是 him」的文法規定。才是正確選項。

**39.題句：Franklin ran away to Philadelphia, ＿＿＿39＿＿＿ he started his own newspaper.

　　　選項：(A) who 誰　(B) which 哪一　(C) where 哪裡　(D) what 什麼

解析

(1)答題關鍵在空格左邊的前述詞也是地方副詞的 Philadelphia 一字。

(2)四個選項中，只有選(C)項、同時也是表示地方的關係副詞 where 才是符合文法的正確選項。

**40.題句：He operated a bookstore and ＿＿＿40＿＿＿ postmaster.

　　　選項：(A) names 取名（現在式）　(B) naming（動名詞）　(C) was named（被動語態）
　　　　　　(D) had named（過去完成式）

解析

(1)答題關鍵在過去式動詞「operated」一字，其後要選(C)項的過去式被動語態 was named，才是

符合對等連接詞「and」前後兩子句動詞時態一致的文法規定，才是正確選項。

⑵考生請注意不可選⒟項的過去完成式 had named，因過去完成式不是被動語態，這兩者的時態公式不同，前者是 had + PP 而後者則是 be + pp。

⑶依題意，開了書店被命名為……，當然要用⒞項的被動語態 was named 才正確。

IV. 閱讀測驗

下面兩篇短文，文後各附 5 個問題，為第 41-50 題，閱讀短文後，請選出每題最適當的答案。

A young man was recently murdered in an apartment in Taipei. The police found no clues except for one fingerprint on the wall. Usually, finding the owner of a fingerprint would take several days or even months because there are millions of fingerprints in the files. In this case, however, the police found the murderer in just a few hours because they had a powerful helper - a computer. The computer compared the fingerprint on the wall with all the fingerprints in the files and told the police whom the fingerprint belonged to.

Computers can store large amounts of information. In a few seconds, they can give us the information stored in them. In one second, computers can do millions of calculations. Through the computer network, we can send information to a faraway place in a moment.

Computers are used in many other situations today. At home, we use small, simple computers to control the washing machine or the microwave oven. At the supermarket, computers read the labels on products and work out the bills. In the library, a computer can tell you, in a second, if a book is there. Many schools use computers to teach students. People may even use computers to make friends on the BBS.

Many people believe that computers will become as smart as or even smarter than human beings and that they will do everything for us. If this happens, what will you do to pass the time? Don't worry. You'll have a lot of computer games.

（一個年輕人最近在臺北的一棟公寓裡被謀殺。警方除了在牆上發現一個指紋外，沒有其他線索。要找出指紋是誰的會花費幾天或甚至幾個月，因為在警方檔案裡有數百萬枚指紋。在本案，然而，警察在僅僅幾小時就找到凶手，因為他們有一個強有力的幫手——一臺電腦。電腦比對牆上的指紋與檔案裡的全部指紋，就告知警察指紋是誰的。

電腦能儲存大數量的訊息。在幾秒之後，它們能給我們儲存在內的訊息。一秒鐘之內，電腦能做出數百萬次的計算。透過電腦網，我們就能馬上能把訊息送到一個遙遠的地方。

電腦今天被用在很多不同的地方。在家，我們使用小、簡單的電腦控制洗衣機或者微波爐。在超市，電腦會讀產品上的條碼並且打出價單。 在圖書館裡，電腦只花一秒鐘就知道這本書在不在。很多學校使用電腦教學。人們甚至可用電腦在 BBS 網上交朋友。

很多人相信電腦將變得和人一樣或更聰明，他們將為我們做所有事情。如果是這樣，

你將做什麼消磨時光？不要擔心，你將會有很多電腦遊戲可玩。）

41. Without the help of the computer, how long does it usually take to find the owner of a fingerprint?

如果沒有電腦的幫助，通常找到指紋所有人要多久時間？

(A) A few minutes. 幾分鐘。　　(B) A few seconds. 幾秒。

(C) A few hours. 幾小時。　　(D) Several days or even months. 幾天或者甚至幾月。

解析

從答題關鍵的「Usually, finding the owner of a fingerprint would take several days or even months」可看出，(D)項的「Several days or even months」才是正確選項。

42. Why could the computer help the police find the murderer so fast?

（電腦為什麼能幫助警方如此迅速地找到凶手？）

(A) Because it could read the labels on products.

因為它能讀產品上的條碼。

(B) Because it helped the police find the person to whom the fingerprint belonged.

因為它幫警方找到指紋所有人。

(C) Because it had a lot of games.

因為它有很多比賽。

(D) Because it could calculate very quickly the number of fingerprints stored in the files.

因為它能非常快速的比對電腦的內存資料。

解析

從答題關鍵的「The computer compared the fingerprint on the wall with all the fingerprints in the files and told the police whom the fingerprint belonged to.」可看出，(B)項的「Because it helped the police find the person to whom the fingerprint belonged.」才是正確選項。

43. Which of the following is the topic sentence of the third paragraph?

（哪一項是本文第3段內容的主題？）

(A) Computers are used in many other situations today.

電腦今天被用在很多其他地方。

(B) At the supermarket, computers read the labels on products and work out the bills.

在超市，電腦讀產品上的條碼並打出帳單。

(C) In the library, a computer can tell you , in a second, if a book is there.

在資料庫裡，電腦在一秒鐘就能告訴你那本書在不在。

(D) Many schools use computers to teach students.

很多學校使用電腦教學。

從答題關鍵的「Computers are used in many other situations today.」可看出，(A) 項的「Computers are used in many other situations today.」才是正確選項。

44. According to the passage, which of the following statements is NOT true?

（根據本文，下列哪一項不屬實？）

(A) At home, computers can help us control some machine.

在家，電腦能幫助我們控制一些機器。

(B) At the supermarket, computers can help us calculate the bills efficiently.

在超市，電腦能幫助我們有效率地計算帳單。

(C) People may use computers to make friends.

人們可使用電腦交朋友。

(D) Computers can replace all the librarians.

電腦能替換全部的圖書館管理員。

解析

看完本文內容都沒提到電腦能替換全部的圖書館管理員之事。因此，(D) 項的「Computers can replace all the librarians」才是不實說法的正確選項。

45. Which of the following can best describe the main idea of this passage?

（下列內容哪一項最能描述本文的主題？）

(A) Finding the owner of a fingerprint is difficult.

發現指紋所有人很困難。

(B) Computers can give us a lot of information.

電腦能給我們很多資料。

(C) We can send information to a faraway place in a minute.

我們能馬上把訊息傳送到遙遠的地方。

(D) Computers are very useful in our daily lives.

電腦在我們的日常生活過程中非常實用。

解析

看完本文內容，可看出 (D) 項的「Computers are very useful in our daily lives.」才是正確選項。

The Retired Senior Volunteer Program (RSVP) offers those aged 55 and older a meaningful life through community volunteer service. Volunteers donate their time and energy regularly to neighborhood watch programs, to helping people recover from natural disasters, and to providing transportation for doctors' appointments, etc. In fact, plenty of other service opportunities exist for RSVP such as visiting nursing home residents, helping in senior nutrition centers, providing service at civic events, serving in health care institutions, and serving at public libraries. The rewards of being a volunteer are countless. For example, each year RSVP volunteers are recognized with a special banquet in **their** honor. The recognition also provides a time for the volunteers to gather together and enjoy a variety of entertainments. Research shows that volunteering promotes physical and psychological well-being. During and after volunteering, 95 percent of people reported feelings of warmth, similar to those who feel happy and excited after exercise.

（退休年長志工計畫（RSVP）透過社區志工服務提供給 55 歲以上的年長者一個有意義的生活，志工定期的貢獻出他們的時間和體力做社區巡守工作，幫助人們自然災害的重建，提供就醫的交通工具等。事實上 RSVP 現有的志工服務機會很多。像是探訪安老院院民、幫助安養中心，提供民政服務、在醫療單位或圖書館幫忙等。 當志工的好處數不完，舉例來說，RSVP 會以志工為榮的名義舉辦一個表揚宴會。這也是所有志工聚會的機會。並有多種娛樂節目。研究顯示這個計畫，對志工身心兩方面都有好處。在此期間，有 95% 的人都反應說有溫暖的感覺，就像運動過後會感覺到很快樂很興奮一樣。）

46. What is the passage mainly about?

（本文主要大意是什麼？）

(A) Opportunities and benefits for student volunteers. 給學生志工的機會和好處。

(B) Services offered by RSVP for elders. 由 RSVP 提供對長輩的服務。

(C) The nature and advantages of joining RSVP. 參加 RSVP 的性質和好處。

(D) The recognition of special senior volunteers. 對年長志工的表揚。

解析
看完本文內容，都是在說明退休後的年長者，如何走出來在社會上提供各種服務。所以，(C) 項的「The nature and advantages of joining RSVP」才是正確選項。

47. According to the passage, at what age can a person become qualified to join RSVP?

（根據本文，在什麼年齡才能合格參加 RSVP？）

(A) 24　(B) 37　(C) 49　(D) 56

解析
從答題關鍵的「offers those aged 55 and older a meaningful life」可看出，(D) 項的「56 歲」才是正確選項。

48. Which of the following is NOT mentioned in the passage as a volunteer work?

（下列有哪些文章裡沒提及志工的工作？）

(A) Reading to children. 對孩子的閱讀。　(B) Serving at libraries. 在圖書館服務。　(C) Offering transportation for the sick. 為病患提供運輸。　(D) Visiting aged citizens at nursing homes. 探訪護理之家的年長者。

看完本文內容都未提到為小孩做閱讀，所以 (A) 項的「Reading to children」才是沒被提到的正確選項。

49. In line 8, the word "**their**" refers to

（在第 8 行的「their」是指哪些人？）

(A) volunteers' 志工　(B) residents' 居民　(C) institutions' 機構　(D) libraries' 圖書館

從答題關鍵的「each year RSVP volunteers are recognized with a special banquet in their honor.」可看出，(A) 項的「volunteers」才是正確選項。

50. Which of the following is true according to the passage?

（下列哪些為真？）

(A) Volunteers give money to nursing home residents. 志工拿錢給老人院的居民。　(B) Volunteering gives one a feeling of happiness. 志工給人愉快的感覺。　(C) Volunteers go to work only when they are invited. 只有被邀請時，志工才去上班。　(D) Volunteering is not rewarding at all. 志願工作根本沒有獎勵。

從答題關鍵的「During and after volunteering, 95 percent of people reported feelings of warmth,」可看出，(B) 項的「Volunteering gives one a feeling of happiness」才是正確選項。

98 年統測（四技二專考試）

I. 字彙題

第 1 至 8 題，每題均有一個劃底線的字詞，請在四個選項中，選擇一個與劃底線的字詞意義最接近的答案。第 9 至 15 題，請選擇一個最適合的答案，以完成該句。

1. In Taiwan, some high school uniforms are symbols of excellence and honor.
   （在臺灣，有些高中制服是優秀與榮譽的象徵。）
   (A) presents 贈品　(B) fashions 流行式樣　(C) signs 記號　(D) restrictions 限制

   解析
   (1)先看底線字的中文意思為「象徵」。
   (2)在四個選項中，只有(C)項的「記號」才是與底線字意思最接近的正確選項。

2. The large number of students quitting schools reflects how serious the drop-out problem has been.
   （很多學生輟學反應出退學的問題有多嚴重。）
   (A) advertises 廣告　(B) shows 顯示　(C) encourages 鼓勵　(D) discusses 討論

   解析
   (1)先看底線字的中文意思為「反映」。
   (2)在四個選項中，只有(B)項的「顯示」才是與底線字意思最接近的正確選項。

3. Taking a one-week vacation in Paris is indeed an unforgettable experience.
   （在巴黎度假一週確實是很難忘的經驗。）
   (A) a possible 可能的　(B) a miserable 悲慘的　(C) a capable 有能力的　(D) a memorable 難忘的

   解析
   (1)先看底線字的中文意思為「忘不了的」。
   (2)在四個選項中，只有(D)項的「難忘的」才是與底線字意思最接近的正確選項。

4. Telling me that he had to take a train home in ten minutes, he vanished into the street.
   （告訴我說他在十分鐘內到趕火車回家，突然消失在街上。）
   (A) disappeared 消失　(B) disappointed 失望　(C) deserved 應得的　(D) ignored 忽視的

解析

(1)先看底線字的中文意思為「突然消失」。

(2)在四個選項中，只有(A)項的「消失」才是與底線字意思最接近的正確選項。

5. With online shopping, one can get hundreds of options when looking for a cell phone.
   （在線上購物，可有數百種選項的手機。）

   (A) choices 選擇　(B) fees 費用　(C) topics 話題　(D) reasons 理由

解析

(1)先看底線字的中文意思為「選項」。

(2)在四個選項中，只有(A)項的「選擇」才是與底線字意思最接近的正確選項。

6. Not knowing what the sales representative was trying to do, the lady looked perplexed .
   （不知售貨員要做什麼，該女士看來很困惑。）

   (A) prepared 準備　(B) bored 無聊　(C) delighted 高興　(D) confused 混淆

解析

(1)先看底線字的中文意思為「困惑」。

(2)在四個選項中，只有(D)項的「混淆」才是與底線字意思最接近的正確選項。

7. She seemed to be out of her mind when we saw her. She was yelling at her little baby.
   （我們見到她時她好像精神不太正常，那時她對她的小嬰孩吼叫。）

   (A) shivering 顫抖　(B) calling 叫喚　(C) swallowing 吞嚥　(D) shouting 大聲吼叫

解析

(1)先看底線字的中文意思為「吼叫」。

(2)在四個選項中，只有選(D)項的「大聲吼叫」才是與底線字意思最接近的正確選項。

8. The restaurant has superb business because it serves 上酒端菜 delicious and healthy food.
   （該餐廳生意極好因為它提供美味的健康食物。）

   (A) works 生效　(B) provides 提供　(C) forwards 向前　(D) strikes 打擊

解析

(1)先看底線字的中文意思為「餐飲之提供」。

(2)在四個選項中，只有選(B)項的「提供」才是與底線字意思最接近的正確選項。

9. May's room is clean and tidy. In contrast, her brother's room is a _____
   （梅的房間乾淨整齊。相反地，她弟弟的房間是 _____ 。）

   (A) mass 大眾　(B) miss 未擊中　(C) mess 雜亂的　(D) math 數學

解析

⑴答題關鍵在題目的前句「梅的房間乾淨整齊」與「相反地」等字句。

⑵四個選項中，只有選 (C) 項的「雜亂」，才可連成「梅的房間乾淨整齊，相反地，她弟弟的房間則是雜亂的」。

10. Water is a precious resource; therefore, we must _____ it or we will not have enough of it in the near future.

（水是珍貴的資源，因此，我們必須 _____ 否則不久就會不夠用。）

(A) conserve 節省　(B) compete 競爭　(C) connect 連結　(D) continue 繼續

解析

⑴答題關鍵在題目前句的的「水是珍貴的資源」。

⑵四個選項中，只有選(A)項的「節省用水」，才可連成「必須節省用水，否則……」。

11. One of the _____ of watching TV is that you can get a lot of information in a short time.

（看電視的 _____ 之一就是你可在短時間內看到很多資訊。）

(A) devices 小裝置　(B) visitors 訪客　(C) attendants 參加者　(D) advantages 獲利 好處

解析

⑴答題關鍵在題目空格左、右方的「看電視的」與「之一」。

⑵四個選項中，只有選(D)項的「獲利 好處」，才可連成「看電視的好處之一……」。

12. Mark and Lisa put an _____ in the newspaper last Saturday, informing their friends and relatives of their wedding.

（馬克和麗莎上週六在報上登一篇 _____ ，告訴親友他們要結婚的事。）

(A) enlargement 放大　(B) announcement 通知、啓事　(C) improvement 改進　(D) amazement 驚奇

解析

⑴答題關鍵在題目空格左「登一篇」。

⑵四個選項中，只有選(B)項的「啓事」，才可連成「登一篇啓事告訴親友……，」。

13. With a big supermarket in his _____ , it is very convenient for him to go grocery shopping.

（有一家大超市在他的 _____ ，他要去購物很方便。）

(A) exhibition 展覽　(B) message 訊息　(C) neighborhood 鄰近地區　(D) prayer 禱告者

解析

⑴答題關鍵在題目空格左方的「在他的……」。

⑵四個選項中，只有選 (C) 項的「鄰近地區」，才可連成「有一家大超市在他的鄰近地區，他要

去購物很方便」。

14. The _____ of Taiwan is over 23 million. That is, there are more than 23 million people living in Taiwan.

（臺灣的 _____ 超過二千三百萬，也就是說，有多於二千三百萬人住在臺灣。）

(A) pollution 汙染　(B) calculation 計算　(C) portion 部分　(D) population 人口數

解析

(1)答題關鍵在題目空格右方的「超過 2300 萬」。

(2)四個選項中，只有選(D)項的「人口數」，才可連成「臺灣的人口數超過二千三百萬」。

15. Joseph is popular at school because of his good _____ .

（由於他的好表現，約瑟夫在學校有名氣。）

(A) performance 表現　(B) attendant 參加者　(C) conductor 管理人　(D) rebellion 反判

解析

(1)答題關鍵在題目空格左方的「由於他的……」。

(2)四個選項中，只有選(A)項的「好表現」，才可連成「由於他的好表現，」。

II. 對話題

第 16 至 25 題，請依對話內容，選出一個最適合的答案，使其成為有意義的對話。

16. Ann：I don't have enough money to buy a birthday cake for my mother.
（我要買生日蛋糕給媽媽但錢不夠。）

Bob：_____

Ann：But I don't know how.
（但我不知要怎麼做。）

Bob：It's not difficult. Let's go to the store to get the ingredients first.
（那不難。我們先去買些做蛋糕的材料。）

(A) How much do you have? 你有多少？　(B) You can buy one for your father. 你可買一個給你爸爸。　(C) Let's make one from scratch. 讓我們自己來做一個。（from scratch 從頭到尾自己做）　(D) I can give you some money. 我可以給你一些錢。

解析

(1)答題關鍵在第三句。

(2)在四個選項中，只有選 (C) 項的「從頭到尾自己來做」，第三句才會接著說「但我不知要怎麼做」。

17.Doctor：How can I help you today?

（今天 我可幫你服務什麼？）

Mary：＿＿＿＿＿＿＿

Doctor：That's because of the cold weather.

（那是因爲天氣冷的關係。）

Mary： How do I take care of my skin in winter?

（在冬天我的皮膚要怎麼保養？）

(A) I have a stomach ache. 我肚子痛。 (B) My face feels dry and itchy. 我的臉感覺很乾很癢。 (C) I need a moisturizer. 我需要潤膚霜。 (D) My arms hurt. 我的手臂痛。

解析

(1)答題關鍵在第三句。

(2)在四個選項中，只有選 (B) 項的「我的臉感覺很乾很癢」，第三句才會接著説「那是因爲天氣冷的關係」。

18.James： What do you like for lunch?

（你的午餐想吃什麼？）

Mandy：I think I'll have a hamburger.

（我要一客漢堡好了。）

James：＿＿＿＿＿＿＿

Mandy：Like what?

（像是哪些？）

(A) Again? You should try something new. 又是漢堡？你應試試其他的。 (B) You always want a hamburger. 你一直都是點漢堡。 (C) Hamburger is your favorite. 漢堡是你最愛吃的。 (D) Pizza is better than hamburger. 披薩比漢堡好。

解析

(1)答題關鍵在第四句。

(2)在四個選項中，只有選 (A) 項的「又是漢堡？你應試試其他的」，第四句才會接著説 「像是哪些？」。

19.Clerk： Here you are. Size 8, purple.

（就是這件。八號，紫色的。）

Customer：Can I try it on?

（我可以試穿嗎？）

Clerk：＿＿＿＿＿＿＿

(A) Fine. I'll take it. 好，我買了。 (B) Sure. The dressing room is right over there. 當然可

以，試衣間就在那邊。　(C) How does it fit? 合身嗎？　(D) Cash or credit?

解析

(1)答題關鍵在第二句。

(2)在四個選項中，只有選 (B) 項的「當然可以，試衣間就在那邊」，才是回應第二句的「我可以試穿嗎」。

20. John：Would you like to go to a movie tonight?

（你晚上想去看電影嗎？）

Gina：＿＿＿＿＿＿

John：I see. What about tomorrow?

（明白，那明天呢？）

(A) Sorry, I can't. I have to study for the test tomorrow. 不行，我要準備明天的考試。

(B) I am glad to. What time? 我很願意，看幾點的？　(C) That's interesting. Thank you. 那有意思。謝謝你。　(D) Which movie do you want to see? 那要看那一片？

解析

(1)答題關鍵在第三句。

(2)在四個選項中，只有選 (A) 項的「不行，我要準備明天的考試」，第三句才會接著說「明白，那明天呢」。

21. Secretary：　Good morning, XYZ Company. May I help you?

（你早，XYZ 公司，我可效勞嗎？）

Mr. Clinton：Yes. Is Mr. Bush there?

（請問布希先生在嗎？）

Secretary：　＿＿＿＿＿＿

Mr. Clinton：Yes, please. This is Bill Clinton. Please tell Mr. Bush to call me back. My phone number is 361-6599.

（我是克林頓先生。請布希先生回我電話。號碼是 3616599。）

(A) Speaking. 我就是，請講。　(B) He is not in now. May I take your message? 他現在不在。我可以寫下你的留言嗎？　(C) I am his secretary. Please wait. 我是他的祕書。請等一下。　(D) Mr. Bush is on the phone. Who is this? 布希先生在電話上。請問你是哪位？

解析

(1)答題關鍵在第二句。

(2)在四個選項中，只有選 (B) 項的「他現在不在 我可以寫下你的留言嗎」，第 句才會接著說「我是克林頓，請布希回電話」。

22. Peter：Hi, Janet. How are you doing?

（嗨，珍妮。妳好嗎？）

Janet：＿＿＿＿＿＿＿＿

Peter：Great. I got a new job last week, and I truly love it.

（很棒，我上週找到工作，我太喜歡這個工作。）

(A) I am a student, and you? 我是學生，你呢？　　(B) I am going shopping. How about you? 我要去購物。你呢？　　(C) I am doing fine. How about you? 我很好。你呢？　　(D) I am doing my homework, and you? 我正在寫功課。你呢？

解析

(1)答題關鍵在第三句。

(2)在四個選項中，只有選 (C) 項的「我很好 你呢？」，第三句才會接著說「很棒，我上週找到工作……」。

23. Billy： I don't feel well today.

（我今天不舒服。）

Nurse：＿＿＿＿＿＿＿＿

Billy： I have a sore throat and a headache.

（我喉嚨痛頭也痛。）

Nurse：Let me take your temperature first. Chang will be with you in a minute.

（我先幫你量體溫，張醫師馬上就幫你看。）

(A) What seems to be the problem? 是什麼樣的問題呢？　　(B) That would be fine. 那很好。

(C) Dr. Chang has an opening at three. 張醫師三點鐘有個會。　　(D) Can you come in then? 你那時可以來嗎？

解析

(1)答題關鍵在第三句。

(2)在四個選項中，只有選 (A) 項的「是什麼樣的問題呢？」，第三句才會接著說「我喉嚨痛頭也痛」。

24. Lisa： Angela, can you keep a secret?

（安琪拉，妳會保密嗎？）

Angela：＿＿＿＿＿＿＿＿

Lisa： I am going to get married next month.

（我下個月結婚。）

(A) Congratulations! 恭喜妳！　　(B) Not at all. 一點也不。　　(C) Of course not. 當然不。

(D) Sure. What is it? 當然會。到底什麼事？

解析
(1)答題關鍵在第三句。
(2)在四個選項中，只有選 (D) 項的「當然會保密，倒底什麼事？」，第三句才會接著說「我下個月結婚」。

25. Mom：Linda, we've got to go. _____

（琳達，我們必須走了。_____）

Linda：I know. I'm tired, too. But it is hard to decide which one to buy.

（我知道，我也累了。但真的很難決定買哪一個。）

Mom：Let's go home first and come again later.

（我們先回家，晚一點再來。）

(A) Which one should I buy? 我應該買哪一個？　(B) I don't have enough money. 我的錢不夠。　(C) Tie your shoelace. 把你的鞋帶綁好。　(D) I'm exhausted. 我累死了。

解析
(1)答題關鍵在第二句。
(2)在四個選項中，只有選 (D) 項的「我累死了」，第二句才會接著說「我知道，我也累了 但是……」。

III. 綜合測驗

以下兩篇短文，共有 15 個空格，為第 26 至 40 題，每題有四個選項，請依各篇短文文意，選出一個最適合該空格的答案。

The Republic of China Consumer Voucher is an economic stimulus package. The vouchers are distributed to every R.O.C. citizen born before March 31st, 2009 _____26_____ holds valid household registrations. The purpose of these vouchers is to halt the economic downturn in Taiwan _____27_____ due to the global financial crisis. The vouchers could be picked up either at voucher-distribution stations on January 18th or at designated post offices between February 7th and April 30th. On the early morning of January 18th, people _____28_____ standing in long lines waiting to receive the vouchers, as they were _____29_____ do some shopping with the vouchers.

According to the Ministry of the Interior, 91.3 percent of the people picked up their vouchers on January 18th, _____30_____ than the voting rate of 76.4 percent in the presidential election held last March. The vouchers may be used to buy just about any item in Taiwan; _____31_____ , they cannot be used to get lottery tickets or plastic surgeries. For _____32_____ still unsure of how to do with their vouchers, some councilors suggested that the public _____33_____ the vouchers to charity. They said the NT$ 3,600 might be an unimportant amount for the rich, but could make a difference to disadvantaged families.

（中華民國的消費券是一種刺激經濟的作法。消費券發給 2009 年 3 月 31 日以前出生，_____26_____ 具有合法戶籍。這些消費券的目的在緩和臺灣的經濟衰退。

_____27_____ 由於全球金融危機。消費券可以在 1 月 18 日在發券站領取，或是在 2 月 7 日和 4 月 30 日期間向指定的郵局領取。在 1 月 18 日一大早，人們 _____28_____ 排了很長隊伍等待領取消費券。他們 _____29_____ 想用消費券去買東西。根據內政部資料，91.3% 的人在 1 月 18 日領取他們的消費券，_____30_____ 年 3 月舉行的總統選舉 76.4% 投票率。消費券可用來買幾乎任何東西，_____31_____ 它不能用來買彩券或做整形手術。對 _____32_____ 仍然不確定要怎樣處理消費券的人，有些議員建議，民眾可 _____33_____ 消費券給慈善機構。他們說 3,600 元臺幣對富人來說可能不是很大的金額，但對貧困家庭卻是極大的幫助。)

**26. 題句：citizen born before March 31st, 2009 _____26_____ holds valid household registrations.

　　選項：(A) when 何時　(B) what 什麼　(C) who 誰　(D) which 哪一

解析

(1)答題關鍵在空格右邊的「holds」一字，因它是動詞，其前須放主格的關係代名詞。

(2)四個選項中，只有選 (C) 項，代表 citizen 的「who」才是主格關係代名詞，才是正確選項。

27. 題句：The purpose of these vouchers is to halt the economic downturn in Taiwan _____27_____ due to the global financial crisis.

　　選項：(A) absolute 絕對　(B) mainly 主要地　(C) daily 每日的　(D) appropriate 恰當

解析

(1)依題意，空格內只能選 (B) 項的「主要地」，才能有意義連成「消費券的目的主要是由於全球的財務危機」。

**28. 題句：people _____28_____ standing in long lines waiting to receive the vouchers,

　　選項：(A) find 發現(現在式)　(B) found 過去式　(C) were found 被發現　(D) who were found 被找到

解析

(1)答題關鍵在句首的「people」一字，而整題題意為「人們被發現正在如何如何」之意。

(2)因此，只有選 (C) 項的過去式被動語態 were found，才是符合題意與文法的正確選項。

29. 題句：as they were _____29_____ do some shopping with the vouchers.

　　選項：(A) eager to 迫切的　(B) similar to 相似　(C) look forward to 盼望　(D) thanks to 幸好

解析

依題意，只有選 (A) 項的「迫切的」放入空格，才可有意義連成「好像他們迫切地想要用消費券去購物」。

**30.題句：91.3 percent of the people... _____30_____ than the voting rate of 76.4 percent in...

選項：(A) which is high　(B) is more high　(C) is higher　(D) higher

解析

(1)答題關鍵在空格右邊的「than」，其前須有「比較級的形容詞」。

(2)四個選項中有比較級形容詞只有 (C), (D) 兩項，但不能選 (C) 項的 is higher（除非它寫成 which is higher 或 it is higher），所以 (D) 項的 higher 才是正確選項。

**31.題句：The vouchers may be used to buy just about any item in Taiwan; _____31_____ , they cannot be used to get lottery tickets or plastic surgeries.

選項：(A) for instance 舉例　(B) however 然而　(C) sometimes 有時　(D) therefore 因此

解析

空格前、後兩句的意思相反，連接詞用 (B) 項的「however」才正確。

**32.題句：For _____32_____ still unsure of how to do with their vouchers,

選項：(A) those who ……的人　(B) who 誰　(C) people who ……的人　(D) those 那些

解析

(1)依題意「For _____32_____ still unsure of how to do with their vouchers,」只有 (D) 項的 those 才是正確選項。

(2)(A) 項的 those who 是陷阱，因其後要有動詞，但題句的 still unsure of how... 都不是動詞。例句 For those who want to go, step forward please.（要去的人請往前站一步）

**33.題句：some councilors suggested that the public _____33_____ the vouchers to charity.

選項：(A) donate 捐獻的現在式　(B) donating 動名詞　(C) to donate 不定詞　(D) is donating 進行式

解析

(1)依文法，suggest 後的 that 子句動詞須用現在式動詞。

(2)四選項中，只有 (A) 項的「donate」才是符合文法的正確選項。

Mount Kilimanjaro, located in Tanzania about 220 miles south of the equator in a very hot region, is the tallest mountain in all of Africa. _____34_____ its location, there are many glaciers and ice fields high up on the mountain. The ice cap was important to the surrounding area and it's also a source of water for the river Nile. Many villages in the Mount Kilimanjaro region _____35_____ the snow and ice melt water.

The appearance of Mount Kilimanjaro is changing. Scientists say that more than 80 percent of its glaciers _____36_____ since 1912. As a result, animals on the plains surrounding the mountain are now dying and many plant species are also in danger. People are beginning to wonder how long it will be before the mountain _____37_____ its snowy white cap. Why is this happening? Some scientists think that the hot weather in this tropical region makes the effects of global warming even worse. For example, the snow melts faster here _____38_____ in cooler parts of the world. ____39____ believe forest reduction on Kilimanjaro may be the strongest human influence on glacial recession. Forest fires, often caused by honey collectors trying to smoke bees out of their hives, ____40____ the air temperature and lower the level of water in the air. These changes cause less snow to fall in the area. Scientists now believe that the mountain's glaciers may be totally gone by the year 2020.

（Kilimanjaro 山，位於坦尚尼亞赤道以南 220 英里的一個炎熱地區裡，是非洲最高的山。 ____34____ 它的位置，在山上高處有很多冰河和冰原。冰冠對周遭地區是重要的，這也是尼羅河的河水來源。在 Kilimanjaro 山區的很多村莊 ____35____ 冰雪。Kilimanjaro 的外貌隨時會改變。科學家說 80% 以上的冰河從 1912 年起 ____36____ 融化了。因此，在平原上區的動物快要滅絕，很多植物種類也處境危險。人們開始懷疑，還要多久山上就會 ____37____ 冰雪大地。為什麼發生這樣的事？某些科學家認為，在這個熱帶地區的熱天氣使全球暖化的影響更大。例如，這裡的雪比世界其他較涼地區的雪 ____38____ 更快。 ____39____ 相信在 Kilimanjaro 森林之減少可能才是人類對冰原減少的最大影響。森林火災，經常是養蜂人以燻煙火方式將蜜蜂趕出蜂巢所引起。 ____40____ 氣溫與空氣中的水份稀少。這些變化會造成更少降雪量前。科學家現在相信高山冰河可能在 2020 年全部消失。）

34. 題句：____34____ 它的位置，在山上高處還是有很多冰河和冰原。
　　選項：(A) Because of 由於　(B) Spite 惡意　(C) Even though 即使　(D) Despite 不管
　　解析
　　依題意只能選(D)項的「不管」，才是正確選項。

35. 題句：Many villages in the Mount Kilimanjaro region ____35____ the snow and ice melt water.
　　選項：(A) belong to 屬於　(B) depend on 依賴　(C) hear from 收到……訊息　(D) figure out 想出
　　解析
　　(1)依題意只能選(B)項的「依賴」，才是正確選項。

**36.題句：Scientists say that more than 80 percent of its glaciers ____36____ since 1912.
　　選項：(A) melted 融化（過去式）　(B) have melted（現在完成式）　(C) is melting（進行式）　(D) will have melted（未來完成式）
　　解析
　　依題意「Scientists say that more than 80 percent of its glaciers ____36____ since 1912.」來看，因空格旁有 since 一字，就知道要用 (B) 項現在完成式的 have melted 才對。
　　所以，(B) 項才是正確選項。

**37.題句：People are beginning to wonder how long it will be before the mountain _____37_____ its snowy white cap.

選項：(A) will lose（未來式）　(B) has lost（現在完成式）　(C) loses（現在式）　(D) will have lost（未來完成式）

解析

(1)答題關鍵在連接詞「before」後的子句。

(2)依文法，連接詞 before 後接子句的動詞要用現在式。因此，(C) 項的 loses 才是符合文法的正確選項。

**38.題句：For example, the snow melts faster here _____38_____ in cooler parts of the world.

選項：(A) than it does 它確實……　(B) as it is 就是　(C) so did they 他們也……　(D) than they are 比他們……

解析

(1)答題關鍵在 snow melts 二字。snow 屬三單主詞，所以 melts 才會加 s。

(2)四個選項中只有(A) 項的 than it does 才是正確選項。

(4)題句的 snow 為三單名詞，所以不能選(D) 項的 ...they are。

**39.題句：_____39_____ believe forest reduction on Kilimanjaro may be the strongest human influence on glacial recession.

選項：(A) Another 另一個　(B) The other 其他一個　(C) Others 其他多個　(D) The others 特定的其他多個

解析

(1)由於本篇短文在第 36 題句提到「Scientists say that ....（有些科學家說）」，因此在本題句四選項中，必須選 (C) 項的「others（其他科學家們）」才可對應前面的「Scientists says...」，才是符合句構的正確選項。

40. 題句：honey collectors trying to smoke bees out of their hives, _____40_____ the air temperature and lower the level of water in the air.

選項：(A) rise 上升　(B) arise 上升不及物動詞　(C) arouse 喚起　(D) raise 升溫、加薪

解析

(1)答題關鍵在題目空格右邊的「the air temperature」。

(2)四個選項中，只有選(D) 項的「raise」放入空格，才是有意義連成整句的正確選項。

IV. 閱讀測驗

以下有兩篇短文，每篇各 5 題，共有 10 個題目，為第 41 至 50 題，請於閱讀短文後，選出最適當的答案。

Say "evolution" and some folks think of dusty archaeologists examining bone fragments.

But, while evidence of previous life forms does play a central part in our understanding of evolution, it is not necessary to go on a dig to see it in action - you might just look inside your mouth.

We all learn that human beings have thirty-two teeth. They are not all the same, though; the <u>pointy</u> incisors in the front are easily distinguished from the flatter, double-edged bicuspids that run along the side. Our teeth serve different functions: those incisors are great for biting and holding on, while the bicuspids do more of a saw-motion for chewing.

Now here is something you may not know: strictly speaking, it is not true that everyone has thirty-two teeth. Even excluding people with dental problems, some folks have only thirty, or even twenty-eight. The ones that are missing are often the farthest back in the mouth. Where did they go?

One likely answer is found in evolution. A long time ago - say ten thousand years - human beings ate much more raw meat. With a rough diet, you need lots of grinding teeth to help prepare your food for digestion. Later, with the gradual advent of cooked foods, not all those teeth are needed anymore. If someone is born without them, he or she does not suffer any ill consequence; a scientist would say there is no evolutionary pressure to keep those teeth.

Source: *http//amos.indiana.edu/library/scripts/mouthevol.html*

（說到「演化」有些人就會想到考古學家在灰塵中檢查骨頭碎片。但是，當先前之生命形式的證據確實在我們的理解演化過程中扮演重要角色，不需要挖掘才看得見行動——你只要看看嘴巴內部就可以。

我們都了解人類有 32 顆牙齒。不過它們不會每顆長得一樣；前面的門牙與平面、雙面的位於兩側的白齒很容易辨識。我們的牙齒各有不同的功能：那些門牙用來咬住東西，而白齒是用來咀嚼。

這裡有些你可能不知道的事：嚴格地說，每人有 32 顆牙齒是不確實的。即使不包括有牙齒問題的人，有些人只有 30 顆，或者甚至 28 顆。缺少的那幾顆經常是長在嘴裡的最內端。它們怎麼不見了？

一個可能答案是與進化過程有關。很久以前——說是 1 萬年前好了，當時人類吃很多很多生肉。對付粗糙的食物，你需要許多咀嚼牙齒（白齒）幫助食物更容易消化。後來，烹煮食品逐漸普遍，那些咀嚼齒不再需要。如果某人出生就沒有咀嚼齒，對他或她不會有任何不利後果；科學家就會說沒有進化的壓力來保有那些牙齒。）

41. According to the passage, which of the following statements is true?

　　（根據本文，下列陳述中的哪個是真實的？）

　(A) Only archaeologists understand evolution.

　　　只有考古學家理解演化。

　(B) Everyone has thirty-two teeth.

　　　每人有 32 顆牙齒。

　(C) Ten thousand years ago, human beings ate much more raw meat than we do now.

1 萬年以前，人類吃的生肉比我們現吃的生肉更多。

(D) With the gradual advent of cooked foods, we need more teeth to chew them.

　　由於烹煮食品逐漸普遍，我們需要更多的牙齒咀嚼他們。

解析

從答題關鍵的「A long time ago-say ten thousand years-human beings ate much more raw meat.」可看出，(C) 項的「Ten thousand years ago, human beings ate much more raw meat than we do now.」才是正確選項。

42. Which of the following is the closest in meaning to the word "pointy" in the second paragraph?

　　（如下內容中的哪個字與第 2 個段文章的「pointy」意思最接近？）

(A) sharp 尖銳的　　(B) round 圓的　　(C) flat 平的　　(D) long 長的

解析

point 是指尖的之意。所以 (A) 項的「sharp」才是正確選項。

43. Which of the following is **NOT** mentioned in the passage?

　　（下列有哪一項沒在文章裡提及？）

(A) Previous life forms play a central part in our understanding of evolution.

　　以前的生命形式在我們的理解演化過程中扮演一個重要角色。

(B) Some people have fewer teeth than others.

　　有些人的牙齒比別人少。

(C) Animals have more teeth than human beings.

　　動物比人有更多的牙齒。

(D) The bicuspids are used mainly for chewing.

　　白齒主要做咀嚼之用。

解析

看完本文內容，只有 (C) 項內容沒被提及。所以 (C) 項的「Animals have more teeth than human beings」才是沒被提及的正確選項。

44. Which of the following can be inferred from the passage?

　　（下列哪一項可從文章中推斷出來？）

(A) Human incisors look much like bicuspids.

　　人的門牙看起來很像二頭齒。

(B) Some people do not need the teeth that are the farthest back in the mouth.

　　有些人不需要用到嘴裡最內端的牙齒。

(C) Today people are born without the teeth that are the farthest back in the mouth.

今天人們出生就沒有是嘴裡最內端的牙齒。

(D) Ancient people have less than thirty-two teeth.

古代人的牙齒少於 32 顆。

解析

從答題關鍵的「　」可看出，(B) 項的「Some people do not need the teeth that are the farthest back in the mouth.」才是正確選項。

45. What is the passage mainly about?

（本文主要大意是什麼？）

(A) Different functions of human teeth. 人類牙齒的不同功能。

(B) People with dental problems 有牙齒問題的人。

(C) The advent of cooked foods. 烹煮食物的到來。

(D) Evolution in terms of human teeth. 人類牙齒的進化。

解析

從整段文章內容都是談論牙齒進化與演變，因此，(D) 項的「Evolution in terms of human teeth.」才是正確選項。

　　We are always trying to understand ourselves by asking "Why did I do that?" Certainly it is true that each human being faces the question of understanding himself, even though he may not put this question in so many words. Part of the answer to "Why did I do that?" is found in the way the individual looks upon himself, or the way he sees himself. This is referred to as the individual's self-concept.

　　It is obvious that we will tend to act with more self-control, and be happier, if we can gradually gain a better understanding of how we ourselves think and act, and what kind of individuals we really are. For example, a young woman may "see herself" as a poor conversationalist and a kind of "wet blanket" when she goes out with her friends. Actually, she is warm and friendly and well liked by all who know her. Here is a case where an individual has formed a "self-concept" which is definitely not in line with the facts. If she could come to realize the true situation, it would in all probability help her overcome this fear of meeting or being with other people. The importance of an individual's "self-concept" in influencing his behavior is plainly evident.

　　（我們總是問說「我爲什麼那麼做」來理解自己當然可以確信每人面臨理解自己的問題，即使他可能不會用太長的句子來問這個問題。對「我爲什麼那麼做？」的部分答案個人怎麼看自己的方法中可以找到。這就是所謂的自我概念。

　　顯然我們傾向於更多的自我控制來行動，如果我們可以漸漸地獲得更多了解我們怎麼看自己的言行，看我們自己眞正的是哪種人，那就會更高興。例如，一年輕婦女可能把自己看成一個不善對話的人，在與朋友出門時，被稱爲「溼毛毯」（掃興的人）。實際上，她是熱情和友好的並且很討人喜歡。這裡有個案例，一個人已形成「自我概念」但這與事實不符。如果她能意識到眞實的情況，它將大有可能幫助她克

服這種懼怕開會或與他人相處的窘境。個人自我概念會影響行爲舉止是很明顯的。）

46. In which subject can this passage be found?

（本文的主題爲何？）

(A) Biology 生物學　(B) Geography 地理　(C) Psychology 心理學　(D) Physics 物理學

解析

從文章的內容來看，所說的都是待人處事的道理，當然 (C) 項的「Psychology」才是正確選項。

47. Which of the following statements is **NOT** true according to the passage?

（下列陳述哪個不眞實？）

(A) If we understand ourselves better, we will be much happier.

　　如果我們理解自己得更好，我們將更愉快。

(B) Why we did the thing that we did never depends on our self-concept.

　　爲什麼我們做事情從未取決於我們的自我概念。

(C) An individual's self-concept evidently influences his or her behavior.

　　一個個人的自我概念明顯地影響他或她的行爲。

(D) We never stop trying to understand our behavior.

　　我們從未停止努力理解我們的行爲。

解析

從答題關鍵的「The importance of an individual's "self-concept" in influencing his behavior is plainly evident.」可看出，(B) 項的「Why we did the thing that we did never depends on our self-concept.」才是不實陳述的正確選項。

48. Based on the context, the phrase "wet blanket" in the second paragraph most likely means "_____".

（基於上下文，在第 2 個段落的片語「潮溼的毯子」可能的意思是）

(A) a blanket that nobody wants 沒人想要的毯子

(B) a blanket that everybody enjoys 每人喜愛的毯子

(C) a person who doubles other people's fun 使他人開心的人

(D) a person who spoils other people's fun 破壞他人開心的人

解析

wet blanket 這個俚語中譯是「不受歡迎的人」，所以 (D) 項的「a person who spoils other people's fun」才是正確選項。

49. According to this passage, which of the following descriptions about the young woman is true?

（根據本文，關於年輕婦女的說法下列哪項敘述為真？）

(A) She identifies herself as an outgoing person, who can make friends easily.

她證實她自己是能容易交到朋友且是外向的人。

(B) She can become more open-minded to socialize with others as long as she changes the way she sees herself.

她更變得能不偏私與其它人一起來往只要她改變對自己的看法。

(C) She has a high self-esteem, and sees herself as a people person.

她有高的自尊，並且把她自己視為一個高高在上的人。

(D) Her "self-concept" is compatible with her true personality.

她的「自我概念」與她的真實的人格是可以並存的。

解析

從答題關鍵的「」可看出，(B) 項的「She can become more open-minded to socialize with others as long as she changes the way she sees herself.」才是正確選項。

50. According to the passage, self-concept is defined as:

（根據本文，自我概念被定義為：）

(A) how the individual looks upon himself 個人怎樣看自己

(B) the way the individual sees other people 個人看他人的模式

(C) the way the individual is respected by others 被人尊重的模式

(D) how the individual is looked upon by others 個人被他人尊重

解析

從答題關鍵的「Part of the answer to "Why did I do that?" is found in the way the individual looks upon himself, or the way he sees himself. This is referred to as the individual's self-concept.」可看出，(A) 項的「how the individual looks upon himself」才是正確選項。

99 年統測（四技二專考試）

I. 字彙題

第 1 至 6 題，每題均有一個劃底線的字詞，請在四個選項中，選擇一個與劃底線的字詞意義最接近的答案。第 7 至 15 題，請選擇一個最適合的答案，以完成該句。

1. In a car accident, you are more likely to <u>escape</u> injury if you are wearing a seatbelt, which prevents you from being thrown out of the car.

（發生車禍時，如果有綁安全帶你比較可避免傷害，或防止被拋出車外。）

　(A) avoid 避免　(B) prepare 準備　(C) damage 傷害　(D) indicate 指出

解析

(1)先看底線字「escape」，中文意思為「逃避、避免」。

(2)在四個選項中，只有(A)項的「避免」才是與底線字意思最接近的正確選項。

2. Some bus drivers might feel sleepy while driving, which can endanger <u>passengers</u> on the bus.

（有些遊覽車司機開車時打瞌睡，這樣會使乘客陷入危險。）

　(A) climbers 攀登者　(B) travelers 旅遊者　(C) retailers 零售商　(D) founders 建立者

解析

(1)先看底線字「passengers」，中文意思為「乘客」。

(2)在四個選項中，只有(B)項的「旅遊者」才是與底線字意思最接近的正確選項。

3. Tom tried to <u>persuade</u> Annie to go on a date with him, but she wouldn't go.

（湯姆試著要說服安妮與他約會，但她不去。）

　(A) supply 供應　(B) convince 使信服　(C) defeat 擊敗　(D) expose 使暴露於

解析

(1)先看底線字「persuade」，中文意思為「說服」。

(2)在四個選項中，只有(B)項的「使信服」才是與底線字意思最接近的正確選項。

4. Sally's mother became very <u>distressed</u> when Sally said she was quitting school, and would work full-time in a restaurant.

（當莎莉說她輟學去擔任餐廳的全職工作時，她母親很憂傷。）

　(A) silent 安靜　(B) unhappy 不愉快　(C) obvious 顯然地　(D) guilty 有罪的

解析
(1) 先看底線字「distressed」，中文意思為「　」
(2)在四個選項中，只有(B)項的「不愉快」才是與底線字意思最接近的正確選項。

5. Andrew is now working at a factory, but his dream is to possess a business run by himself.
　　（安德魯在工廠上班，但他的夢想是擁有自己的事業。）
　　(A) allow 允許　(B) hit 打擊　(C) depend 信賴　(D) own 自己的

解析
(1)先看底線字「possess」，中文意思為「擁有」。
(2)在四個選項中，只有(D)項的「自己的」才是與底線字「擁有」意思最接近，才是正確選項。

6. You might fail in pursuit of your goals, but the lessons you learn from each failure will help you to eventually succeed.
　　（你可能沒有追求到目標，但失敗中的教訓使你最後會成功。）
　　(A) easily 容易地　(B) readily 樂意地　(C) finally 終於　(D) simply 簡單地

解析
(1)先看底線字「eventually」，中文意思為「最後」。
(2)在四個選項中，只有(C)項的「終於」才是與底線字意思最接近的正確選項。

7. As airplane pilots fly for many long hours, they are ＿＿＿＿＿＿ for the safety of hundreds of people on board.
　　（當駕駛員多為長時數飛行，他們要為機上數百位乘客的安全＿＿＿＿＿＿。）
　　(A) understandable 可理解的　(B) changeable 可變的　(C) believable 可信的　(D) responsible 負責任的

解析
(1)答題關鍵在題目空格左、右方的「are」與「for」。
(2)四個選項中，只有選(D)項的「負責」，才可有意義地連成「要為機上數百位乘客的安全負責」。
(3)本題是考片語「be responsible for 為～負責」。

8. Based on their study results, scientists have found that there is a close ＿＿＿＿＿＿ between stressful jobs and increased illness.
　　（根據研究結果，科學家發現壓力大的工作與疾病的增加有密切的＿＿＿＿＿＿。）
　　(A) reflection 反射　(B) connection 關聯　(C) attention 注意　(D) medication 藥物治療

解析
(1)答題關鍵在題目空格左方的「密切的」。
(2)四個選項中，只有選(B)項的「關聯」，才可有意義地連成「……壓力大的工作與疾病的增加

有密切的關聯」。

9. A producer for a popular television show is always looking for people with unusual _____ to perform on the show.

（有名的電視節目製作人一直都會找具有不尋常 _____ 的人上電視。）

(A) reasons 理由　(B) courts 法庭　(C) platforms 平臺　(D) talents 才能

解析

(1)答題關鍵在題目空格左方的「不尋常」。

(2)四個選項中，只有選 (D) 項的「才能」，才可有意義地連成「……會找具有不尋常才能的人上電視」。

10. More and more students _____ that with a good knowledge of English, they will have more opportunities to find a good job.

（越來越多的學生 _____ 英文程度更好的人會有更多的工作機會。）

(A) delay 延誤　(B) launch 開始　(C) realize 體會到　(D) bother 打擾

解析

(1)答題關鍵在題目空格左、右方的「越多的學生」與 that 子句「英文程度更好的人會有……」

(2)四個選項中，只有選 (C) 項的「體會到」，才可有意義地連成「越來越多的學生體會到英文程度更好的人會有更多的」。

(3)that 子句是「連接詞 that+從屬子句」之謂。同理，連接詞 who+子句稱為「who 子句」連接詞 what+子句稱為 what 子句……以此類推。

(4)主要子句要敘述的句子太長時，通常用從屬子句的方式寫出來。

11. Some students might be expelled from schools for _____ their computers, such as illegal downloads.

（有些學生可能被退學是為了 _____ 電腦，像是非法下載。）

(A) improving 改進　(B) entering 進入　(C) remaining 剩餘的　(D) misusing 濫用

解析

(1)答題關鍵在題目空格左、右方的「為了」與「他們的電腦」。

(2)四個選項中，只有選 (D) 項的「濫用」放入空格，才可有意義地連成「……被退學是為了濫用他們的電腦」。

12. Doctors point out that stress, _____ , and lack of friends can have a negative influence on sick people.

（醫生們指出，壓力 _____ 與缺少朋友等，對病人有負面的影響。）

(A) fitness 健康　(B) kindness 仁慈　(C) goodness 善良　(D) loneliness 孤獨

解析

(1)答題關鍵在題目空格左、右方的「壓力」與「缺少朋友」。

(2)四個選項中，只有選 (D) 項的「孤獨」，才可有意義地連成「……壓力、孤獨與缺少朋友等，對病人有負面的影響。」

13. David is now the best student in high school. It's ＿＿＿＿＿＿ that he will get a scholarship to the state university.

（大衛是校內最好的學生。那是 ＿＿＿＿＿＿，他會獲得大學獎學金。）

(A) available 可用的　(B) various 不同的　(C) certain 確定的　(D) doubtful 懷疑的

解析

(1)答題關鍵在題目空格左、右方的「It's」與「that 子句」。

(2)四個選項中，只有選 (C) 項的「確定之事」，才可有意義地連成「那是確定之事：他會獲得大學獎學金。」

(3)子句的說明，請參閱上文第 10 題。

14. The weather changes so ＿＿＿＿＿＿ that no one can accurately predict what it will be like the next day.

（氣候如此 ＿＿＿＿＿＿ 變化，沒有人能正確預測第二天氣候會如何。）

(A) properly 恰當的　(B) skeptically 懷疑的　(C) rationally 理性的　(D) constantly 不斷地

解析

(1)答題關鍵在題目空格左方的「如此變化」與「that...」。

(2)四個選項中，只有選 (D) 項的「不斷地」，才可有意義地連成「氣候如此不斷地變化，沒有人能正確預測……」。

15. If you want to eat in that popular restaurant on weekend, you'd better make a reservation in ＿＿＿＿＿＿ .

（如果你想週末去那家餐聽吃飯，你最好要 ＿＿＿＿＿＿ 訂位。）

(A) advance 先前　(B) address 地址　(C) amount 數額　(D) account 帳

解析

(1)答題關鍵在題目空格左方的「訂位」。

(2)四個選項中，只有選 (A) 項的「預先」，才可有意義地連成「……你最好要預先訂位」，才是正確選項。

(3)本題是考片語「in advance」預先。

II. 對話題

第 16 至 25 題，請依對話內容，選出一個最適合的答案，使其成為有意義的對話。

16. Cashier： Your total is NT $ 699.
   （總價是 699 元。）

   Customer：＿＿＿＿＿＿＿＿

   Cashier： Yes, Ma'am. Then that's NT $ 599.
   （好的，那麼就是 599 元。）

   Customer：Do you take credit card?
   （妳收信用卡嗎？）

   Cashier： Sure.
   （當然有收。）

   (A) I don't have cash. 我沒有現金。　(B) Do you need a bag? 妳要購物袋嗎？

   (C) I have these coupons. 我這裡有折價券　(D) May I use the shopping cart? 我可使用購物車嗎？

   解析
   (1)答題關鍵在第三句。
   (2)在四個選項中，第二句只有選 (C) 項的「我這裡有折價券」，第三句才會接著說「好的，那麼就是 599 元」。

17. Bill： Jean, I'm sorry. I can't come over today. I have a sore throat.
   （抱歉。我今天不能過來，喉嚨痛。）

   Jean：Oh, no! Your voice sounds funny. When did you get sick?
   （你的聲音很怪，什麼時候生病的？）

   Bill：＿＿＿＿＿＿＿＿

   Jean：I'm sorry to hear that.
   （真遺憾。）

   (A) Just this morning. 就在今天早上。　(B) I guess I have a fever. 我恐怕發燒了。

   (C) I'll go to the doctor later. 我晚一點去看醫生。　(D) I don't think it's funny. 那不好笑。

   解析
   (1)答題關鍵在第二句。
   (2)在四個選項中，第三句只有選 (A) 項的「就在今天早上」，才可回應第二句「什麼時候生病的？」。

18. Boy： Mom, can we ride on the roller coaster?
   （媽，我們可以坐雲霄飛車嗎？）

Mother：Of course, we can.

（當然可以。）

Boy：　　Can we go on the Ferris wheel, too?

（我們也可坐摩天輪嗎？）

Mother：_____

Boy：　　What? Mom, that's for babies!

（什麼，媽，那是嬰兒坐的！）

(A) You can go alone if you really want to. 真想坐的話就去吧。　(B) Sure. But let's try the merry-go-round first. 好，我們先坐旋轉木馬。　(C) I am afraid that we don't have time for that. 恐怕時間不夠喔。　(D) Sorry. It is under construction. 抱歉，那在整修中。

解析

(1)答題關鍵在第五句。

(2)在四個選項中，第四句只有選 (B) 項的「我們先坐旋轉木馬」，第五句才會接著說 「媽，那是嬰兒坐的」。

19. Manager：_____

Kelly：　　Pretty much, sir, but I am wondering if there is a dress code.

（相當多，但不曉得有沒有規定穿什麼衣服。）

Manager：Yes, the company wants all the employees to look their best and represent the company well.

（有，公司要所有員工穿起來最能代表公司。）

(A) Is everything clear so far? 情況都解決了嗎？　(B) The dress looks great on you. 這件衣服你穿得很好看。　(C) Do you have any questions? 有任何問題嗎？　(D) Welcome to the Sales Department. 歡迎到業務部門來。

解析

(1)答題關鍵在第二句。

(2)在四個選項中，第一句只有選 (A) 項的「情況都解決了嗎？」，第二句才會接著說「相當多……」。

20. Roger：I am off to the post office.

（我要去郵局。）

Rich：　Can you mail this airmail for me?

（可以幫我寄這封信嗎？）

Roger：Sure. _____

（沒問題。_____）

Rich： Yes, you can simply throw it into the mailbox

（有，只要丟入郵筒就好了。）

(A) You can fax it to me. 你可以傳真給我。　(B) Why don't you mail it yourself? 為什麼不自己寄。　(C) Have you stamped it? 郵票貼了嗎？　(D) I'm also going to the bank. 我同時要去銀行。

解析

(1)答題關鍵在第四句。

(2)在四個選項中，第三句只有選 (C) 項的「郵票貼了嗎」，第四句才會接著說「只要丟入郵筒就好了」。

21. Mother：You look tired. Why don't you go to bed earlier today?

（你看起來很累。為何不早點睡？）

Jimmy： I can't. I have an English test tomorrow.

（不行。明天要考英文。）

Mother：＿＿＿＿＿＿＿

Jimmy： I haven't finished reviewing yet. I don't want to take any chances.

（還沒溫習完，我不想冒考不上的險。）

(A) Don't worry. You'll be fine. 不用擔心你不會有問題的。　(B) You should study earlier. 你應早點準備。　(C) How about a cup of coffee? 想要來杯咖啡嗎？　(D) Is that the only test tomorrow? 明天只考那一科嗎？

解析

(1)答題關鍵在第 句。

(2)在四個選項中，第三句只有選 (A) 項的「不用擔心你不會有問題的」，第四句才會接著說「我不想冒考不上的險」。

22. Teacher：Peter, I think we need to talk.

（彼得，我們需要談談。）

Peter： Yes, Ma'am.

（好的，老師。）

Teacher：＿＿＿＿＿＿＿

Peter： I forgot to bring it to school.

（我忘了帶來學校。）

(A) What's wrong with you? 有什麼不妥嗎？　(B) Are you feeling alright? 你感覺還好吧

(C) You didn't come to class yesterday. 你昨天沒來上課。　(D) You didn't turn in your assignment today. 你今天作業沒交。

解析

(1)答題關鍵在第四句。

(2)在四個選項中，第三句只有選 (D) 項的「你今天作業沒交」，第四句才會接著說「我忘了帶來學校」。

23.Jim： Are we going to have a vacation this summer?

（今年夏天我們要去度假嗎？）

Molly：Where do you like to go?

（你會想去哪裡？）

Jim：＿＿＿＿＿＿＿＿

Molly：Sounds great!

（太好了！）

(A) I have no idea. What do you think? 我不知道。妳認為呢？ (B) It seems that weather will be good. 天氣好像會不錯。 (C) Let's go somewhere near the beach. 我們去海邊好了。 (D) It depends on how much money we have. 這要看看我們還有多少錢。

解析

(1)答題關鍵在第四句。

(2)在四個選項中，第三句只有選(C) 項的「我們去海邊好了」，第四句才會接著說「太好了」。

24.Helen：Do you want me to bring you something for lunch?

（要我買些午餐給妳嗎？）

Nancy：＿＿＿＿＿＿＿＿

Helen：No problem, whatever you ask for.

（妳要什麼都沒問題。）

(A) No bother. I am not hungry at all. 不必了我一點都不餓。 (B) A hamburger, small coffee, and an apple pie. 一份漢堡一小杯咖啡及一份蘋果派。 (C) Where are you going to eat? 你要去哪裡用餐？ (D) Are you going alone or with friends? 自己去還是跟朋友去？

解析

(1)答題關鍵在第三句。

(2)在四個選項中，第二句只有選 (B) 項的「一份漢堡一小杯咖啡……」，第三句才會接著說「妳要什麼都沒問題」。

25.Milly：I have a reservation for two at 6:30.

（我有六點半兩個人的訂位。）

Host：＿＿＿＿＿＿＿＿

Milly：It's Milly Chang.

（名字叫米莉‧張）

Host：Thank you. Please follow me.

（謝謝。請跟我來。）

(A) Where are you from? 妳是哪裡人？　(B) May I have your name? 可以告訴我名字嗎？

(C) Can you wait for a minute? 請稍等一下。　(D) May I take your order? 妳要點菜了嗎？

解析

(1)答題關鍵在第三句。

(2)在四個選項中，第二句只有選 (B) 項的「可以告訴我名字嗎」，第三句才會接著說「名字叫米莉‧張」。

III. 綜合測驗

以下三篇短文，共有 15 個空格，為第 26 至 40 題，每題有四個選項，請依各篇短文文意，選出一個最適合該空格的答案。

▲下篇短文共有 5 個空格，為第 26-30 題，請依短文文意，選出一個最適合該空格的答案。

　　Opinions are strongly divided about the type of clothing which is appropriate for worship. According to some religious leaders, people who come to pray should wear clothing that shows respect and ____26____ for their religion. They shouldn't be wearing clothes that are for jogging, shopping, or attending a ball game. On the other hand, there are many religious leaders who don't care about such ____27____ issues. They believe that religion, ____28____ is a spiritual matter, isn't concerned with clothing. They welcome everyone who attends religious services. Most people think that the issue actually goes ____29____ clothing. More formal clothing usually accompanies an atmosphere which is more traditional and ____30____. Informal clothing, however, is more acceptable in religious services that are more contemporary and informal.

　　（關於祭拜時要穿哪一類服裝較為恰當的意見強烈分歧。根據宗教領袖的說法，來祈禱的人應穿對他們的宗教能表示尊敬與 ____26____ 的服裝。他們不應穿慢跑、購物或參加球賽的衣服。反之，也有不少宗教領袖不在乎這樣 ____27____ 議題。他們相信宗教 ____28____，是精神層面的事，與穿衣服無關。他們歡迎每一個人來參加宗教活動。大多數人認為該議題實際上 ____29____ 服裝。較正式服裝通常穿於傳統與 ____30____ 的場合。然而，非正式服裝在更當代和非正式的宗教活動裡更會被接受。）

26. 題句：people who come to pray should wear clothing that shows respect and ____26____ for their religion.

選項：(A) limitation 限制　(B) admiration 欽佩　(C) restriction 限定　(D) comparison 比較

解析

(1)答題關鍵在題目空格左、右邊的「shows respect」與「for their religion」。

(2)四個選項中，只有選 (B) 項的「admiration」放入空格，才是有意義連成整句的正確選項。

27. 題句：there are many religious leaders who don't care about such ＿＿＿27＿＿＿ issues.

　　選項：(A) healthy 健康　(B) diligent 勤勉的　(C) sincere 真誠的　(D) material 物質的

解析

(1)答題關鍵在題目空格左、右邊的「many religious leaders don't care about such」與「issues」。

(2)四個選項中，只有選(D)項的「material」放入空格，才是有意義連成整句的正確選項。

**28.題句：They believe that religion, ＿＿＿28＿＿＿ is a spiritual matter,

　　選項：(A) who 誰　(B) what 什麼　(C) which 哪一　(D) why 為何

解析

(1)答題關鍵在題目空格左邊的「religion」一字，它是前置詞。

(2)四個選項中，只有選(C)項的「which」才是代表「事、物」的關係代名詞。將之放入空格，才是符合文法的正確選項。

**29.題句：Most people think that the issue actually goes ＿＿＿29＿＿＿ clothing.

　　選項：(A) beyond 越過　(B) along 沿著　(C) against 反對　(D) between 兩者之間

解析

(1)答題關鍵在題目空格左邊的「goes」。

(2)四個選項中，只有選(A)項的「beyond」放入空格，連成 go beyond（超越、超出範圍）的片語。它才是有意義連成整句的正確選項。

30. 題句：More formal clothing usually accompanies an atmosphere which is more traditional and ＿＿＿30＿＿＿

　　選項：(A) playful 愛玩的　(B) naughty 頑皮的　(C) serious 嚴肅的　(D) casual 偶然的

解析

(1)答題關鍵在題目空格左邊的「more traditional and」。

(2)四個選項中，只有選(C)項的「serious」放入空格，才是有意義連成整句的正確選項。

▲下篇短文共有 5 個空格，為第 31-35 題，請依短文文意，選出一個最適合該空格的答案。

　　Vincent Willem van Gogh (30 March, 1853-29 July, 1890) was a Dutch Post-Impressionist painter whose work had a far-reaching influence on 20th century art. Little ＿＿＿31＿＿＿ during his lifetime, his fame grew in the years after his death. Today, he is widely regarded as one of history's greatest painters and an important ＿＿＿32＿＿＿ to the foundations of modern art. Van Gogh did not begin painting ＿＿＿33＿＿＿ his late twenties, and most of his bestknown works were produced during his final two years. He produced more than 2,000 artworks, ＿＿＿34＿＿＿ of around 900 paintings and 1,100 drawings and sketches. He was little known during his lifetime; however, his work was a strong influence on the Modernist art ＿＿＿35＿＿＿ , and today many of his pieces - including his numerous self portraits, landscapes, portraits and sunflowers - are among the world's most recognizable and expensive works of art.

　　文森‧梵谷（1853.03.30.~1890.07.29）是荷蘭後印象派畫家。他的作品對二十世

紀藝術有深遠的影響。在他有生之年少有　　31　　，他在死後才成名。今天，他被公認是史上最偉大的畫家與對現代藝術打下基礎的重要　　32　　。梵谷　　33　　近 30 歲時才開始作畫，而他的多數名作是在死前兩年內畫的。他的畫作超過 2,000 件，　　34　　約 900 件油畫與 1,100 件素描和草圖。他在生前幾乎沒有人認識他，不過，他的畫作對　　35　　現代藝術有深遠的影響。今天他的多數作品——包括他的許多自畫像、風景、其他畫像、向日葵等，都是世上公認為最昂貴的藝術作品。

**31. 題句：Little ＿＿31＿＿ during his lifetime,

　　選項：(A) appreciate 讚賞（原形動詞）　(B) appreciates（現在式）　(C) appreciated（過去式）　(D) appreciating（動名詞）

解析

(1)答題關鍵在空格左邊的「Little」。在此指「很少人」。

(2)四個選項中，只有選 (C) 項的「appreciated（讚賞）」放入空格，才符合題意的「在他有生之年很少人讚賞他的作品」。才是正確選項。

32. 題句：he is widely regarded as one of history's greatest painters and an important ＿＿32＿＿ to the foundations of modern art.

　　選項：(A) generator 發電機　(B) contributor 貢獻者　(C) distributor 分配者　(D) tractor 牽引機

解析

(1)答題關鍵在題目空格左、右邊的「an important」與「to the foundations of modern art」。

(2)四個選項中，只有選 (B) 項的「contributor」放入空格，才是有意義連成整句的正確選項。

**33. 題句：Van Gogh did not begin painting ＿＿33＿＿ his late twenties,

　　選項：(A) until 直到……　(B) with 與　(C) than 比……　(D) rather 相當

解析

(1)答題關鍵在題句前段的「did not」。

(2)四個選項中只有選 (A) 項的「until」，才符合文法「not~until」的正確選項。

34. 題句：He produced more than 2,000 artworks, ＿＿34＿＿ of around 900 paintings and 1,100 drawings and sketches.

　　選項：(A) covering 覆蓋　(B) containing 包含　(C) composing 組成　(D) consisting 組成

解析

(1)答題關鍵在題目空格右邊的「of」。

(2)四個選項中，只有選 (D) 項的「consisting」放入空格，連成 consist of 片語用法，才是有意義連成整句的正確選項。

**35.題句：his work was a strong influence on the Modernist art _____35_____ ,

選項：(A) that followed 跟隨　(B) be followed 被跟隨　(C) follows 跟隨（現在式）　(D) followed（過去式）

解析

(1)答題關鍵在題目空格左邊的整句。

(2)四個選項中，只有選(A)項的「that followed」放入空格，才是有意義連成整句的正確選項。

▲下篇短文共有 5 個空格，為第 36-40 題，請依短文文意，選出一個最適合該空格的答案。

　　The tiger may be more ancient and distinct than we thought. Tigers are less closely related to lions, leopards and jaguars _____36_____ these other big cats are to each other, according to a new study. The genetic analysis also reveals that the tiger began evolving 3.2 million years ago, and its closest living _____37_____ is the equally endangered snow leopard. _____38_____ the popularity and endangered status of tigers, much remains to be discovered about them, including how they evolved. It has long been known that the five species of big cat - the tiger, lion, leopard, jaguar and snow leopard - and the two species of clouded leopard are more closely related to each other than to other smaller cats. But it has been difficult to pin _____39_____ the exact relationships between them. So to find out more, scientists _____40_____ an analysis of the DNA of all these species.

　　（老虎可能比我們想像的更古老與其差異性。根據一項新研究，老虎與獅子、花豹、美洲豹的關聯性 _____36_____ 這三種大貓之間的關聯性還少。基因分析也顯示老虎在 320 萬年前就開始進化，牠與近親雪豹都屬瀕臨絕種。不論牠的普及性與瀕臨絕種的狀況，還有很多都有待研究，包括牠們怎麼進化。人們早知 5 種大貓——老虎、獅子、豹、美洲豹和雪豹——兩種雲豹比較體型較小貓科關係更密切。但是要把牠們明確劃分有些困難。為了查明更多，科學家進行一個所有這些品種的 DNA 分析。）

**36.題句：Tigers are less closely related to lions, leopards and jaguars _____36_____ these other big cats are to each other,

選項：(A) than 比……　(B) while 當……　(C) before……之前　(D) since 自從

解析

(1)答題關鍵在空格左右方的兩個子句，特別是句首出現的「less closely（更少關聯）」，這就表示空格前後是兩子句比較。（看了題句的中譯就更清楚）

(2)四個選項中只有(A)項的 than 才是符合文法的正確選項。

37. 題句：and its closest living _____37_____ is the equally endangered snow leopard.

選項：(A) demand 要求　(B) battery 蓄電池　(C) method 方法　(D) relative 親戚

解析

(1)答題關鍵在空格左方的 its closest living~（牠最有關聯且仍存活的……）。

(2)四個選項中，只有選(D)項的「relatives」才是符合文法的正確選項。

**38.題句：_____38_____ the popularity and endangered status of tigers,

　　選項：(A) Both 兩者　(B) Despite 不論　(C) Without 無　(D) From 從

解析

(1)四個選項中，只有選(B)項的「Despite 不論」才符合題意與文法規定。才是正確選項。

**39.題句：But it has been difficult to pin _____39_____ the exact relationships between them.

　　選項：(A) to 到　(B) on 在……之上　(C) down 下方　(D) under 在……之下

解析

(1)答題關鍵在題目空格左邊的「pin」。

(2)四個選項中，只有選(C)項的「down」放入空格，連成 pin down（ ）的片語用法，才是有意義連成整句的正確選項。

40. 題句：scientists _____40_____ an analysis of the DNA of all these species.

　　選項：(A) conducted 主導、引導　(B) mistreated 虐待　(C) ridiculed 嘲笑　(D) neglected 疏忽

解析

(1)答題關鍵在題目空格右邊的「an analysis of the DNA」。

(2)四個選項中，只有選(A)項的「conducted」放入空格，才是有意義連成整句的正確選項。

IV. 閱讀測驗

以下有三篇短文，共有 10 個題目，為第 41 至 50 題，請於閱讀短文後，選出最適當的答案。

▲閱讀下文，回答第 41-43 題

One summer afternoon when I went to visit grandmother, she was busy with her pottery. She was sitting on the floor on her green shawl, with her property all around her. In her hand was a small bowl, which she was polishing.

I sat beside grandmother to watch her smooth and polish the pottery. To smooth out the rough edges, she used a pad used for cleaning pots. Then dampening the pottery, she rubbed it with a small, smooth stone until it shone.

Her hands at times would move swiftly and then slow down. While working, she sometimes hummed a song to herself. As I was sitting beside grandmother, she didn't even glance at me for a long time because she was concerning on her pottery.

After completing the pottery, she glanced up at me over her eyeglasses and asked, "When did you come?" I said, "I came a long time ago." Then we both laughed and sat there on the floor chatting for a few minutes.

（某夏天的下午我去拜訪祖母時，她正忙於她的陶瓷。她當時圍著綠色披肩坐在地板上，旁邊都是她的寶貝陶瓷。她正在磨亮手裡的小碗。

　　我坐在祖母旁邊看她順利的磨亮這件陶瓷。爲了刷平粗糙的邊緣，她用清潔用的襯墊來磨亮。然後把陶瓷弄溼，她用一塊小且光滑的石頭擦它，直到發亮。

　　她的手有時會迅速移動然後慢下來。在工作時，她有時對她自己哼一首歌。當我坐在祖母旁邊時，她甚至沒看我一眼，因爲她只專心在她的陶瓷。

　　在完成這件陶瓷之後，她在她的眼鏡上方瞄我並問「你什麼時候來的？」我說，「我來很久了。」然後我們兩個笑著並且坐在那裡在地板上聊天幾分鐘。）

41. What was the grandmother doing when the author visited her?
　　（當作者去看她時，祖母在做什麼？）
　(A) She was rubbing a shawl. 她正擦一條披肩。
　(B) She was writing a song. 她正寫一支歌。
　(C) She was washing her eyeglasses. 她正洗她的眼鏡。
　(D) She was polishing her pottery. 她正擦亮她的陶瓷。

解析
從答題關鍵的「One summer afternoon when I went to visit grandmother, she was busy with her pottery.」可看出，(D) 項的「She was polishing her pottery.」才是正確選項。

42. What would the grandmother do while she was working?
　　（當她工作時，祖母能做什麼？）
　(A) She sometimes hummed a song. 她有時哼唱一支歌。
　(B) She always laughed loudly. 她總是高聲笑。
　(C) She waved her hand all the time. 她一直揮動她的手。
　(D) She chatted most of the time. 她多數時間聊天。

解析
從答題關鍵的「While working, she sometimes hummed a song to herself.」可看出，(A) 項的「She sometimes hummed a song」才是正確選項。

43. Why did the author and the grandmother laugh?
　　（作者和祖母爲什麼笑？）
　(A) The grandmother made beautiful pottery. 祖母做美麗的陶瓷。
　(B) They both loved singing a song to themselves. 他們兩個喜歡對他們自己唱一首歌。
　(C) The author brought the grandmother some pottery. 作者爲祖母帶來一些陶瓷。
　(D) The grandmother didn't notice the author was there. 祖母沒注意到作者在那裡。

解析
從答題關鍵的「"When did you come?" I said, "I came a long time ago." Then we both laughed and sat

there...」可看出，(D) 項的「The grandmother didn't notice the author was there」才是正確選項。

▲閱讀下文，回答第 44-47 題

Cacao beans (from which chocolate is made) were brought to Spain from Central America in the 16th century. The Indians of Central America had been making hot chocolate drinks for many years. They made their hot chocolate with water, not milk, and it was dark brown, spicy and bitter. At first, the Spanish people were not impressed with this strange drink. However, someone came up with the idea of adding sugar. As a result, drinking hot chocolate became popular in Spain, and quickly spread to England, France, Italy and beyond.

Because cacao beans had to be shipped such a long distance, chocolate was an expensive drink and only the rich could afford it. The ordinary people generally drank beer, cheap wine or water. They probably wondered how this special chocolate drink tasted. As drinking chocolate became popular, chocolate houses grew up in England. Rich men spent hours in them, drinking chocolate while they played cards for money, read the newspapers and shared the latest gossip. Rich ladies did not generally go to the chocolate houses, but enjoyed their hot chocolate at home, usually for breakfast.

（可可豆〔做巧克力的豆〕在 16 世紀從中美洲被帶到西班牙。中美洲的印第安人做熱巧克力已經多年。他們用水做他們的熱巧克力，並非用牛奶，並且它是暗褐色、辣和苦味的。最初，西班牙人對這種奇怪的飲料沒有好印象。不過，某人提出加糖的想法。因此，喝熱巧克力在西班牙變得受歡迎，並且迅速傳到英國、法國、義大利，和其他地方。

因為可可豆必須被運送到這麼遙遠的距離，巧克力是一種昂貴的飲料，只有富人能付得起。普通的人們一般喝啤酒、便宜的酒或者水。他們或許想知道這種特別的巧克力味道如何。當喝巧克力變得流行時，巧克力屋在英國興盛起來。有錢男人會好幾個小時玩牌、看報紙、分享最新八卦新聞時，都會喝巧克力。富有的女士一般不去巧克力屋，而是在家喜喝她們的熱巧克力，通常是當早餐用。）

44. What is the best title for this passage?
（這段文章最好的標題是什麼？）

(A) What Did Rich People Do in Europe? 富人在歐洲做什麼？

(B) Why Did People Drink Hot Chocolate? 人們為什麼喝熱巧克力？

(C) Where Did Hot Chocolate Come from? 熱巧克力來自哪裡？

(D) How Did the Indians Grow Cacao Beans? 那些印第安人怎樣種可可豆？

解析

從本文內容來看，談的都是有關可可豆的發源與發展等，只有 (C) 項的「Where Did Hot Chocolate Come from?」才是正確選項。

45. What did the Spanish people like to add to their hot chocolate?

（西班牙人喜歡加入什麼在熱巧克力？）

(A) Butter. 黃油。　(B) Eggs. 蛋。　(C) Wine. 酒。　(D) Sugar. 糖。

解析

從答題關鍵的「　」可看出，(D)項的「Sugar.」才是正確選項。

46. According to the passage, why was chocolate so expensive?

（根據本文，爲什麼巧克力如此昂貴？）

(A) Because growing cacao beans took a lot of time.

因爲種可可豆占用許多時間。

(B) Because shipping cacao beans cost a lot of money.

因爲裝運可可豆花費許多錢。

(C) Because drinking chocolate was affordable for everyone.

因爲喝巧克力對每人來說是付得起的。

(D) Because going to chocolate houses became popular in Europe.

因爲去巧克力屋在歐洲變得很風行。

解析

從答題關鍵的「Because cacao beans had to be shipped such a long distance, chocolate was an expensive drink」可看出，(B)項的「Because shipping cacao beans cost a lot of money.」才是正確選項。

47. According to the passage, which of the following statements is true?

（根據本文，下列陳述中的哪個是眞？）

(A) Only the wealthy could afford hot chocolate.

只有富人能買得起熱巧克力。

(B) Rich ladies enjoyed their hot chocolate in cafes.

富有的女士在咖啡館喜愛他們的熱巧克力。

(C) Sometimes beer was added to the hot chocolate.

有時啤酒被增加到熱巧克力。

(D) Chocolate houses became popular all over Europe.

巧克力屋遍及歐洲變得受歡迎。

解析

從答題關鍵的「Because cacao beans had to be shipped such a long distance, chocolate was an expensive drink and only the rich could afford it.」可看出，(A)項的「Only the wealthy could afford hot chocolate.」才是正確選項。

▲閱讀下文，回答第 48-50 題

　　Last year, when Daniel decided to buy a bicycle, it was a serious matter to him. He intended to buy a good one, but knew that it would be expensive. After looking at different types of bicycles in many bike shops, he decided to buy a mountain bike. However, that was not all. He also had to get many accessories for it. Since he couldn't afford to buy them all at once, he bought a helmet and gloves first. Then, he purchased tools, bags to hang on the bike, special bike shoes and light. After that, he found that all of the accessories were actually more expensive than the bike.

　　With this bike, he started to train himself to be a bike racer, which might take a lot of time and **stamina**. This was going to be a very difficult process and could be extremely exhausting at first. However, in order to be a competitive racer, it was necessary. He had to ride an average of 200-300 miles each week. In addition, he had to be very cautious about what he ate and drank. Whenever he ate or drank something unhealthy, such as candy or coffee, he was slowed down and his training was disrupted. What was even more challenging for Daniel was that he also had to work full-time to support himself.

　　（去年，當丹尼爾決定買一輛腳踏車時，這對他是一件認真的事。他打算買好一點的，但是知道好的腳踏車很昂貴。在看過很多腳踏車店的不同款式腳踏車後，他決定買越野腳踏車。但是，並非只有這些。他也必須買很多零配件。因爲無法一下全部都買，他先買一頂鋼盔和手套。然後，他購買工具，腳踏車袋掛，特別的腳踏車鞋和照明燈。在那之後，他發現所有零配件實際上比腳踏車還貴。

　　有了這輛腳踏車，他開始訓練自己成爲腳踏車選手，這需要花許多時間和耐力。這將是一個非常難的過程，而一開始非常耗體力。但是，爲了成爲有競爭力的參賽者，那是必要的。他必須每週騎平均 200-300 英里。另外，他必須非常注意飲食。每當他吃或喝不健康的東西時，例如糖果或者咖啡，他的車速變慢，他的訓練被中斷。給丹尼爾更挑戰的是，他也必須全職工作來養活自己。）

48. According to the passage, what did Daniel buy first?

　　（根據本文，丹尼爾首先買什麼？）

　(A) A helmet and gloves. 一頂鋼盔和手套。

　(B) A mountain bike. 越野腳踏車。

　(C) Bags to hang on the bike. 腳踏車上的掛袋。

　(D) Bike shoes and light. 腳踏車鞋和照明燈。

解析

從答題關鍵的「After looking at different types of bicycles in many bike shops, he decided to buy a mountain bike.」可看出，(B) 項的「A mountain bike.」才是正確選項。

49. Which of the following is the closest in meaning to the word "stamina" in the second paragraph?

　　（下列哪項與第 2 個段落 stamina 單字的意思最接近 stamen？）

(A) muscle 肌肉　(B) obstacle 障礙　(C) energy 能量　(D) breath 氣息

解析

stamina 為精力、耐力之意。只有(C)項的「energy 活力」才是與其意思最接近的正確選項。

50. According to the passage, which of the following statements is **NOT** true?

（根據本文，下列陳述中哪項不實？）

(A) Eating candy and drinking coffee was helpful to Daniel.

吃糖果喝咖啡對丹尼爾有幫助。

(B) Daniel received training and worked full-time at the same time.

丹尼爾須受訓練並全職工作。

(C) Daniel had to ride 200 to 300 miles each week.

丹尼爾必須每週騎 200 到 300 英里。

(D) After buying a bike, Daniel trained himself to be a bike racer

買了腳踏車後，丹尼爾自我訓練要成為賽車選手。

解析

從答題關鍵的「Whenever he ate or drank something unhealthy, such as candy or coffee, he was slowed down and his training was disrupted.」可看出，(A) 項的「Eating candy and drinking coffee was helpful to Daniel」才是本題的答案。

100年統測（四技二專考試）

I. 字彙題

第 1 至 8 題，每題均有一個劃底線的字詞，請在四個選項中，選擇一個與劃底線的字詞意義最接近的答案。第 9 至 15 題，請選擇一個最適合的答案，以完成該句。

1. Don't park your car here because it is reserved for the <u>handicapped</u>.
   （不要在這裡停車，因為它是殘障車位。）
   (A) fascinated 使著迷　(B) twisted 扭曲　(C) disabled 生理殘障的　(D) endangered 瀕臨絕種

   解析
   (1)先看底線字的中譯為「殘障者」。
   (2)只有(C)選項的「生理殘障的」，才是與底線字意思最接近的正確選項。

2. In <u>conventional</u> farming, chemicals are frequently used to kill insects and fight diseases.
   （在傳統農作裡，化學製品經常被用來殺死昆蟲並對抗農作病變。）
   (A) geographical 地理的　(B) traditional 傳統的　(C) accidental 偶然的　(D) environmental 環境

   解析
   (1)先看底線字的中譯為「傳統式的」。
   (2)只有(C)選項的「傳統的」才是與底線字意思最接近的正確選項。

3. In preparation for the wedding anniversary party, the couple invited an outstanding designer to remodel the <u>interior</u> of the house.
   （為婚禮週年慶聚會作準備，夫婦邀請一個傑出的設計師重作房子的內部裝潢。）
   (A) inside 裡面　(B) decoration 裝飾　(C) invasion 侵略　(D) price 價格

   解析
   (1)先看底線字的中譯為「內部的」。
   (2)只有(A)選項的「裡面的」，才是與底線字意思最接近的正確選項。

4. After sharing an apartment with a friend for two years, you should be able to <u>recognize</u> him by his voice.
   （與朋友共住公寓兩年後，你應該能認出他的聲音。）
   (A) reveal 揭示　(B) identify 識別出　(C) allow 允許　(D) 擾亂 disturb

解析
(1)先看底線字的中譯為「認出」。
(2)只有(B)選項的「識別出」，才是與底線字意思最接近的正確選項。

5. There is a strong <u>resemblance</u> between the man and the boy. They must be father and son.
　（那個人和男孩長得很像。他們一定是父親和兒子。）
　　(A) liking 愛好　(B) likelihood 可能　(C) likewise 同樣　(D) likeness 相像

解析
(1)先看底線字的中譯為「相似」。
(2)只有(D)選項的「相像」，才是與底線字意思最接近的正確選項。

6. When the potato was first brought to Europe, many people thought it was a <u>weird</u> vegetable.
　（當馬鈴薯首次被帶到歐洲時，很多人認為它是一種怪異的菜蔬。）
　　(A) underground 在地下　(B) poisonous 有毒的　(C) nutritious 有營養的　(D) strange 奇怪

解析
(1)先看底線字的中譯為「怪異的」。
(2)只有(D)選項的「奇怪的」，才是與底線字意思最接近的正確選項。

7. She was fully attracted by the novel; therefore, when her mother asked her to run an errand, she. put the book down <u>reluctantly</u>.
　（她完全被小說情節吸引，因此，當她母親要她做家事時，她不情願地放下書。）
　　(A) genuinely 真實　(B) rapidly 迅速　(C) unwillingly 不情願　(D) definitely 明確地

解析
(1)先看底線字的中譯為「勉強地」。
(2)只有(C)選項的「不情願地」，才是與底線字意思最接近的正確選項。

8. In some cultures, giving someone a letter opener <u>implies</u> that the relationship will be cut.
　（在某些文化裡，遞給某人一把開信刀暗示關係將被切斷。）
　　(A) suggests 建議　(B) includes 包括　(C) impresses 給留下印象　(D) bargains 特價品

解析
(1)先看底線字的中譯為「暗示」。
(2)只有(A)選項的「建議」，才是與底線字意思最接近的正確選項。

9. She wasted so much money on luxuries that she ran into ＿＿＿＿＿＿ very soon.
　（她在奢侈品上浪費太多錢，很快她就陷入 ＿＿＿＿＿＿ 。）
　　(A) doubt 懷疑　(B) date 日期　(C) debt 欠債　(D) dirt 灰塵

解析

(1)答題關鍵在「在奢侈品上浪費太多錢」。

(2)只有(C)選項的「欠債」放入空格，才是符合題意的正確選項。

10. Whenever I am in trouble, he always helps me out. I really _____ his assistance

（每當我遇到麻煩時，他總是幫助我度過難關。我真的 _____ 他的幫助。）

(A) accomplish 完成　(B) associate 同事　(C) achieve 取得　(D) appreciate 感激

解析

(1)答題關鍵在「我真的 _____ 他的幫助」。

(2)只有(D)選項的「感激」放入空格，才是符合題意的正確選項。

11. He is filling out a visa application _____ because he is going to visit South Africa next month.

（他正填寫簽證申請 _____ 因為他下個月將要訪問南非。）

(A) farm 農場　(B) firm 堅定的　(C) form 表格　(D) fame 名氣

解析

(1)答題關鍵在「正填寫簽證申請 _____ 」。

(2)只有(C)選項的「表格」放入空格，才是符合題意的正確選項

12. Studying should be the _____ of a student, not working part-time.

（研習功課應該是學生的 _____ ，不是兼差工作。）

(A) priority 優先事務　(B) resume 簡歷　(C) margin 邊　(D) variation 變化

解析

(1)答題關鍵在「研習功課應該是學生的 _____ 」。

(2)只有(A)項的「優先事務」放入空格，才是符合題意的正確選項。

13. A university president has a high social _____ , and (s)he is highly respected by the people.

（大學校長有崇高的社會 _____ 而他或她受高度尊重。）

(A) stage 階段　(B) status 地位　(C) statue 雕像　(D) station 車站

解析

(1)答題關鍵在「大學校長有崇高的社會 _____ 」。

(2)只有(B)選項的「地位」放入空格，才是符合題意的正確選項。

14. Since water shortage in many regions is getting worse, it is predictable that the world will be facing water _____ soon.

（由於很多地區的缺水情況惡化，不久世界將是是可預測的面對水 _____ 。）

(A) leve 水準1　(B) energy 能量　(C) crisis 危機　(D) sink 下沉

解析
(1)答題關鍵在「面對水 ＿＿＿＿＿」。
(2)只有(C)選項的「危機」放入空格，才是符合題意的正確選項。

15.The ＿＿＿＿＿ between the government and the general people of Egypt led to an eighteen-day. demonstration, which caused the President to step down
（埃及政府和人民的 ＿＿＿＿＿ 導致 18 天的遊行示威，導致總統辭職。）
(A) cabinet 內閣　(B) conflict 衝突　(C) captain 隊長　(D) company 公司

解析
(1)答題關鍵在「埃及政府和人民的 ＿＿＿＿＿ 導致 18 天的遊行示威……」
(2)只有(B)選項的「衝突」放入空格，才是符合題意的正確選項。

II. 對話題

第 16 至 25 題，請依對話內容，選出一個最適合的答案，使其成為有意義的對話。

16.Paul: Hi, I wonder if you could help me. I have a fever and a sore throat. Can you give me something for it?
（保羅：喂，我想知道你可否幫我。我發燒且喉嚨痛。你可給我一些藥嗎？）
Pharmacist: ＿＿＿＿＿
（藥劑師：＿＿＿＿＿）
Paul: Thank you.
（保羅：感謝你。）
(A) Did you want to try our delicious doughnuts? 你想要嘗我們的美味甜甜圈嗎？　(B) Smoking or nonsmoking? 吸煙還是不吸煙？　(C) OK.You can take these medicines twice a day. 沒問題。你拿這些藥，一天吃兩次。　(D) That's very kind of you. 你太好了。

解析
(1)答題關鍵在第 1 句的「你可給我一些藥嗎？」。
(2)只有(C)選項的「沒問題。你拿這些藥，一天吃兩次」放入空格，才是有意義回應第 1 句的正確選項。

17.Jenny: So, how was your first date with Mark?
（珍妮：那麼，妳與馬克的第一次約會如何？）
Tina: Terrible! Can you believe he asked me how much I weighed?
（田娜：可怕！你能相信他問我有多重嗎？）
Jenny: ＿＿＿＿＿

（珍妮：_____）

(A) He doesn't know your age? 他不知道你的年齡嗎？　(B) Exercise could help him keep in shape. 鍛鍊能幫助他保持身材。　(C) Why don't you wear that pink dress? 你為什麼不穿那件粉紅色女裝？　(D) Hmm. That's a little personal. 噢。那是有點個人隱私的問題。

解析

(1)答題關鍵在第 2 句的「可怕！你能相信他問我有多重嗎？」。

(2)只有 (D) 選項的「那是有點個人隱私的問題。」放入空格，才是有意義回應第 2 句的正確選項。

18. Daniel: Are you ready to play tennis?

（丹尼爾：你準備打網球嗎？）

Andy: _____ And you're not going to win today!

（安迪：_____ 並且你今天不會贏！）

Daniel: Don't say things you're not sure about. You might have to eat your words.

（丹尼爾：不要說你沒把握的事。你可能會食言。）

(A) What's the matter with you? 你發生了什麼事？　(B) No, I'm still thinking. 不，我仍然想。　(C) You bet! 當然！　(D) Sorry, but I've got other plans. 抱歉，但是我有其他計畫。

解析

(1)答題關鍵在第 2 句的後半句「你今天不會贏！」。

(2)只有 (C) 選項的「當然」放入空格，才是做為第 2 句前半句的正確選項。

19. Rita: Hello. What time do you close today?

（莉達：你好。你們今天什麼時候打烊？）

Tony: We close at 10:00 p.m. every day. And we open at 9:00 in the morning.

（湯尼：我們在下午 10：00 打烊，早上 9：00 開門。）

Rita: Oh, OK.

（莉達：噢，沒問題。_____）

Tony: Yeah, same hours as on the weekdays.

（湯尼：是的，週末的營業時間也一樣。）

(A) And are you open on the weekends? 你們週末營業嗎？　(B) I'll come down tonight. 我今晚將下來。Thanks. 感謝。　(C) Your sale is still on, isn't it? 你們的促銷還有，對不對？　(D) How long does it take? 要多久時間？

解析

(1)答題關鍵在第 2 句。但並沒提到週末的營業時間。

(2)所以只有 (A) 選項的「你們週末營業嗎？」放入空格，才是符合題意的正確選項。

20.Jessica: Could you call me a taxi, please?

（傑西嘉：請幫我叫一輛計程車好嗎？）

Bell Captain: Yes, ma'am.

（行李領班：是的，太太。＿＿＿＿＿＿＿＿ ）

Jessica: The airport.

（傑西嘉：我要去機場。）

Bell Captain: Sure, take a seat in the lobby. I'll let you know when it's here.

（行李領班：好的，請在大廳坐一下。車來時我會叫妳。）

(A) What model do you like? 你喜歡什麼款式？　(B) Where are you going? 你去哪兒？

(C) Let me get your car. 我去取你的車。　(D) When are you going to leave? 你何時要離開？

解析

(1)答題關鍵在第 3 句的「我要去機場。」。

(2)只有(B)選項的「你去哪兒」放入空格，第 3 句才會說「我要去機場」。

21.Lucy: You'll never guess what happened downtown.

（露西：你絕猜不到在下城發生什麼事。）

Brian: What?

（布賴恩：什麼事？）

Lucy: While I was driving home, a man ran out in front of me...with a gun!

（露西：當我駕車回家時，一個人拿了槍在我的前面跑出來）

Brian: He had a gun? It's really scary

（布賴恩：他拿了槍？真的很可怕。）

Lucy: ＿＿＿＿＿＿＿＿

（露西：＿＿＿＿＿＿＿＿ ）

(A) I'm a real fan of scary movies. 我是恐怖電影迷。　(B) You're telling me. 你才知道！

(C) Good for you. 做得不錯。　(D) That's why he is worried. 那是他焦慮的原因。

解析

(1)答題關鍵在第 5 句的「他拿了槍？真的很可怕。」。

(2)只有(B)選項的「你才知道！」放入空格，才是符合題意的正確選項。

(3)You are telling me! 不可照字面翻譯，它最接近的中譯是「你才知道！」

22.Albert: Has the 5:30 showing of the movie started yet?

（艾伯特：5：30 的電影開演了嗎？）

Clerk: ＿＿＿＿＿＿＿＿

（辦事員：＿＿＿＿＿＿＿＿ ）

Albert: Then I'll come back for the eight o'clock showing.

（艾伯特：那我回來看 8 點那一場。）

I hate to miss the beginning of a film.

（我不喜歡錯過電影的開始情節。）

(A) I don't think so. 我不這樣想。　(B) No, not yet.不，還沒開演。　(C) Yes, sir, about ten minutes ago. 是的，大約 10 分鐘以前開演了。　(D) You can hardly wait? 你不能等嗎？

解析

(1)答題關鍵在第 3 句的「那我回來看 8 點那一場。」。

(2)只有(C)選項的「大約 10 分鐘以前開演了」放入空格，之後才會有第 3 句的說法。

23. Terry: What kind of a seat do you request when you fly?

（泰利：你搭飛機時，會要求哪種座位？）

Susie: I prefer an aisle seat.

（蘇西：我較喜歡走道座位。）

Terry: Why?

（泰利：為什麼？）

Susie: _____

（蘇西：_____ ）

(A) So I can stretch my legs. 我可以伸伸腿。　(B) Sitting in the back of the plane is exciting. 坐在飛機的後段令人興奮。　(C) It doesn't usually take much time. 通常不會花很多時間。　(D) I like to sleep, and I need something to lean against. 我想睡，並且我需要東西可倚靠。

解析

(1)答題關鍵在第 3 的「為什麼」。

(2)只有(A)選項的「我可以伸伸腿。」放入空格，才是解釋為什麼想坐走道座位的原因。

24. Amy: Are there any interesting jobs in the paper today?

（艾咪：今天報紙有刊登有趣的徵才廣告嗎？）

Peter: Well, here's one for salesperson.

（彼得：這裡有一個是要徵銷售員的。）

Amy: _____

（艾咪：_____ ）

Peter: You have to make an appointment for an interview.

（彼得：你必須預約面談。）

(A) What are the qualifications? 要求什麼樣的資格？　(B) What's the salary? 薪水多少錢？

(C) Is it expensive? 它很昂貴嗎？　(D) How can I apply for the job? 我要怎樣應徵那份工作？

解析

(1)答題關鍵在第 4 句的「你必須預約面談」。

(2)只有(D) 選項的「我要怎樣應徵那份工作？」放入空格，才是符合題意的正確選項。

25. Mary: Hello. Steve?

（瑪莉：你好，史蒂夫）

David: I'm sorry, but Steve is out right now. ＿＿＿＿＿＿

（大衛：對不起，但是史蒂夫外出。＿＿＿＿＿＿）

Mary: Mary, his friend from work.

（瑪莉：瑪莉，是工作上的朋友。）

David: May I take a message?

（大衛：我可以傳個口信嗎？）

(A) Who is calling? 是哪一位？　(B) Thanks for calling. 謝謝您的來電。　(C) Why don't you call his office? 你可打到他的辦公室　(D) He will be back in ten minutes. 他10 分鐘內就會回來。

解析

(1)答題關鍵在第 3 句的「瑪莉，是工作上的朋友。」。

(2)只有(A) 選項的「是哪一位？」放入空格，第 3 句才會說「瑪莉，是工作上的朋友。」

III. 綜合測驗

以下三篇短文，共有 15 個空格，為第 26 至 40 題，每題有四個選項，請依各篇短文文意，選出一個最適合該空格的答案。

▲下篇短文共有 5 個空格，為第 26-30 題，請依短文文意，選出一個最適合該空格的答案。

　　Strolling through the streets in Taiwan, people often see a convenience store within a short walking distance. Taiwan is ＿＿＿26＿＿＿ first in the world for having the greatest number of convenience immediacy and convenience. The shelves in the stores, which reflects Taiwanese's craze ＿＿＿27＿＿＿ stores are fully stocked for consumers to pick up ＿＿＿28＿＿＿ day or night. City life is seen carrying on at the convenience store when day ends and night starts, making the store a standardized image of the city that never ＿＿＿29＿＿＿ . Nowadays, the term 7-Eleven, the name of a convenience store, ＿＿＿30＿＿＿ as a metaphor for the non-stop working pattern. Convenience stores are not only a source of wonder to foreign visitors but also one of the things that Taiwanese who go abroad miss most about hometown.

　　（漫步走在台灣的街道，人們經常看到到處都有的便利商店。在提供最直接與便利性來說，台灣是世界 ＿＿＿26＿＿＿ 第一的。店裡的貨架子，可反應出台灣的時尚 ＿＿＿27＿＿＿ 這些商店存貨齊全，以讓顧客 ＿＿＿28＿＿＿ 白天或晚上都可來購物。便

利商店也是都市生活的寫照，給人的印象好像人們晚上從不 ___29___ 。而現在，「7-Eleven」這個名詞原為便利商店的店名，已 ___30___ 「不斷工作型態」的比方。對外國人而言，便利商店不僅一個美好事物的來源，而且也是台灣人出國後，最懷念的家鄉事物之一。）

26. 題句：在提供最直接與便利性來說，台灣是世界 ___26___ 第一的。
    選項：(A) ranked 排名　(B) famous 著名的　(C) popular 受歡迎的　(D) favored 贊同

解析

(1)答題關鍵在「台灣是世界 ___26___ 第一的。」。

(2)只有(A)選項的「ranked」放入空格，才是符合題意的正確選項。

27. 題句：which reflects Taiwanese's craze ___27___ stores are fully stocked ...
    這反映出台灣的時尚 ___27___ 這些商店存貨齊全……
    選項：(A) at 在　(B) in　(C) of　(D) for 因為

解析

(1)答題關鍵在「這反映出台灣的時尚 ___27___ 這些商店存貨齊全……」。

(2)只有(D)選項的「因為」放入空格，才是符合題意的正確選項。

28. 題句： ___28___ 白天或晚上顧客都可來購物。
    選項：(A) even so 雖然如此　(B) no matter 不論　(C) because of 由於　(D) at best 充其量

解析

(1)答題關鍵在「 ___28___ 白天或晚上顧客都可來購物。」。

(2)只有(B)選項的「不論」放入空格，才是符合題意的正確選項。

29. 題句：the city that never ___29___ （城市的居民晚上從不 ___29___ ）
    選項：(A) sleep 睡的原形動詞　(B) had slept 過去完成式　(C) slept 過去式　(D) sleeps 主詞三單時睡的現在式

解析

(1)答題關鍵在「the city that never ___29___ （城市的居民晚上從不 ___29___ 」。

(2)只有(D)選項的「sleeps」放入空格，才符合「主詞 the city 是三單主詞，其普通動詞須＋s」的文法規定。

30. 題句：「7-Eleven」這個名詞原為便利商店的店名，已 ___30___ 「不斷工作型態」的比方。
    選項：(A) used 過去式　(B) uses 主詞三單時的現在式　(C) is used 被動語態　(D) is using 現在進行式

解析

(1)答題關鍵在「已_____30_____」不斷工作型態「的比方。」。

(2)只有(C)選項的「is used」放入空格，才符合題意是被動語態的文法規定。

▲下篇短文共有5個空格，為第31-35題，請依短文文意，選出一個最適合該空格的答案。

　　The little country school house was heated by an old-fashioned coal stove. A little boy had the job of coming to school early each day to start the fire and _____31_____ the room before his teacher and his classmates arrived. One morning they arrived to find the schoolhouse in flames. They dragged the unconscious little boy out of the building more dead than _____32_____ . The doctor told his mother that her son would surely die — which was for the best, really — for the terrible fire had destroyed the _____33_____ half of his body. But the brave boy didn't want to die. He made up his mind that he would survive. Ultimately through his daily massages, his iron persistence, _____34_____ his resolute determination, he did develop the ability to stand up, then to walk with others' help, then to walk by himself — and then — to run. He began to walk to school, then to run to school, and to run for the sheer joy of running. _____35_____ in college he made the track team. This determined young man, Dr. Glenn Cunningham, ran the world's fastest mile!

　　（一間鄉下學校使用煤爐加熱提供暖氣。一個小男孩之前的工作是，在全校師生還沒到校之前，他要每天提早到校啓動火爐_____31_____房間。 有一天早上，他們到校時發現校舍起火。 他們把已無意識的小男孩拖出屋外_____32_____。醫生告訴他的母親說，她的兒子一定會死去，也許這樣才是最好的結果，因爲惡火已嚴重燒傷了小孩身體的_____33_____半身。但是勇敢的男孩不想要死。他決定要存活下去。最後透過他的每日按摩，他的鋼鐵般的毅力，_____34_____他的堅決的決心，他確最後已能站起來，有了別人協助他也能開始走路。接著也能自己走，最後還可自己跑步。他開始走路去上學，然後跑步到學校，最後變成純粹爲快樂而跑。_____35_____在大學裡他參加田徑隊。這個堅決的年輕人，葛倫孔寧漢博士跑出世界上最快的成績。）

31. 題句：他要每天提早到校啓動火爐_____31_____房間。

　　選項：(A) paint 油漆　(B) warm 溫暖　(C) tear down 撕下　(D) design 設計

解析

(1)答題關鍵在「啓動火爐_____31_____房間。」。

(2)只有(B)選項的「溫暖」放入空格，才是符合題意的正確選項。

32. 題句：他們把已無意識的小男孩拖出屋外_____32_____。

　　選項：(A) live 生活　(B) lively 活生生的　(C) livable 適合居住的　(D) alive 活著

解析

(1)答題關鍵在「more dead than～」。

(2)只有選(D)項的「alive」放入空格，才符合「more dead than alive」的片語説法。

(3)more dead than alive 之中譯爲「快死了、奄奄一息」之意。

33. 題句：惡火已嚴重燒傷了小孩身體的 ____33____ 半身
　　選項：(A) first 第一　　(B) lower 低一點　　(C) other 其他　　(D) one 一個

解析

(1)答題關鍵在第　句的「嚴重燒傷了小孩身體的 ____33____ 半身」。

(2)只有(B)選項的「lower」放入空格，才是符合題意的正確選項。

(3)lower half of the body 指「下半身」之意。

34. 題句：他的鋼鐵般的毅力，____34____ 他的堅決的決心，他確最後已能站起來
　　選項：(A) and 和　　(B) next to 在隔壁　　(C) then 之後　　(D) or 或

解析

(1)答題關鍵在「他的鋼鐵般的毅力，____34____ 他的堅決的決心」。

(2)只有(A)選項的「和」放入空格，才是符合題意的正確選項。

35. 題句：____35____ 在大學裡他參加田徑隊
　　選項：(A) Otherwise 否則　　(B) Sadly 悲傷地　　(C) Later 之後　　(D) Rarely 稀少地

解析

(1)答題關鍵在第　句的「____35____ 在大學裡他參加田徑隊」。

(2)四個選項中，只有(C)選項的「之後」放入空格，才是符合題意的正確選項。

▲下篇短文共有 5 個空格，為第 36-40 題，請依短文文意，選出一個最適合該空格的答案。

　　For years scientists suspected that people with strong emotional ties to families, friends and community enjoy longer lives than loners do. But this had ____36____ influence on cancer care until 1989 when Dr. David Spiegel published a study involving two groups of women with breast cancer. ____37____ groups received standard medical care. Patients in one group also attended a weekly support -group meeting for one year. Those women, Dr. Spiegel found, fought cancer better and ____38____ an average of 18 months longer. ____39____ , a study showed that skin cancer patients who participated ____40____ a support group survived significantly longer than those who had received only standard care.

　　（多年來，科學家懷疑與家庭、朋友與社會感情強烈的人，比性格孤癖的人享受更長的生命。但是這對癌症影響 ____36____ 。一直到 1989 年大衛史比博士出版了有關兩組婦女罹患乳癌的研究報告之後，____37____ 組接受標準醫療護理。其中一組的病患也參加了每週一次的會議，為期一年。那些婦女，史比博士發現到，對抗癌症效果較好，而平均多 ____38____ 18個月。____39____ ，有研究報告顯示，____40____ 支援團隊會議的皮膚癌病患，比僅接受標準療程的病患，存活率明顯延長。）

36. 題句：但是這對癌症影響 ____36____ 。
　　選項：(A) little 小　　(B) much 非常　　(C) any 任何　　(D) great 大

解析

(1)答題關鍵在「但是這對癌症影響_____36_____。」。

(2)只有(A)選項的「小」放入空格，才是符合題意的正確選項。

37. 題句：_____37_____組都接受標準醫療護理

選項：(A) Each 每　(B) One 一　(C) Both 兩　(D) None 沒有一個

解析

(1)答題關鍵在「～組都接受標準醫療護理」。

(2)只有(C)選項的「both」放入空格，才符合「both 兩者都……」的文法規定。

38. 題句：對抗癌症效果較好，而平均多_____38_____18 個月

選項：(A) survive 存活　(B) surviving　(C) to survive　(D) survived

解析

(1)答題關鍵在「而平均多_____38_____18 個月」。

(2)只有(D)選項的「survived」放入空格，才是符合題意的文法規定。

39. 題句：_____39_____，有研究報告顯示，參加支援團隊會議的皮膚癌病患，比僅接受標準療程的病患，存活率明顯延長。

選項：(A) To our surprise 使我們驚奇的是　(B) Similarly 相同地　(C) Nonetheless 不過

(D) Ridiculously 可笑

解析

(1)答題關鍵在「參加支援團隊的病患比僅接受標準療程的病患，存活率明顯延長。」。

(2)只有(B)選項的「相同地」放入空格，才是符合題意的正確選項。

40. 題句：who participated _____40_____ a support group.

選項：(A) for 因　(B) at 在　(C) on 在上　(D) in 在內

解析

(1)答題關鍵在「who participated _____40_____ a support group」。

(2)只有(D)選項的「in」放入空格，才符合「participated in」的文法規定。

IV. 閱讀測驗

以下有三篇短文，共有 10 個題目，為第 41 至 50 題，請於閱讀短文後，選出最適當的答案。

▲閱讀下文，回答第 41-43 題

　　Everywhere we look there is color, from the blue sky to the green grass, from the gray concrete of a city to the black of a moonless night. Colors have a direct and powerful impact on the way we feel and react to our surroundings. When we decorate our homes, we choose colors that welcome us and make us feel good. Some colors excite us while others soothe and calm us. For example, when the Blackfriar Bridge in London was painted green, suicide jumps from the bridge decreased by 34 %. Research reveals that people have similar emotional responses to specific colors and in general, the brighter the color, the stronger the response.

（目光所及之處都有顏色，從藍天到綠草，從城市的灰色水泥到無月光夜晚的黑色。顏色對我們的感覺有直接和強力的影響。也會影響我們對週邊環境的反應。當我們裝飾我們的家時，我們會選擇適合我們且讓我們感覺不錯的顏色。一些顏色使我們興奮，也有一些顏色有助我們平靜。例如，當倫敦的布雷克橋被漆成綠色時，跳橋自殺比率降低了34%。研究顯示，人們對某特定的顏色有相似的情緒反應，一般來說，顏色越鮮艷，反應越強大。）

41. What is the best title for this passage?

（本文最佳標題是什麼？）

(A) Emotional Responses to Color 對顏色的情緒回應

(B) Color and Decoration 顏色和裝璜

(C) Suicide Jumps and Color 跳橋自殺和顏色

(D) The Importance of Color 顏色的重要性

解析

根據文章內容，(A) 項的「對顏色的情緒回應」才是最佳標題。

42. According to the passage, what color has a soothing effect on people?

（根據本文，什麼顏色對人有令人舒適影響？）

(A) Red 紅　(B) Blue 藍色　(C) Green 綠色　(D) Gray 灰色

解析

從答題關鍵的「當倫敦的布雷克橋被漆成綠色時，跳橋自殺比率降低了34%。」可看出，(C) 項的「綠色」才是正確選項。

43. According to the passage, which of the following statements is NOT true?

（根據本文，下列陳述中哪項為非？）

(A) Colors have an impact on how people react to the surroundings.

顏色對人們對環境的反應有影響。

(B) Some colors excite people while others soothe and calm them.

一些顏色刺激人們而其它顏色則使人平靜

(C) The brighter the color, the stronger the response to it.

越鮮艷的顏色，對它的反應越強烈。

(D) People's emotional responses to specific colors are different.

人們對特定顏色的反應會有所不同。

解析

根據文章內容「研究顯示，人們對某特定的顏色有相似的情緒反應，」的敘述，(D)項的「 」才是不實的陳述。

▲閱讀下文

In my science and math classes, I always have to memorize lists of things for science and all kinds of math formulas. Since my memory is not that great, I've had to learn ways to improve my memory. Maybe you could benefit from some of the tips that I've picked up for memorizing things. Or maybe you already do these things anyway. Of course, the first rule of memorizing something is to repeat it in your mind. For example, the first day of class, sometimes the teacher will ask all the students to introduce themselves. I use this class time as a chance to exercise my memory skills. As we go around the room, I try to memorize each student's name by repeating his or her name to myself. Most of the time, by the end of the class, I've memorized everyone's name. Another trick I have learned for memorizing things is to build on small pieces in order to learn longer things. This idea comes from the fact that a person's short term memory can only hold eight or nine pieces of information at a time. So those pieces of information in short term memory have to be moved to long term memory by repeating them again and again before more information can go into short term memory.

（在我的自然與數學課裡，我總是要記許多自然科的目錄事項及多種數學公式。因為我的記憶不那麼好，我必須學習能幫我記憶的方法。 或許你能從一些訣竅中獲益，或者你也許早就這 麼做了。當然，記憶的第一個規則就是在你的頭腦裡重複要記的事。例如，有時，上課的第一天，老師會要求學生自我介紹。我就利用這一堂課的時間，作為運用我練習記憶技巧的機會。當時我們繞著房間走，我用重複同學名字的方式努力記住每個人的名字。多數情況是，在課程結束時，我已經記住每人的名字。另一個我學到的技巧是，用小紙片幫我記憶較複雜的事。這想法有事實根據，一個人的短期記憶一次只能記住 8 件或 9 件訊息。所以那些短期記憶區的訊息必須在新訊息進來之前，用不斷重複的方式將之移至長期記憶區。）

44. What is the main idea of this passage?

（本文的大意是什麼？）

(A) Ways of memorizing things 記住事情的方法

(B) Learning experiences in science classes 在自然課方面的學習經驗

(C) The importance of short term memory 短期記憶的重要性

(D) The importance of memorizing names 記住名字的重要性

解析

根據文章內容(A)項的「記住事情的方法」才是本文大意。

45. According to the passage, how many pieces of information can a person's short term memory hold at most?

（根據本文，人們的短期記憶區裡一次可存放多少則訊息？）

(A) Four or five4 或 5 則　(B) Eight or nine 8 或 9 則

(C) Eleven or twelve(D) Six or seven 11 或 12 則　(D) 6 或 7 則

解析

從答題關鍵的「一個人的短期記憶一次只能記住 8 件或 9 件訊息。」可看出，(B) 選項的「8 或 9 則」才是正確選項。

46. Based on the passage, how many ways has the author learned to improve his memory?

（根據本文，作者學習改進記憶的方式有己種？）

(A) One 一種　(B) Two 兩種　(C) Three 三種　(D) Four 四種

解析

從答題關鍵的「記憶的第一個規則就是……另一個我學到的技巧是……」可看出，(B) 選項的「兩種」才是正確選項。

47. According to the passage, which of the following statements is NOT true?

（根據本文，下列陳述中哪項非真？）

(A) People memorize things by repeating them in their minds.

人們在心裡不斷重複來記事情。

(B) Memorizing things is to build on small pieces in order to learn longer things.

做成小片來學習更長的事物

(C) The information in short term memory has to be moved to long term memory.

短期記憶區的訊息必須要移到長期記憶區。

(D) People's capacity for memorizing things is usually unlimited.

人們的記憶通常是無限的。

解析

根據文章內容，(D) 項的「人們的記憶通常是無限的」陳述非真。

▲ 閱讀下文，回答第 48-50 題

Have you ever thought of making a family album? The first thing to do is to find an album. A nice, big, and strong album is the best. Make sure that the album has pages made of paper, not plastic.It's hard to paste things onto plastic. The next thing to do is to collect family treasures to paste in the album. Some treasures you might collect are photographs, tickets, programs from special events, or postcards. After that, you'll want to organize the treasures.

You could give each family member one page, or try to put things in time order. Finally, label each treasure and write something about it Ask a family member to help you finish it.

（你曾想過製造一本家庭像簿嗎？要做的第一件事是找一本像簿。一本品質好，

大本一點，與耐用的像簿才是最好的。要確定這本像簿的內頁是紙做的頁而非塑膠頁。在塑膠上粘東西很較。再來就是找出家裡的寶物，再黏到像簿裡。你搜集的寶物可能是照片，各種票券，特別活動的節目表或明信片等。之後，你應該組合一下這些寶物。把同一人的東西放在同一頁，或是按日期的先後順序排列。最後，給每件寶物貼上標籤並簡述相關訊息。請家人幫妳完成吧。）

48. What is the best title for this passage?

　　（本文的最佳標題是什麼？）

　　(A) Taking a Family Picture 拍一張家庭照片

　　(B) Making a Family Album 做一本家庭像簿

　　(C) Planning a Family Trip 計畫一次家庭旅行

　　(D) Making a Family Dinner 做一頓家庭晚餐

解析

根據文章內容，(B) 項的「做一本家庭像簿」才是最佳標題。

49. What is the first step in the process of making a family album?

　　（在製做家庭像簿的第一步驟是什麼？）

　　(A) Putting things in order 將東西安排好　　(B) Talking to the family 與家人交談

　　(C) Pasting things onto paper 粘貼東西到紙上　　(D) Finding an album 找一本像簿

解析

從答題關鍵的「要做的第一件事是找一本像簿。」可看出，(D) 項的「找一本像簿」才是正確選項。

50. What is the third step in the process?

　　（過程裡的第 3 步驟是什麼？）

　　(A) Organizing the treasures 分類組合寶物　　(B) Asking for treasures 去要一些寶物

　　(C) Collecting treasures 搜集寶物　　(D) Labeling each treasure 給每筆寶物貼標籤

解析

從答題關鍵的「之後，你應該組合一下這些寶物。」可看出，(A) 項的「分類組合寶物」才是正確選項。

學測（學科能力測驗）

（97～100年學測）

97 年學測（學科能力測驗）

一、詞彙（15%）

說明：第 1 至 15 題，每題選出最適當的一個選項，標示在答案卡之「選擇題答案區」。每題答對得 1 分，答錯不倒扣。

1. Amy did not ＿＿＿＿＿＿ changes in the course schedule and therefore missed the class.
   艾咪沒 ＿＿＿＿＿＿ 在課程表方面的變化因此曠課。
   (A) arrest 逮捕　(B) alarm 警報　(C) notice 注意到　(D) delay 延遲

   解析
   (1)答題關鍵在「艾咪沒 ＿＿＿＿＿＿ 在課程表方面的變化」。
   (2)只有(C)選項的「注意到」放入空格，才是符合整句題意的正確選項。

2. It is not easy for old people to ＿＿＿＿＿＿ their backs, so they need help when their backs itch.
   老年人 ＿＿＿＿＿＿ 他們的背有困難，因此當背癢時他們需要幫助。
   (A) label 標籤　(B) scratch 搔癢　(C) lighten 減輕　(D) squeeze 壓縮

   解析
   (1)答題關鍵在「老年人 ＿＿＿＿＿＿ 他們的背有困難」。
   (2)只有(B)選項的「搔癢」放入空格，才是符合整句題意的正確選項。

3. Mary is suffering from a stomachache and needs to eat food which is easy to ＿＿＿＿＿＿.
   瑪莉遭受胃痛之苦並且需要吃容易 ＿＿＿＿＿＿ 食品。
   (A) launch 啟動　(B) invade 侵入　(C) adopt 採用　(D) digest 消化

   解析
   (1)答題關鍵在「需要吃容易 ＿＿＿＿＿＿ 食品。」
   (2)只有(D)選項的「消化」放入空格，才是符合整句題意的正確選項。

4. Since our classroom is not air-conditioned, we have to ＿＿＿＿＿＿ the heat during the hot summer days.
   由於我們的教室沒裝空調，我們必須 ＿＿＿＿＿＿ 炎夏的熱氣。
   (A) consume 消費　(B) tolerate 忍受　(C) recover 恢復　(D) promote 推廣

解析

(1)答題關鍵在「我們必須 ＿＿＿＿＿ 炎夏的熱氣。」

(2)只有(B)選項的「忍受」放入空格，才是符合整句題意的正確選項。

5. Sue is so ＿＿＿＿＿ that she always breaks something when she is shopping at a store.

蘇是如此 ＿＿＿＿＿ 當她在一家商店採買時，她總會弄壞一些東西。

(A) religious 宗教的　(B) visual 視覺的　(C) clumsy 笨拙的　(D) intimate 親密

解析

(1)答題關鍵在「蘇是如此 ＿＿＿＿＿ ……她總會弄壞一些東西。」

(2)只有(C)選項的「笨拙」放入空格，才是符合整句題意的正確選項。

6. Ann enjoyed going to the flower market. She believed that the ＿＿＿＿＿ of flowers refreshed her mind.

安喜歡去花市。她相信花的 ＿＿＿＿＿ 使她的心情愉快。

(A) instance 實例　(B) dominance 支配　(C) appliance 器具　(D) fragrance 芳香

解析

(1)答題關鍵在「她相信花的 ＿＿＿＿＿ 使她的心情愉快」。

(2)只有(D)選項的「芳香」放入空格，才是符合整句題意的正確選項。

7. The profits of Prince Charles's organic farm go to ＿＿＿＿＿ to help the poor and the sick.

查理斯王子的有機農場利潤捐給 ＿＿＿＿＿ 幫助貧病者。

(A) charities 慈善機構　(B) bulletins 公報　(C) harvests 農作收成　(D) rebels 叛亂者

解析

(1)答題關鍵在「有機農場利潤捐給 ＿＿＿＿＿ 幫助貧病者」。

(2)只有(A)選項的「慈善機構」放入空格，才是符合整句題意的正確選項。

8. Jack was given the rare ＿＿＿＿＿ of using the president's office, which made others quite jealous.

傑克被給予難得的 ＿＿＿＿＿ 使用總統府，使其它人十分妒忌。

(A) mischief 惡作劇　(B) privilege 特權　(C) involvement 介入　(D) occupation 職業

解析

(1)答題關鍵在「傑克被給予難得的 ＿＿＿＿＿ 使用總統府」。

(2)只有(B)選項的「特權」放入空格，才是符合整句題意的正確選項。

9. This new computer is obviously ＿＿＿＿＿ to the old one because it has many new functions.

這台新款電腦比舊款電腦 ＿＿＿＿＿ 因為它有很多新功能。

　(A) technical 技術　(B) suitable 合適　(C) superior 較高的　(D) typical 典型

解析

(1)答題關鍵在「新款電腦比舊款電腦 _____」。

(2)只有(C)選項的「superior」放入空格，才是符合整句題意的正確選項。

(3)片語 superior to 中譯為「比～優、好、年長」之意。

10. Simon loves his work. To him, work always comes first, and family and friends are
_____.

　　賽門熱愛他的工作。對他來說，工作總是優先而家庭和朋友是 _____。

　(A) secondary 第二　(B) temporary 暫時的　(C) sociable 愛交際的　(D) capable 有能力

解析

(1)答題關鍵在「工作總是優先而家庭和朋友是 _____」。

(2)只有(A)選項的「第二」放入空格，才是符合整句題意的正確選項。

11. Although your plans look good, you have to be _____ and consider what you can
actually do.

　　雖然你的計畫看起來好，但是你必須 _____ 並考慮你實際上能做多少。

　(A) dramatic 戲劇化　(B) realistic 務實地　(C) stressful 緊張的　(D) manageable 可管理的

解析

(1)答題關鍵在「但是你必須 _____ 並考慮你實際上能做多少。」

(2)只有(B)選項的「務實地」放入空格，才是符合整句題意的正確選項。

12. Built under the sea in 1994, the _____ between England and France connects the UK
more closely with mainland Europe.

　　1994年在海底建造，在英國和法國之間的 _____ 使英國更靠近歐洲大陸。

　(A) waterfall 瀑布　(B) temple 寺廟　(C) tunnel 隧道　(D) channel 海峽

解析

(1)答題關鍵在「在英國和法國之間的 _____ 使英國更靠近歐洲大陸。」

(2)只有(C)選項的「隧道」放入空格，才是符合整句題意的正確選項。

13. This tour package is very appealing, and that one looks _____ attractive. I don't know
which one to choose.

　　這個旅遊套餐很有魅力，而那個看起來 _____ 有吸引力。我不知要選哪一
個。

　(A) equally 同樣地　(B) annually 每年　(C) merely 僅僅　(D) gratefully 充滿感激

解析

(1)答題關鍵在「而那個看起來 _____ 有吸引力。」

(2)只有(A)選項的「同樣地」放入空格，才是符合整句題意的正確選項。

14. Hsu Fang-yi, a young Taiwanese dancer, recently ＿＿＿＿＿＿ at Lincoln Center in New York and won a great deal of praise.

　　徐芳宜，一位年輕的台灣舞蹈家，最近在紐約的林肯中心 ＿＿＿＿＿＿ 且贏得很多讚揚。

　　(A) performed 表演　　(B) pretended 假裝　　(C) postponed 延期　　(D) persuaded 說服

解析

(1)答題關鍵在「最近在紐約的林肯中心 ＿＿＿＿＿＿ 且贏得很多讚揚」。

(2)只有(A) 選項的「表演」放入空格，才是符合整句題意的正確選項。

15. The police searched the house of the suspect ＿＿＿＿＿＿ They almost turned the whole house upside down.

　　警察 ＿＿＿＿＿＿ 搜查嫌犯的房子。他們幾乎把整個房子裡裡外外都搜遍了。

　　(A) relatively 相對地　　(B) thoroughly 徹底地　　(C) casually 隨意的　　(D) permanently 永久地

解析

(1)答題關鍵在「警察 ＿＿＿＿＿＿ 搜查嫌犯的房子」。

(2)只有(B) 選項的「徹底地」放入空格，才是符合整句題意的正確選項。

二、綜合測驗（15%）

> 說明：第 16 至 30 題，每題一個空格，請依文意選出最適當的一個選項，標示在答案卡之「選擇題答案區」。每題答對得 1 分，答錯不倒扣。

　　What is so special about green tea? The Chinese and Indians ＿＿＿16＿＿＿ it for at least 4,000 years to treat everything from headache to depression. Researchers at Purdue University recently concluded that a compound in green tea ＿＿＿17＿＿＿ the growth of cancer cells. Green tea is also helpful ＿＿＿18＿＿＿ nfection and damaged immune function. The secret power of green tea is its richness in a powerful anti-oxidant.

　　為什麼綠茶如此特別？中國人與印第安人至少已經 ＿＿＿16＿＿＿ 4,000 年的綠茶來治病，從頭痛到精神沮喪都會有幫助。珀杜大學的研究人員最近斷定，在綠茶裡的一種化合物會 ＿＿＿17＿＿＿ 癌細胞的成長。綠茶也 ＿＿＿18＿＿＿ 對感染或受損的免疫功能有幫助。綠茶的祕密的是，它是很強效的抗氧化劑。

　　Green tea and black tea come from the same plant. Their ＿＿＿19＿＿＿ is in the processing. Green tea is dried but not fermented, and this shorter processing gives it a lighter flavor than black tea. It also helps retain the tea's beneficial chemicals. That is ＿＿＿20＿＿＿ green tea is so good for health. The only reported negative effect of drinking green tea is a possible allergic reaction and insomnia due to the caffeine it contains.

　　綠茶和紅茶來自相同的植物。他們的 ＿＿＿19＿＿＿ 在於處理過程。綠茶是乾燥且烘焙、不發酵，而在更短的處理過程中，它的味道比紅茶淡。它也有助於保留茶的有

益化學物質。那是 _____20_____ 綠茶是如此有益健康的原因。喝綠茶的唯一的負面報
告是，它本身的咖啡因，會有過敏反應與失眠的可能性。

16. 題句：The Chinese and Indians _____16_____ it for at least 4,000 years to treat ...

中國人與印第安人至少已經 _____16_____ 4,000 年的綠茶來治病……

選項：(A) would use 使用　(B) are using　(C) had used　(D) have been using

解析

(1)答題關鍵在，「已經 _____16_____ 4,000 年的綠茶來治病……」。

(2)只有選 (D) 項的「have been using」放入空格，才符合現在完成進行式的文法規定。

17. 題句：在綠茶裡的一種化合物會 _____17_____ 癌細胞的成長。

選項：(A) looks after 照料　(B) slows down 減慢　(C) takes over 接手　(D) turns out 變成

解析

(1)答題關鍵在「在綠茶裡的一種化合物會 _____17_____ 癌細胞的成長」。

(2)只有 (B) 選項的「減慢」放入空格，才是符合題意的正確選項。

18. 題句：Green tea is also helpful _____18_____ infection and damaged immune function.

選項：(A) for 為　(B) from 從　(C) at 在　(D) inside 裡邊

解析

(1)答題關鍵在「Green tea is also helpful _____18_____ infection and damaged immune function」。

(2)只有選 (A) 項的「for」放入空格，才是符合題意的正確選項。

19. 題句：他們的 _____19_____ 在於處理過程。

選項：(A) weight 重量　(B) purpose 目的　(C) difference 不同之處　(D) structure 結構

解析

(1)答題關鍵在「他們的 _____19_____ 在於處理過程」。

(2)只有 (C) 選項的「不同之處」放入空格，才是符合題意的正確選項。

20. 題句：That is _____20_____ green tea is so good for health.

(A) whether 是否　(B) whenever 何時　(C) what 什麼　(D) why 為什麼

解析

(1)答題關鍵在「That is _____20_____ green tea is so good for health」。

(2)只有 (D) 選項的「why」放入空格，才符合「That is way」的正確選項。

　　A wise woman traveling in the mountains found a precious stone. The next day she met
another traveler who was hungry. The wise woman generously opened her bag to _____21_____
her food with the traveler. When the hungry traveler saw the precious stone, he asked her to give

it to him.　The woman did _____22_____ without hesitation.　The traveler left, rejoicing.

一名聰明婦女在山中旅行時檢到一塊寶石。第二天她遇見一名飢餓的旅遊者。聰明的婦女慷慨地打開她的包包與旅遊者 _____21_____ 她的食品。當飢餓的旅遊者看見寶石時，要求她把寶石送給他。該婦女毫不猶豫地 _____22_____ 。旅遊者高興地離開。

If he sold the stone, he thought, he _____23_____ enough money for the rest of his life. But in a few days he came back to find the woman. When he found her, he said, "I know how valuable this stone is, but I'm giving it back to you, _____24_____ that you can give me something even more precious. You gave me the stone without asking for anything _____25_____ .Please teach me what you have in your heart that makes you so generous."

如果他出售這塊寶石，他這一輩子都會 _____23_____ 足夠的錢。但是在幾天之後他回來找到了那婦女。，他說，「我知道這塊石頭多麼有價值，但是我要把它還給你， _____24_____ 你能給我更寶貴的東西。當初你給我石頭時並沒要求任何 _____25_____ 。請教教我，你的內心有些什麼會讓妳那麼慷慨」。

21. 題句：打開她的包包與旅遊者 _____21_____ 她的食品
　　選項：(A) give給　(B) bring攜帶　(C) share分享　(D) earn賺取
　[解析]
　(1)答題關鍵在「與旅遊者 _____21_____ 她的食品」。
　(2)只有(D)選項的「分享」放入空格，才是符合題意的正確選項。

22. 題句：該婦女毫不猶豫地 _____22_____ 。
　　選項：(A) so 因此　(B) such 如此　(C) as 當　(D) thus 因此
　[解析]
　(1)答題關鍵在「該婦女毫不猶豫地 _____22_____ 」。
　(2)只有(A)選項的「so」放入空格，才是符合題意的正確選項。

23. 題句：如果他出售這塊寶石，他這一輩子都會 _____23_____ 足夠的錢。
　　選項：(A) had 過去式的有　(B) had had 過完式的有　(C) would have 現在式的有
　　　　　(D) would have had 假設語氣的過去事實
　[解析]
　(1)答題關鍵在「他這一輩子都會 _____23_____ 足夠的錢」。
　(2)只有(C)選項的「would have」放入空格，才是符合題意的正確選項。

24. 題句： _____24_____ that you can give me something even more precious.
　　　　　(A) hope 希望　(B) hoping 動名詞　(C) hoped 過去式　(D) to hope 不定詞

解析

(1)答題關鍵在「＿＿＿＿24＿＿＿＿ that you can give me something...」。

(2)只有(B)選項的「Hoping」放入空格，才符合「動名詞當主詞」的文法規定。

25. 題句：當初你給我石頭時並沒要求任何＿＿＿＿25＿＿＿＿

　　選項：(A) on leave 請假　(B) by surprise 驚喜　(C) off record 非正式的　(D) in return 回報

解析

(1)答題關鍵在「當初你給我石頭時並沒要求任何＿＿＿＿25＿＿＿＿」。

(2)只有(D)選項的「回報」放入空格，才是符合題意的正確選項。

Prague, the capital of the Czech Republic, is a very beautiful city. Situated on both banks of the winding River Vltava, Prague is like one big open-air museum. ＿＿＿＿26＿＿＿＿ some six hundred years of architecture nearly untouched by natural disaster or war, the city retains much of its medieval appearance. ＿＿＿＿27＿＿＿＿ you go, there are buildings in Romanic, Baroque, and Rococo styles that were popular hundreds of years ago. All of them successfully ＿＿＿＿28＿＿＿＿ the destruction of postwar redevelopment and remained unchanged. While the Iron Curtain was still in place under the communist government, Prague was ＿＿＿＿29＿＿＿＿ visited by foreigners. Since the 1990s, ＿＿＿＿30＿＿＿＿ all that has changed. Prague is now one of the most popular tourist attractions in Europe.

布拉格，捷克共和國的首都，是一座非常美麗的城市。位於蜿蜒沃他瓦河的兩岸，布拉格看起來象一座大型的戶外博物館。一些＿＿＿＿26＿＿＿＿600年歷史的古建築，沒有遭受天災或戰爭的破壞。城市盡量保留它的中世紀風貌。＿＿＿＿27＿＿＿＿你走到那裡，都會看到數百年前流行的羅馬式、巴洛克與洛克克式等建築。所有這些都幸運地＿＿＿＿28＿＿＿＿戰火的破壞，保留原樣不變。

在以前的鐵幕共產時代，＿＿＿＿29＿＿＿＿外國人造訪布拉格。然而，從20世紀90年代＿＿＿＿30＿＿＿＿，所有的都改變了。布拉格現在是歐洲最受歡迎的旅遊勝地之一。

26. 題句：＿＿＿＿26＿＿＿＿ some six hundred years of architecture

　　選項：(A) For 為　(B) With 有　(C) Upon 由於　(D) Along 沿著

解析

(1)答題關鍵在「some six hundred years...」。

(2)只有(B)選項的「with 有」放入空格，才符合 with 的正確用法。

27. 題句：＿＿＿＿27＿＿＿＿ you go, there are buildings in Romanic...

　　選項：(A) Since 自從　(B) Before 之前　(C) Whatever 不論什麼　(D) Wherever 不論何處

解析

(1)關鍵字在「you go」。

(2)只有選(D)項的「wherever」連成 wherever you go「不論你走到何處」才是正確答案。

28. 題句：All of them successfully＿＿＿28＿＿＿ the destruction of postwar
　　選項：(A) escaped 逃過、避過　(B) featured 有特色　(C) defended 防衛　(D) inspired 受啟發

解析

(1)答題關鍵在「destruction of postwar...」。

(2)只有(A)選項的「逃過、避過」放入空格，才是符合整句題意的正確選項。

29. 題句：Prague was ＿＿＿29＿＿＿ visited by foreigners.
　　選項：　(A) ever 以前　(B) seldom 很少　(C) nearly 近於　(D) wholly 全部

解析

(1)答題關鍵在「visited by foreigners」。

(2)只有(B)選項的「seldom」放入空格，才是符合整句題意的正確選項。

30. 題句：Since the 1990s, ＿＿＿30＿＿＿ all that has changed.
　　選項：(A) afterwards 之後　(B) therefore 所以　(C) however 然而　(D) furthermore 而且

解析

(1)答題關鍵在「空格左右兩邊的兩句」。

(2)只有(C)選項的「however」放入空格，才符合「however 當連接詞的用法」的文法規定。

三、文意選填（10%）

說明：第 31 至 40 題，每題一個空格，請依文意在文章後所提供的(A) 到 (J) 選項中分別選出最適當者，並將其英文字母代號標示在答案卡之「選擇題答案區」。每題答對得 1 分，答錯不倒扣。

　　One day, a guru foresaw in a vision what he would be in his next life. Then he called his favorite disciple and asked him, "What would you do to thank me for all you have received from me?" The disciple said he would do whatever his guru asked him to do. Having received this ＿＿＿31＿＿＿ , the guru said, "Then this is what I'd like you to do for me. I've just ＿＿＿32＿＿＿ that I'll die very soon and I'm going to be reborn as a pig. Do you see that sow eating garbage there in the yard? I'm going to be the fourth piglet of its next litter. You'll ＿＿＿33＿＿＿ me by a mark on my brow. After that sow gives birth, find the fourth piglet with a mark on its brow and, with one ＿＿＿34＿＿＿ of your knife, slaughter it. I'll be ＿＿＿35＿＿＿ from a pig's life. Will you do this for me?"

　　The disciple felt sad to hear this, but he agreed to do as he was told. Soon after their ＿＿＿36＿＿＿ , the guru died and the sow did have a litter of four little pigs. Then the disciple ＿＿＿37＿＿＿ his knife and picked out the little pig with a mark on its brow. When he was about to cut its throat, the little pig suddenly _____38_____ , "Stop!" Before the disciple could recover from the _____39_____ of hearing the little pig speak in a human voice, it continued, "Don't kill me. I want to live on as a pig. When I asked you to kill me, I didn't know what a pig's life would be _____40_____ . It's great! Just let me go".

　　有一天，一名印度教導師看到了他未來生命裡的樣子。然後他打電話給他最喜愛的弟子並且問他，「你要怎麼謝我你從我這裡所學到的全部？」弟子說他將會做到導師要他做的任何事情。得到這個 ___31___ 後，導師繼續說：「以下就是我要你為我做的事：我剛剛才 ___32___ 我很快就會死，然後投胎為豬。你有看到那頭母豬在院子裡吃垃圾嗎？我將會是牠的下一窩仔豬裡的第4頭小豬。你會看到我眉上的標記 ___33___ 我。在母豬分娩之後，找到那頭眉上有記號的仔豬，用你的刀子 ___34___ 殺了牠。這樣我就可以 ___35___ 繼續當做豬。你會幫我這個忙嗎？」

　　聽到這麼說這名弟子很悲哀，但是他同意導師的要求去做。就在他們 ___36___ 之後，導師死了，而母豬確實生出一窩有4隻的仔豬。然後弟子 ___37___ 他的刀，挑出那隻眉上有標記的小豬。當他正要割斷小豬的咽喉時，小豬突然 ___38___ ，「停止！」在弟子還沒有能從小豬講人話的 ___39___ 中恢復過來之前，牠繼續說，「不要殺死我。我還是想要繼續當作豬活下去。先前當我要求你殺死我時，我並不知道豬的生活是 ___40___ 樣子。太棒了！就讓我去吧。」

(A) shock 驚嚇　(B) conversation 談話　(C) like 像什麼　(D) promise 承諾
(E) released 豁免　(F) screamed 大聲尖叫　(G) learned 獲知　(H) recognize 認出
(I) stroke 劃一下　(J) sharpened 磨利

31. 題句：得到這個 ___31___ 後，導師繼續說……
解析
(1)答題關鍵在「得到這個 ___31___ 後」。
(2)只有(D)選項的「承諾」放入空格，才是符合題意的正確選項。

32. 題句：我剛才 ___32___ 我很快就會死，
解析
(1)答題關鍵在「剛才 ___32___ 我很快就會死，」。
(2)只有(F)選項的「獲知」放入空格，才是符合題意的正確選項。
(3)I have learned … 中譯為「我剛才獲知……」之意。

33. 題句：你會看到我眉上的標記＿＿＿＿33＿＿＿＿我。

解析

(1) 答題關鍵在「你會看到我眉上的標記＿＿＿33＿＿＿我。」。

(2) 只有(H)選項的「認出」放入空格，才是符合題意的正確選項。

34. 題句：用你的刀子＿＿＿＿34＿＿＿＿殺了牠。

解析

(1)答題關鍵在「用你的刀子＿＿＿34＿＿＿殺了牠。」。

(2)只有(D)選項的「劃一下」放入空格，才是符合題意的正確選項。

35. 題句：這樣我就可以＿＿＿＿35＿＿＿＿繼續當做豬

解析

(1)答題關鍵在「我就可以＿＿＿35＿＿＿繼續當做豬」。

(2)只有(E)選項的「豁免」放入空格，才是符合題意的正確選項。

36. 題句：就在他們＿＿＿＿36＿＿＿＿之後，導師死了

解析

(1)答題關鍵在「就在他們＿＿＿36＿＿＿之後，導師死了」。

(2)只有(B)選項的「對話」放入空格，才是符合題意的正確選項。

37. 題句：然後弟子＿＿＿37＿＿＿他的刀……

解析

(1)答題關鍵在「然後弟子＿＿＿37＿＿＿他的刀……」。

(2)只有(J)選項的「磨利」放入空格，才是符合題意的正確選項。

38. 題句：小豬突然＿＿＿＿38＿＿＿＿，「停止！」

解析

(1)答題關鍵在「停止」。

(2)只有(F)選項的「大聲尖叫」放入空格，才是符合題意的正確選項。

39. 題句：還沒有能從小豬講人話的＿＿＿＿39＿＿＿＿中恢復過來之前

解析

(1)答題關鍵在「還沒有能從小豬講人話的＿＿＿39＿＿＿中恢復過來之前」。

(2)只有(A)選項的「驚嚇」放入空格，才是符合題意的正確選項。

40. 題句：先前當我要求你殺死我時，我並不知道豬的一生是 ___40___ 樣子

解析

(1)答題關鍵在「我並不知道豬的一生是 ___40___ 樣子」。

(2)只有(D)選項的「like」放入空格，才是符合題意的正確選項。

(3)what a pig's life would be like. 中譯為豬的一生是什麼樣子

＝豬隻過什麼樣的生活

四、閱讀測驗（32%）

> 說明：第 41 至 56 題，每題請分別根據各篇文章之文意選出最適當的一個選項，標示在
> 答案卡之「選擇題答案區」。每題答對得 2 分，答錯不倒扣。

41-44 為題組

Howler monkeys are named for the long loud cries, or howls, that they make every day. They are the loudest land animal and their howls can be heard three miles away through dense forests. Male howler monkeys use their loud voices to fight for food, mates, or territory. Everyone starts and ends the day by howling to check out where their nearest competitors are.

吼猴是因有又長又大的吼叫聲而得名，他們每天都會吼叫。他們是陸上叫聲最大的動物，而牠們的吼叫聲在濃密森林三哩外的地方都聽得到。公吼猴利用牠們的吼聲來搶食物、交配或爭地盤。每隻吼猴在清晨與黃昏都會用吼叫聲來查出最接近的競爭者在哪裡。

Interestingly, when there are few howler monkeys in an area, the howling routine takes on a different pattern. In Belize, where howler monkeys were newly reintroduced into a wildlife sanctuary, the howler monkeys were heard only a few times a week rather than every day.

Apparently, with plenty of space and no other howler monkeys around, there was no need to check on the whereabouts of their competitors.

有趣的是，一個地區如果吼猴不多時，吼叫的模式會不一樣。在貝里斯，在那裡吼猴是最近才被引進到某一個野生動物禁獵區，這些吼猴一周才吼叫幾次而不是每天吼叫。

顯然，在很大的空間且附近沒有其他吼猴出現，沒有必要檢查他們的競爭者在哪裡。

At the sanctuary, keepers now use recorded howler sounds from a distance so that the monkeys feel the need to make the territorial calls as they would do in the wild. In the future when the population grows, there will be no need for the recording because the howler monkeys will have more reason to check in with the neighbors to define their own territories.

在禁獵區，動物管理人使用預錄的吼猴聲，拿到遠處播放，使園區裡的這些猴子感到，還是有必要像在荒野一樣的吼叫。將來，區內的吼猴數量增加時，就不會再用預錄的聲音，到時眾多的吼猴有更多的理由去清查競爭者與地盤。

41. Why do howler monkeys howl?

　　吼猴為什麼吼叫？

　(A) To claim their territory.

　　　聲稱他們的地盤。

　(B) To check how popular they are.

　　　查看他們有多麼受歡迎。

　(C) To tell others they are going to leave.

　　　告訴它猴他們將要離開。

　(D) To show friendliness to their neighbors.

　　　向鄰居表示友好。

解析

從答題關鍵的「公吼猴利用他們的吼聲來搶食物、交配或爭地盤」可看出，只有 (A) 選項的「聲稱他們的地盤」才是符合題意的正確選項。

42. Why did the howler monkeys in Belize howl less often?

　　吼猴為什麼在貝里斯吼叫的次數少？

　(A) They lived too close to each other.

　　　他們住得太接近。

　(B) There was enough food for all of them.

　　　他們有足夠的食物。

　(C) There were no other competitors around.

　　　在周遭沒有其他競爭者。

　(D) They were not used to the weather there.

　　　他們不習慣當地天氣。

解析

從答題關鍵的「在很大的空間且附近沒有其他吼猴出現，沒有必要檢查他們的競爭者在哪裡。」可看出，只有 (C) 選項的「在周遭沒有其他競爭者。」才是符合題意的正確選項。

43. Why do the keepers at the sanctuary use recorded howls?

　　在園區的看護人為什麼用預錄吼猴聲？

　(A) To prevent the howler monkeys from getting homesick.

　　　不讓吼猴有思家之苦。

　(B) To help howler monkeys maintain their howling ability.

　　　為了幫助吼猴保持吼叫的能力。

　(C) To trick the monkeys into the belief that there is plenty of space around.

誘騙猴子周遭土地空間很大。

(D) To teach the monkeys how to make the loudest cries to scare people away.

教猴子怎樣叫出最大聲來嚇人。

解析

從答題關鍵的「使園區裡的這些猴子感到，還是有必要像在荒野一樣的吼叫。」可看出，只有(B)選項的「為了幫助吼猴保持吼叫的能力。」才是符合題意的正確選項。

44. According to the passage, which of the following is true about howler monkeys?

根據本文，如下內容中哪項關於吼猴說法才是屬實？

(A) They howl most often at noon.

他們最常在中午吼叫。

(B) They originally came from Belize.

他們最初來自貝里斯。

(C) People can hear their howls three miles away.

人們在 3 英里外就能聽到吼猴叫聲。

(D) Female monkeys howl to protect their babies.

母猴吼叫來保護嬰兒。

解析

從答題關鍵的「牠們的吼叫聲在濃密森林三哩外的地方都聽得到。」可看出，只有 (C) 選項的「人們在 3 英里外就能聽到吼猴叫聲。」才是正確選項。

45-48為題組

After the creation of the Glacier National Park in Montana, the growing number of park visitors increased the need for roads. Eventually, the demand for a road across the mountains led to the building of the Going-to-the-Sun Road. The construction of the Going-to-the-Sun Road was a huge task. After 11 years of work, the final section of the road was completed in 1932. The road is considered an engineering feat. Even today, visitors to the park marvel at how such a road could have been built. It is one of the most scenic roads in North America.

The construction of the road has changed the way visitors experience the Glacier National Park. Visitors now can drive over sections of the park that previously took days of horseback riding to see. Just across the border, in Canada, is the Waterton Lakes National Park. In 1931, members of the Rotary Clubs of Alberta and Montana suggested joining the two parks as a symbol of peace and friendship between the two countries. In 1932, the United States and Canadian governments renamed the parks the Waterton-Glacier International Peace Park, the world's first. More recently, the parks have received several international honors. They were named as a World Heritage Site in 1995. This international recognition highlights the importance of this area, not just to the United States and Canada, but to the entire world.

在蒙大拿有了冰河國家公園之後，日益增多的公園訪客數量使當地道路需求增加。最後，會需要一條穿過山脈的道路，導致「通向太陽之路」的興建。通向太陽之

路是一項巨大工程。施工 11 年之後，道路的末段部分在 1932 年完工。這條道路被認為爲一項英勇工程。即使今天，去公園訪客對還感到驚訝，這樣的道路是怎麼建造起來的。這是在北美洲風景最美的道路之一。

　　道路的建設已經改變參觀者觀賞冰河國家公園的方式。參觀者現在已能開車越過以前要騎馬好幾天才看得到的公園景色。只需穿過邊境，在加拿大這一邊是沃特頓湖國家公園。在 1931 年，亞伯特和蒙大拿的扶輪社會員建議，結合這兩個國家公園，作爲在兩個國家之間的一個和平和友誼的象徵。到了 1932 年，美國和加拿大政府給公園重新命名沃特頓冰河國際和平公園，世界的第一個這一類公園。近年來，公園已經獲得幾種國際榮譽，在 1995 年被列爲世界文化遺產。這個國際榮譽強調的是這個地區的重要性，不屬美國和加拿大，而是屬於全世界。

45. What made it necessary to build a road through the Glacier National Park?

　　爲什麼要穿過冰河國家公園建造道路？

(A) There were too many parks in Montana.

　　在蒙大拿有太多公園。

(B) The park was not sunny enough for visitors.

　　公園對參觀者來說不夠晴朗。

(C) The existing mountain roads were destroyed.

　　現有的山區道路被破壞。

(D) More visitors were interested in going to the park.

　　更多的參觀者有興趣去公園。

解析

根據文章內容，只有 (D) 選項的「更多的參觀者有興趣去公園。」才是符合題意的正確選項。

46. How has the Going-to-the-Sun Road influenced the way people experience the Glacier National Park?

　　「通向太陽之路」怎樣影響人們觀賞冰河國家公園的方式？

(A) The scenery along the road is too beautiful for visitors to drive carefully.

　　沿著道路的風景太美麗，參觀者無法小心駕駛。

(B) It has become a marvelous experience for people to ride horses on this road.

　　人們在這條道路上騎馬賞景已成爲一種奇妙的經驗。

(C) The road has allowed people to see more of the park in a shorter period of time.

　　道路的便捷使人們在更短的時間期看到更多的公園美景。

(D) The transportation on the road was so difficult that few people could really enjoy the trip.

　　在道路上的運輸很困難以致很少人能眞正享受旅行的樂趣。

解析

從答題關鍵的「參觀者現在已能開車越過以前要騎馬好幾天才看得到的公園景色。」可看出，只有 (C) 選項的「道路的便捷使人們在更短的時間期看到更多的公園美景。」才是符合題意的正確選項。

47. What does "an engineering feat" mean?

　　是指何意？

(A) A big success in construction.

　　建築史上的大成功。

(B) A magical building machine.

　　一台有魔法的造路機。

(C) A great disaster for the travelers.

　　對旅遊者的大災難。

(D) An enjoyable process for engineers.

　　給工程師的愉快過程。

解析

根據文章內容，只有(A)選項的「建築史上的大成功。」才是符合題意的正確選項。

48. What is special about the Waterton-Glacier International Peace Park?

　　沃特頓冰河國際和平公園有何特別？

(A) It is where the glacier runs to the lake.

　　冰河在此流向湖泊。

(B) It is the first park funded by the whole world.

　　這是被全世界提供資金的第一個公園。

(C) It is a special park built to protect wild animals.

　　它是一個特別的公園建造來保護野生動物。

(D) It is composed of two parks located in two countries.

　　它由兩個國家的兩個公園組成。

解析

從答題關鍵的「到了 1932 年，美國和加拿大政府給公園重新命名沃特頓冰河國際和平公園，世界的第一個這一類公園。」可看出，只有 (D) 選項的「它由兩個國家的兩個公園組成。」才是符合題意的正確選項。

49-52 為題組

　　Ice sculpting is a difficult process. First, ice must be carefully selected so that it is suitable for sculpting. Its ideal material is pure, clean water with high clarity. It should also have the minimum amount of air bubbles. Perfectly clear ice blocks weighing 140 kg and measuring 100 cm × 50 cm × 25 cm are available from the Clinebell Company in Colorado. Much larger clear blocks are produced in Europe and Canada or harvested from a frozen river in Sweden. These large ice blocks are used for large ice sculpting events and for building ice hotels.

　　冰雕是一個艱難的過程。首先，必須仔細挑選適於雕刻的冰塊。它的理想材料不要有雜質、乾淨透明的水。它也應該有最小數量的氣泡。完全的冰塊重 140 公斤，尺寸約 100 公分 × 50 公分 × 25 公分，這些都來自科羅拉多的 Clinebell 公司。超大且透明的冰塊產自歐洲與加拿大或來自瑞典的結冰河川。這些超大冰塊用於大規模的冰雕場合或用來建設冰凍旅館。

　　Another difficulty in the process of ice sculpting is time control. The temperature of the environment affects how quickly the piece must be completed to avoid the effects of melting. If the sculpting does not take place in a cold environment, then the sculptor must work quickly to finish his piece. The tools used for sculpting also affect when the task can be accomplished. Some sculptures can be completed in as little as ten minutes if power tools are used. Ice sculptors also use razor-sharp chisels that are specifically designed for cutting ice. The best ice chisels are made in Japan, a country that, along with China, has a long tradition of magnificent ice sculptures.

　　另一個冰雕過程中的困難是時間的控制。環境的溫度影響冰雕必須在多少時間內完成，以避免融化掉。如果雕刻不在低溫的環境裡進行，那麼雕刻師必須快速完成他的作品。用於雕刻的工具也會影工作進度。如果使用電動工具，有些雕刻品可能在10分鐘內就可完成。冰雕師也會用像剃刀那樣鋒利的鑿刀，用來切割特定花樣。最好的冰雕鑿刀產自日本，跟中國一樣，都有冰雕悠久傳統。

　　Ice sculptures are used as decorations in some cuisines, especially in Asia. When holding a dinner party, some large restaurants or hotels will use an ice sculpture to decorate the table. For example, in a wedding banquet it is common to see a pair of ice-sculpted swans that represent the union of the new couple.

　　冰雕作品多半用做爲菜餚的裝飾品，特別是亞洲。當舉行晚宴時，一些大的餐廳或者飯店將使用冰雕品來裝飾桌子。例如，在婚宴場合用一對冰雕天鵝是很普遍的，牠們代表新婚夫婦的結合。

49. What kind of ice is ideal for sculpting?

　　哪種冰做冰雕最理想？

　　(A) Ice from ice hotels.

　　　　來自冰飯店的冰。

　　(B) Ice from clean water.

　　　　來自淨水的冰。

　　(C) Ice with lots of bubbles in it.

　　　　裡頭有很多水泡的冰。

　　(D) Ice weighing over 100 kilograms.

　　　　重量超過 100 公斤的冰。

從答題關鍵的「它的理想材料不要有雜質、乾淨透明的水。」可看出，只有 (B) 選項的「來自淨水的冰」才是符合題意的正確選項。

50. Why is ice sculpting difficult?

冰雕爲什麼很難？

(A) It is hard to control the size and shape of the ice.

不容易控制冰的大小與形狀。

(B) The right theme for ice sculpting is not easy to find.

不容易找到冰雕的的正確主題。

(C) The appropriate tools are only available in some countries.

只有某些國家才有合適的工具。

(D) It is not easy to find the right kind of ice and work environment.

不容易找到合適的冰塊與工作環境。

解析

根據文章內容，只有 (D) 選項的「不容易找到合適的冰塊與工作環境。」才是符合題意的正確選項。

51. What is paragraph 3 mainly about?

第 3 段落的大意爲何？

(A) The uses of ice sculptures.

冰雕品的用途。

(B) The places where ice is sculpted.

冰塊被雕刻的地方。

(C) The quality of ice sculptures.

冰雕的品質。

(D) The origin of ice sculpting parties.

冰雕聚會的起源。

解析

根據文章第3段內容來看，只有(A)選項的「冰雕品的用途。」才是符合題意的正確選項。

52. Which of the following statements is true about the process of sculpting ice?

有關冰雕過程，下列陳述哪項爲眞？

(A) It takes more time to carve with razor-sharp chisels.

用剃刀式鑿刀雕刻須花更多的時間。

(B) It can be finished in 10 minutes if the right tools are used.

　　如果使用合適的工具，可能在 10 分鐘內完成冰雕。

(C) Larger blocks of ice from Sweden are easier to handle for sculptors.

　　來自瑞典的大型冰塊使雕刻師更容易於處理。

(D) The carver must work fast in a cold environment to avoid catching cold.

　　雕刻師在冰冷的環境裡工作動作要快以免感冒。

解析

從答題關鍵的「如果使用電動工具，有些雕刻品可能在10分鐘內就可完成。」可看出，只有(B)選項的「如果使用合適的工具，可能在10分鐘內完成冰雕。」才是符合題意的正確選項。

53-56 為題組

beforehand that the pain won't be so bad, you might not suffer as much. According to a recent study, the part of your brain that reacts to severe pain is largely the same part that reacts to expectation of pain. Researchers in this study worked with 10 volunteers, ages 24 to 46. Each volunteer wore a device that gave out 20-second-long pulses of heat to the right leg. There were three levels of heat, producing mild, moderate, or strong pain. During training, the volunteers would first hear a tone, followed by a period of silence, and then feel a heat pulse. They then learned to associate the length of the silent pause with the intensity of the upcoming heat pulse. The longer the pause, the stronger the heat pulse would be, causing more severe pain.

　　如果你的手指破觸到熱爐，那會很痛。不過，如果你事先說服你自己，疼痛不會那麼糟，你可能就不會那麼痛苦。根據一項最近的研究，你大腦內反應劇痛的部分，與想像會很痛的部分基本上兩者是相同的部分。研究人員與 10 位志願者合作，年齡 24到 46 歲。每位志願者穿一套能夠傳遞 20 秒長振動熱度到右腿的裝置，有三種等級的熱，會產生溫和、適度、或強烈的疼痛。這期間志願者會先聽到一個音調，隨後會寂靜一段時間，然後感到熱振動。他們然後要學習處理靜止的長度，與即將到來的熱脈衝的強度。 靜止時間越長，熱脈衝越強，疼痛越劇烈。

A day or two later, the real experiment began. The researchers found that the parts of the brain involved in learning, memory, emotion, and touch became more active as the volunteers expected higher levels of pain. These were mainly the same areas that became active when participants actually felt pain. Interestingly, when the volunteers expected only mild or moderate pain but experienced severe pain, they reported feeling 28 percent less pain than when they expected severe pain and actually got it. The new study emphasizes that pain has both physical and psychological elements. Understanding how pain works in the mind and brain could eventually give doctors tools for helping people cope with painful medical treatments.

　　一兩天後，真正的實驗開始。那些研究人員發現，當那些志願者想像會更痛時，他們大腦內負責學習、記憶、情感與觸覺的部分，活動變得更積極。 這與參加者實際感到痛苦時的腦部反應是同一部分。有趣的是，當那些志願者只期待溫和或適度痛苦時，卻也會感到劇痛。當他們期待劇痛也實際感到劇痛時，他們的報告卻顯示有百分之28的較少疼痛。新研究強調痛苦有身體和心理兩要素。了解疼痛怎樣在精神上與大腦裡運作，在將來會讓醫師做些有助人們處理疼痛醫療之事。

53. What is the main idea of the passage?

本文的大意是什麼？

(A) We should learn to be sensitive to pain.

我們應該學習對痛苦敏感些。

(B) Our feeling of pain is decided by our environment.

我們對痛苦的感覺由週遭環境決定。

(C) How people feel pain remains unknown to scientists.

人們怎樣感到疼痛在科學上還是未知。

(D) Our reaction to pain is closely related to our expectation of pain.

我們對疼痛的反應與我們對疼痛預期密切相關。

解析

根據文章內容，只有 (D) 選項的「我們對疼痛的反應與我們對疼痛預期密切相關。」才是本文大意。

54. Which of the following is true about the pulses of heat in the study?

如下內容中的哪些在研究過程中關於熱脈衝是真實的？

(A) Each heat pulse lasted for 20 seconds.

每一熱脈衝持續20秒。

(B) The pulses were given to the arms of the volunteers.

脈衝被傳到那些志願者的手臂。

(C) Different devices gave out different levels of heat pulses.

不同的設備發出熱漲落的不同的水準。

(D) There were two levels of heat intensity given to the volunteers.

有給那些志願者的熱強度的兩步。

解析

從答題關鍵的「每位志願者穿一套能夠傳遞 20 秒長振動熱度到右腿的裝置」可看出，只有 (A) 選項的「每一熱脈衝持續 20 秒。」才是符合題意的正確選項。

55. How did the volunteers learn to expect different levels of heat?

那些志願者怎樣學習期待不同等級的熱度？

(A) From the loudness of the tone they heard.

從他們聽到音調的音量。

(B) From the instruction given to them by the researchers.

從研究人員給他們的指示。

(C) From the color of a light flashing on the device they wore.

從他們所穿裝置上閃燈的顏色。

(D) From the length of the pause between a tone and the heat pulse.

從音調和熱脈衝之間的中止長度。

解析

從答題關鍵的「他們然後要學習處理靜止的長度，與即將到來的熱脈衝的強度。」可看出，只有 (D) 選項的「從音調和熱脈衝之間的中止長度。」才是符合題意的正確選項。

56. According to the passage, what may be the author's advice to a doctor before a surgery?

根據本文，在手術作者對醫生的建議可能是什麼？

(A) To provide the patient with more pain killers.

為病患提供更多的止痛藥。

(B) To talk to the patient and ease his/her worries.

和病患交談以緩和他／她的耽心。

(C) To give the patient strong heat pulses beforehand.

事先給病患強壯的熱脈衝

(D) To emphasize the possible severe pain to the patient.

對病患強調可能的劇痛。

解析

從答題關鍵的「了解疼痛怎樣在精神上與大腦裡運作，在將來會讓醫師做些有助人們處理疼痛醫療之事。」可看出，只有 (B) 選項的「和病患交談以緩和他／她的耽心。」才是符合題意的正確選項。

第貳部分：非選擇題

一、翻譯題（8%）

說明：1. 請將以下兩句中文譯成正確而通順達意的英文，並將答案寫在「答案卷」上。
　　　2. 請依序作答，並標明題號。每題 4 分，共 8 分。

1. 聽音樂是一個你可以終生享受的嗜好。

解析

本題的重要字彙如下：

聽音樂 Listening to the music　是一個 is a / an　你可以 you may / can　終身享用的 enjoy the lifetime　嗜好 a hobby

整句英譯

Listening to the music is a hobby that you may enjoy the livetime.

2. 但能彈奏樂器可以為你帶來更多的喜悅。

解析

本題的重要字彙如下：

但 but　能彈奏樂器 to be able to play musical instruments　可以 may / can　為你帶來 bring you
更多的喜悅 more joy

整句英譯

But it will bring you more joy if you are able to play musical instruments.

二、英文作文（20%）

說明：1.依提示在「答案卷」上寫一篇英文作文。
　　　2.文長 120 個單詞（words）左右。

提示：你（英文名字必須假設為 George 或 Mary）向朋友（英文名字必須假設為 Adam 或
　　　Eve）借了一件相當珍貴的物品，但不慎遺失，一時又買不到替代品。請寫一封
　　　信，第一段說明物品遺失的經過，第二段則表達歉意並提出可能的解決方案。

請注意：為避免評分困擾，請使用上述提示的 George 或 Mary 在信末署名，<u>不得使用自
　　　己真實的中文或英文姓名</u>。

解析

(1)先將題句內相關字詞寫出中譯：

借 borrow　　　相當 pretty　　　珍貴的 precious　　物品 article　　但是 but
不慎遺失 lost it carelessly / by accident　　一時 in the meantime　買不到 not able to buy
替代品 substitution / replacement　表達歉意 to express one's apology　　提出 offer
可能的解決方案 possible solution

第一段：說明物品遺失的經過

　　Dear Adam:
　　I am terribly sorry that I have lost the camera that I borrowed from you last week. It was last weekend when my wife and I went to Taipei 101 for our wedding anniversary. we took quite a few pictures there, especially the largest damper in the world on the 88th floor. But when I wanted to take more pictures after we came down the ground floor, I suddenly realized that my camera has gone. And my wife said that she didn't see me carrying the camera ever since I came out the men's room on the 89th floor. I dashed back to the toilet, and even checked with the Lost & Found Desk. It wasn't my day, the camera has gone for sure.

　　（親愛的亞當：）

　　很抱歉我把上個禮拜向你借的照相機弄丟了。上一個週末我和我太太慶結婚週年去了台北 101 大樓，我們在那裡拍了很多照片，特別是 88 樓的全世界最大的阻尼。

但是當我們回到一樓想要再拍幾張照片時，我突然發現照相機不見了。我太太說我從89樓的男廁出來後就沒有看到我揹照相機。我趕快衝回廁所，甚至於也問了失物招領處的人，照相機確定被人撿走了。

I've checked with the camera shop, wish to buy you a new one but the clerk said the factory has stopped producing the model of your camera. In the meantime there is no way of getting the same model camera in Taiwan. Adam my friend, can I buy you the same brand but different model camera instead? Hope to hear from you soon.

Your friend,

George

我去了相機店，想要買一台新的相機還你，但店員說工廠已停產你那一款相機了。而一時之間在台灣又買不到同款相機。亞當我的好友，我可否買一台同廠牌但不同款式的相機還給你呢？請儘快回覆。

你的好友　喬治　上

98 年學測（學科能力測驗）

第壹部分：選擇題（72分）

一、詞彙（15分）

1. Steve's description of the place was so _____ that I could almost picture it in my mind.

   史蒂夫對該地方的描述相當 _____ 我幾乎可以在我腦海中想像得到。

   (A) bitter 苦味　(B) vivid 生動　(C) sensitive 敏感　(D) courageous 英勇的

   解析

   (1)答題關鍵在題目空格左、右方的「描述相當」與「我幾乎可以」。

   (2)四個選項中，只有選(B)項的「生動」，才可有意義連成「描述相當生動我幾乎可以⋯⋯」。

2. When people feel uncomfortable or nervous, they may _____ their arms across their chests as if to protect themselves.

   當人們感到不舒服或緊張時，他們可能會在胸前 _____ 雙臂好像來保護自己

   (A) toss 拋出　(B) fold 摺疊　(C) veil 戴面紗　(D) yield 出產

   解析

   (1)答題關鍵在題目空格右方的「在胸前」與「雙臂」。

   (2)四個選項中，只有選(B)項的「摺疊」，才可有意義連成「在胸前摺疊雙臂」。

3. The doors of these department stores slide open _____ when you approach them. You don't have to open them yourself.

   當你踏觸到時百貨公司的門都是打開 _____ 。你不必自己打開。

   (A) necessarily 必須地　(B) diligently 勤勉地　(C) automatically 自動地　(D) intentionally 有意地

   解析

   (1)答題關鍵在題目空格左方的「打開」。

   (2)四個選項中，只有選(C)項的「自動地」，才可有意義連成「那些門會自動打開」（自動打開的英文說法是「打開自動open automatically」與中文順序想反）。

4. Nicole is a _____ language learner. Within a short period of time, she has developed a good command of Chinese and Japanese.

妮可是一個 _____ 的語言學習者。短期間內她就能流利地說華語和日語。

(A) convenient 方便　(B) popular 流行　(C) regular 規律的　(D) brilliant 優秀的

解析

(1)答題關鍵在題目空格右方的「語言學習者」。

(2)四個選項中，只有選(D)項的「優秀的」，才可有意義連成「是一個優秀的語言學習者」。

5. With rising oil prices, there is an increasing _____ for people to ride bicycles to work.

隨著油價的上升，騎腳踏車上班的人有增加的 _____ 。

(A) permit 允許　(B) instrument 工具　(C) appearance 出現　(D) tendency 趨勢

解析

(1)答題關鍵在題目空格左方的「增加的」。

(2)四個選項中，只有選(D)項的「趨勢」，才可有意義連成「……增加的趨勢」。

6. This information came from a very _____ source, so you don't have to worry about being cheated.

這消息來自 _____ 來源，你不用擔心被騙。

(A) reliable 可靠的　(B) flexible 有彈性的　(C) clumsy 笨拙的　(D) brutal 殘酷的

解析

(1)答題關鍵在題目空格左、右方的「來自」與「來源」。

(2)四個選項中，只有選(A)項的「可靠的」，才可有意義連成「來自可靠的來源」。

7. We hope that there will be no war in the world and that all people live in peace and _____ with each other.

希望世界上沒有戰爭而人們有和平的生活並且互相 _____ 相處。

(A) complaint 抱怨　(B) harmony 和諧　(C) mission 任務　(D) texture 結構

解析

(1)答題關鍵在題目空格左、右方的「互相」與「相處」。

(2)四個選項中，只有選(B)項的「和諧地」，才可有意義連成「互相和諧相處」。

8. To have a full discussion of the issue, the committee spent a whole hour _____ their ideas at the meeting.

為了對該議題有全面的討論，委員會花了整整一小時 _____ 他們的想法。

(A) depositing 寄存　(B) exchanging 交換　(C) governing 管理　(D) interrupting 干擾

解析

(1)答題關鍵在題目空格右方的「他們的想法」。

(2)四個選項中，只有選(B)項的「交換」，才可有意義連成「交換他們的想法」。

9. While adapting to western ways of living, many Asian immigrants in the US still try hard to ＿＿＿＿＿＿ their own cultures and traditions.

在適應西式生活的同時，很多移美的亞洲人仍努力地 ＿＿＿＿＿＿ 他們自己的文化與傳統。

(A) volunteer 志願者　(B) scatter 分散　(C) preserve 保留　(D) motivate 有動機

解析

(1)答題關鍵在題目空格左、右方的「努力地」與「他們自己的」。

(2)四個選項中，只有選 (C) 項的「保留」，才可有意義連成「努力地保留他們自己的文化與傳統」。

10. With the worsening of global economic conditions, it seems wiser and more ＿＿＿＿＿＿ to keep cash in the bank rather than to invest in the stock market.

有了全球經濟的惡化，在銀行存款比投資股票應該是比較 ＿＿＿＿＿＿ 。

(A) sensible 明智的　(B) portable 手提的　(C) explicit 清楚地　(D) anxious 焦慮地

解析

(1)答題關鍵在題目空格左、右方的「比較」與「在銀行存款」 ＿＿＿＿＿＿ 。

(2)四個選項中，只有選 (A) 項的「明智的」，才可有意義連成「在銀行存款……是比較明智的」。

11. Under the ＿＿＿＿＿＿ of newly elected president Barack Obama, the US is expected to turn a new page in politics and economy.

在新當選的歐巴馬總統 ＿＿＿＿＿＿ 之下，人們期待美國在政經方面會有新的做法。

(A) adoption 採用　(B) fragrance 香味　(C) identity 身分　(D) leadership 領導

解析

(1)答題關鍵在題目空格左、右方的「歐巴馬總統」與「之下」。

(2)四個選項中，只有選(D)項的「領導」，才可有意義連成「在歐巴馬總統領導之下……」。

12. Rapid advancement in motor engineering makes it ＿＿＿＿＿＿ possible to build a flying car in the near future.

機動工程的快速進步 ＿＿＿＿＿＿ 可能在不久將來就可以建造飛行車輛。

(A) individually 個別的　(B) narrowly 狹窄的　(C) punctually 準時地　(D) technically 技術上來說

解析

(1)答題關鍵在題目空格右方的「可能」。

(2)四個選項中，只有選 (D) 項的「技術上來說」，才可有意義連成「技術上來說有可能在不久的將來……」。

13. When you take photos, you can move around to shoot the target object from different _____ .

拍照時你可從不同的 _____ 拍攝影像。

(A) moods 心情　(B) trends 趨勢　(C) angles 角度　(D) inputs 輸入

解析

(1)答題關鍵在題目空格左方的「不同的」與「拍攝影像」。

(2)四個選項中，只有選(C) 項的「角度」，才可有意義連成「從不同的角度拍攝影像」。

14. Students were asked to _____ or rewrite their compositions based on the teacher's comments.

學生被要求 _____ 或依老師的意見重寫作文。

(A) revise 修改　(B) resign 辭職　(C) refresh 使清新　(D) remind 提醒

解析

(1)答題關鍵在題目空格左、右方的「被要求」與「或依老師的意見」。

(2)四個選項中，只有選 (A) 項的「修改（作文）」，才可有意義連成「被要求修改或依老師的意見重寫作文」。

15. Besides lung cancer, another _____ of smoking is wrinkles, a premature sign of aging.

除了肺癌外，另一個吸菸的 _____ 是有皺紋，提前老化的現象。

(A) blessing 祝福　(B) campaign 活動　(C) consequence 後果　(D) breakthrough 突破

解析

(1)答題關鍵在題目空格左、右方的「另一個」與「吸菸的」。

(2)四個選項中，只有選(C) 項的「後果」，才可有意義連成「另一個吸菸的後果是有皺紋」。

二、綜合測驗（15分）

說明：第 16 至 30 題，每題一個空格，請依文意選出最適當的一個選項，標示在答案卡之「選擇題答案區」。每題答對得 1 分，答錯不倒扣。

　　Art Fry was a researcher in the 3M Company. He was bothered by a small irritation every Sunday as he sang in the church choir. That is, after he _____16_____ his pages in the hymn book with small bits of paper, the small pieces would invariably fall out all over the floor. One day, an idea _____17_____ Art Fry. He remembered a kind of glue developed by a colleague that everyone thought _____18_____ a failure because it did not stick very well. He then coated the glue on a paper sample and found that it was not only a good bookmark, but it was great for writing notes. It would stay in place _____19_____ you wanted it to. Then you could remove it

_____20_____ damage. The resulting product was called the Post-it, one of 3M's most successful office products.

　　阿特‧福萊是 3 M 公司的研究員。他每個星期日在教堂唱詩班唱歌時，都會有點困擾。那就是，在他用小紙片在唱詩書內 _____16_____ 頁數後，小紙片總是掉落滿地。有一天，阿特 _____17_____ 一個辦法。他記得一位同事開發的一種膠水，每人都認為那 _____18_____ 一次敗筆，因為它黏不牢。他之後將紙板樣品塗上膠並且發現它不但是一個好書籤，而且作筆記也很好用。它會黏在 _____19_____ 你想黏的地方，也可以把它拿下來 _____20_____ 損壞。這種有效的產品被叫作「方便貼」，是 3 M 最暢銷的辦公用品之一。

16. 題句：after he _____16_____ his pages in the hymn book with small bits of paper,
　　　　在他用小紙片在唱詩書內 _____16_____ 頁數後，小紙片總是掉落滿地。
　　選項：(A) marked 做標記　(B) tore 撕毀　(C) served 保留　(D) took 攜帶

解析

依題意只有選 (A) 項的「做標記」（把某頁做標記之意）才是正確選項。

17. 題句：One day, an idea _____17_____ Art Fry.
　　　　有一天，阿特 _____17_____ 。
　　選項：(A) threw at 投擲　(B) occurred to 有……想法　(C) looked down upon 看不起　(D) came up with 想出辦法

解析

(1) 依題意只有選 (B) 項的「occurred to」才是正確選項。

(2) occurred to 為「想起」之意。當及物動詞用時，其後受詞是「某人」。如 A good idea occurred to me.

(3) (D) 選項的 come up with 是陷阱選項，它與 occurred to 兩片語的差別是，前一片語之前，要有「人」的主詞，後一片語的人稱主詞，是放片語後當受詞。如：He came up with a good idea. 與 A good idea occurred to me.

**18. 題句：that everyone thought _____18_____ a failure because it did not stick very well.
　　　　每個人都認為那 _____18_____ 一次敗筆，因為它黏不牢。
　　選項：(A) is 是　(B) was （過去式）　(C) will be （未來式）　(D) has been （現在完成式）

解析

(1) 答題關鍵在連接詞 because 的前後兩個子句。從屬子句已有 did not 二字。

(2) 因此四選項中要選 (B) 項過去式動詞的 was，才是符合文法的正確選項。

**19. 題句：It would stay in place _____19_____ you wanted it to.

它會黏在 _____19_____ 你想黏的地方。

選項：(A) despite that 不管…… (B) rather than 而不是 (C) as long as 只要 (D) no matter what 不論什麼

解析

(1)空格左右方是兩個子句，需要連接詞放入空格。

(2)依題意只有選(C)項的從屬片語連接詞的「as long as只要」，才能有意義連成「只要你要它留（黏）在哪裡它就黏在哪裡」，才是正確選項。

20. 題句：Then you could remove it _____20_____ damage.

也可以把它拿下來 _____20_____ 損壞。

選項：(A) into 到……裡 (B) out of 自……離開 (C) within…… 之內 (D) without 不會、沒有

解析

依題意只有選(D)項的「不會、沒有」才是正確選項。

　　The pineapple, long a symbol of Hawaii, was not a native plant. _____21_____ , pineapples did not appear there until 1813. The pineapple was _____22_____ found in Paraguay and in the southern part of Brazil. Natives planted the fruit across South and Central America and in the Caribbean region, _____23_____ Christopher Columbus first found it. Columbus brought it, along with many other new things, back to Europe with him. From there, the tasty fruit _____24_____ throughout other parts of civilization. It was carried on sailing ships around the world because it was found to help prevent scurvy, a disease that often _____25_____ sailors on long voyages. It was at the end of one of these long voyages that the pineapple came to Hawaii to stay.

　　鳳梨，長久以來一直是夏威夷的象徵，但它不是本地植物。 _____21_____ 鳳梨直到1813年才出現在那裡。鳳梨 _____22_____ 巴拉圭與巴西南方。當地人在美國中、南部及加勒比海地區栽種鳳梨， _____23_____ 哥倫布首先發現了鳳梨。哥倫布帶了鳳梨與其他新奇的東西回歐洲。此後，這個可口的水果 _____24_____ 整個文明國度。載送鳳梨的船運一直不停因為鳳梨被發現可以預防壞血病，那是一種經常使長程航行船員 _____25_____ 疾病。這些長程航行最後把鳳梨運到夏威夷。

21. 題句：The pineapple... was not a native plant. _____21_____ , pineapples did not appear there until 1813.

它不是本地植物。 _____21_____ 鳳梨直到1813年才出現在那裡。

選項：(A) For example 舉例 (B) In fact 事實上 (C) As a result 結果 (D) Little by little 漸漸地

解析

依題意只有選(B)項的「事實上」才是正確選項。

22. 題句：The pineapple was ＿＿＿22＿＿＿ found in Paraguay and in the southern part of Brazil.

鳳梨 ＿＿＿22＿＿＿ 巴拉圭與巴西南方。

選項：(A) nearly 幾乎　(B) recently 最近地　(C) originally 原先、源自　(D) shortly 短時間

解析

依題意只有選(C)項的「原先、源自」才是正確選項。

**23. 題句：Natives planted the fruit across South and Central America and in the Caribbean region, ＿＿＿23＿＿＿ Christopher Columbus first found it.

當地人在美國中、南部及加勒比海地區栽種鳳梨，＿＿＿23＿＿＿ 哥倫布首先發現了鳳梨。

選項：(A) that 那個　(B) what 什麼　(C) which 哪一　(D) where 何處

解析

(1) 答題關鍵在空格左邊的前述詞也是地方副詞的 region 一字，其後接關係副詞 where。

(2) 四個選項中，只有選(D)項、同時也是表示地方的關係副詞，才是符合文法的正確選項。

**24. 題句：From there, the tasty fruit ＿＿＿24＿＿＿ throughout other parts of civilization.

此後，這個可口的水果 ＿＿＿24＿＿＿ 整個文明國度。

選項：(A) spread 散布、普及　(B) to spread（不定詞）　(C) should spread 應該散布　(D) will spread（未來式）

解析

依本題句是在敘述一件事實，所以選(A)項現在式動詞的「spread」才是正確選項。

25. 題句：it was found to help prevent scurvy, a disease that often ＿＿＿25＿＿＿ sailors on long voyages.

鳳梨被發現可以預防壞血病，那是一種經常使長程航行船員 ＿＿＿25＿＿＿ 疾病。

選項：(A) bothered 受困擾　(B) contacted 接觸　(C) suffered 受苦　(D) wounded 受傷

解析

依題意只有選(A)項的「受困擾」才是正確選項。

　　The Paralympics are Olympic-style games for athletes with a disability. They were organized for the first time in Rome in 1960. In Toronto in 1976, the idea of putting together different disability groups ＿＿＿26＿＿＿ sports competitions was born. Today, the Paralympics are sports events for athletes from six different disability groups. They emphasize the participants' athletic achievements ＿＿＿27＿＿＿ their physical disability. The games have grown in size gradually. The number of athletes ＿＿＿28＿＿＿ in the Summer Paralympic Games has increased from 400 athletes from 23 countries in 1960 to 3,806 athletes from 136 countries in 2004.

The Paralympic Games have always been held in the same year as the Olympic Games. Since the Seoul 1988 Paralympic Games and the Albertville 1992 Winter Paralympic Games, they have also _____ 29 _____ in the same city as the Olympics. On June 19, 2001, an agreement was signed between the International Olympic Committee and the International Paralympics Committee to keep this _____ 30 _____ in the future. From the 2012 bid onwards, the city chosen to host the Olympic Games will also host the Paralympics.

殘障奧運會是殘障人士的奧運形式的競賽。這種比賽在 1960 年於羅馬第一次舉辦。1976 年在多倫多，_____ 26 _____ 不同的殘障團體參加比賽的想法落實了。今天，殘奧會是由六種不同的殘障團體組成的比賽。他們強調參加者的運動成就，_____ 27 _____ 他們的身體殘障。比賽規模逐漸擴大。_____ 28 _____ 夏季殘奧會從 1960 年的 23 個國家 400 名運動員增加到 2004 年的 136 個國家 3,806 名。

殘奧會都會與一般奧運會同年舉行。自 1988 年的首爾殘奧會與 1992 年的阿爾貝維爾的冬季殘奧會以來，1992 年冬季殘奧會，他們就改在與奧運會相同的城市_____ 29 _____。到了 2001 年 6 月 19 日，一項由國際奧運會與國際殘奧會委員們簽署一項同意書，以後要繼續的舉辦這類 _____ 30 _____。且自 2012 年以後被選為主辦奧運會的城市，也要同時舉辦殘奧會。

**26. 題句：the idea of putting together different disability groups _____ 26 _____ sports competitions was born.

_____ 26 _____ 不同的殘障團體參加比賽的想法落實了。

選項：(A) for 為了　(B) with 與　(C) as 當　(D) on 在……上

解析

依題意只有選(A)項的「for」（為了讓不同……參加之意）才是正確選項。

27. 題句：They emphasize the participants' athletic achievements _____ 27 _____ their physical disability.

他們強調參加者的運動成就，_____ 27 _____ 他們的身體殘障。

選項：(A) in terms of 就……而論　(B) instead of 取代、而不是　(C) at the risk of 冒……險　(D) at the cost of 以……為代價

解析

依題意只有選(B)項的「取代、而不是」才是正確選項。

**28. 題句：The number of athletes _____ 28 _____ in the Summer Paralympic Games has increased....

選項：(A) participate 參加　(B) participated （過去式）　(C) participating （動名詞）　(D) to participate （不定詞）

解析

(1)依題意只有選(C)項的「participating」才是正確選項。

(2)參加者從1960年的多少人到2004年的多少人，已不是單純的過去式用法，因此，在緊接athletes（運動員）字後就用分詞片語「athletes participating in the Summer Paralympic...」來修飾 athletes，所以(C)項的 participating 才是正確選項。

29. 題句：they have also _____29_____ in the same city as the Olympics 1992

　　　1992年冬季殘奧會，他們就改在與奧運會相同的城市 _____29_____ 。

　選項：(A) taken turns 輪流　(B) taken place 舉行　(C) taken off 脫下　(D) taken over 接管

解析

依題意只有選(B)項「舉行」才是正確選項。

30. 題句：International Olympic Committee and the International Paralympics Committee to keep this _____30_____ in the future.

　　　將來，國際奧委會與國際輪椅奧運會都會保持這類的 _____30_____ 。

　選項：(A) piece 一片　(B) deadline 最後期限　(C) date 日期　(D) practice 練習、訓練

解析

依題意只有選 (D) 項的「練習、訓練」才是正確選項。

三、文意選填（10分）

説明：第 31 至 40 題，每題一個空格，請依文意在文章後所提供的(A) 到 (J) 選項中分別選出最適當者，並將其英文字母代號標示在答案卡之「選擇題答案區」。每題答對得 1 分，答錯不倒扣。

Familiar fables can be narrated differently or extended in interesting and humorous ways. The end of the famous fable of "The Tortoise and the Hare" is well known to all: the tortoise wins the race against the hare. The moral lesson is that slow and steady wins the race. We all have grown up with this popular version, but the _____31_____ fable can be extended with different twists. At the request of the hare, a second race is _____32_____ and this time, the hare runs without taking a rest and wins. The moral lesson is that _____33_____ and consistent will always beat slow and steady. Then it is the tortoise that _____34_____ the hare to a third race along a different route in which there is a river just before the final destination. This time, the tortoise wins the race because the hare cannot swim. The moral lesson is "First _____35_____ your strengths, and then change the playing field to suit them."

But the story continues. Both _____36_____ know their own drawbacks and limitations very well; therefore, they jointly decide to have one last race-not to decide who the winner or loser is, but just for their own pleasure and satisfaction. The two _____37_____ as a team. Firstly, the hare carries the tortoise on its back to the river. Then, the tortoise carries the hare and swims to the _____38_____ bank of the river. Lastly, the hare carries the tortoise again on its back. Thus they reach the _____39_____ line together. Overall, many moral lessons from the last match are highlighted. The most obvious one is the importance of _____40_____ . Another moral which also means a great deal is "competition against situations rather than against rivals."

熟悉的寓言可以有不同的詮釋，或者在有趣和幽默的模式裡誇張一些。著名寓言

「龜兔賽跑」的結局眾所皆知：烏龜贏得比賽。寓意所說的是，緩慢但穩定者贏！我們都是在這種版本的環境中長大。但是　　31　　寓言也會有不同的詮釋。應兔子的要求，第二場比賽　　32　　，這次，兔子沒有休息所以跑贏。寓意則是指　　33　　和一致性贏過緩慢與穩定。然後是烏龜　　34　　兔子要跑第三次比賽，但是路線不同，且在抵達終點前會有一條小河。這次，烏龜贏得比賽，因為兔子不能游泳。這則的寓意是「首先要　　35　　你的力量，然後改變運動場適應它」。

但是故事繼續著。兩個　　36　　都非常了解自己的缺點和限制；因此，他們共同決定有最後一場比賽不是用來決定誰勝誰敗，只要比賽快樂和滿意就好。這兩個　　37　　成為一個團隊。首先，兔子把烏龜背到河邊，然後，烏龜背著兔子游到　　38　　岸。最後，兔子再次背著烏龜。因此他們一同到達　　39　　線。總的來說，來自最後比賽的很多寓意被強調出來。最明顯的一種是　　40　　的重要性。另一種意義重大的寓意是，「為所處環境競爭而不是為對手競爭」。

(A) arranged 安排的　(B) challenges 挑戰　(C) competitors 競爭者
(D) cooperate 合作　(E) fast 快　(F) finishing 完成、終點　(G) identify 確認
(H) opposite 相反地　(I) same 相同　(J) teamwork 團隊

31. 題句：We all have grown up with this popular version, but the ____31____ fable can be extended with different twists.

　　但是　　31　　寓言也會有不同的詮釋。

解析

依題意只有選(I)項的「相同的」才是正確選項。

32. 題句：a second race is ____32____ and this time, the hare runs without taking a rest and wins.

　　應兔子的要求，第二場比賽　　32　　。

解析

依題意只有選(A)項的「被安排了」才是正確選項。

33. 題句：The moral lesson is that ____33____ and consistent will always beat slow and steady.

　　寓意則是指　　33　　和一致性贏過緩慢與穩定。

解析

依題意只有選(E)項的「快」才是正確選項。

34. 題句：Then it is the tortoise that _____34_____ the hare to a third race.

　　　　　然後是烏龜 _____34_____ 兔子要跑第三次比賽。

解析

依題意只有選(B)項的「挑戰」才是正確選項。

35. 題句：Then it is the tortoise that _____34_____ the hare to a third race along a different route.

　　　　　首先要 _____35_____ 你的力量，然後改變運動場適應它。

解析

依題意只有選(G)項的「確認」才是正確選項。

36. 題句：Both _____36_____ know their own drawbacks and limitations very well;

　　　　　兩個 _____36_____ 都非常了解自己的缺點和限制。

解析

依題意只有選(C)項的「競爭者」才是正確選項。

37. 題句：The two _____37_____ as a team.

　　　　　這兩個 _____37_____ 成為一個團隊。

解析

依題意只有選(D)項的「合作」才是正確選項。

38. 題句：The tortoise carries the hare and swims to the _____38_____ bank of the river.

　　　　　然後，烏龜背著兔子游到 _____38_____ 岸。

解析

依題意只有選(H)項的「相反的」（即對岸之意）才是正確選項。

39. 題句：Thus they reach the _____39_____ line together.

　　　　　因此他們一同到達 _____39_____ 線。

解析

依題意只有選(F)項的「完成」（終點線之意）才是正確選項。

40. 題句：The most obvious one is the importance of _____40_____ .

　　　　　最明顯的一種是 _____40_____ 的重要性。

解析

依題意只有選 (J) 項的「團隊配合」才是正確選項。

四、閱讀測驗（32分）

41-44 為題組

To Whom It May Concern:

　　Your address was forwarded to us by Why Bother Magazine. All of us here think The International Institute of Not Doing Much is the best organization in the world. You know how to avoid unnecessary activities!

　　We closely followed the advice in your article. First, we replaced all our telephones with carrier pigeons. Simply removing the jingle of telephones and replacing them with the pleasant sounds of birds has had a remarkable effect on everyone. Besides, birds are cheaper than telephone service. After all, we are a business. We have to think of the bottom line. As a side benefit, the birds also fertilize the lawn outside the new employee sauna.

　　Next, we sold the computers off to Stab, Grab, Grit, and Nasty, a firm of lawyers nearby. Our electricity bill went way down. Big savings! The boss is impressed. We have completely embraced paper technology. Now that we all use pencils, doodling is on the increase, and the quality of pencilwomanship is impressive, as you can tell from my handwriting in this letter. By the way, if you can, please send this letter back to us. We can erase and reuse it. Just tie it to **Maggie**'s leg and she'll know where to take it.

　　Now it's very calm and quiet here. You can notice the difference. No more loud chatter on the telephones! All we hear is the scratching of pencil on paper, the sound of pigeons, and the delivery of inter-office correspondence by paper airplane.

　　Wonderful! I've always wanted to work for an insurance company ever since I was a little girl. Now it's perfect.

　　Sincerely yours,

　　Eleanor Lightly

　　Spokeswoman and Company Hair Stylist

　　ABC Activity Insurance: Insure against overdoing it

敬啟者（敬啟有關的人）

　　Why Brother 雜誌將您的演講內容給了我們，我們認為，「不必多做國際機構」是世界上最好的組織。你們知道如何避免不必要的活動。

　　我們採用你們文章裡的建言。首先，我們用信鴿替代我們的全部電話。僅僅用鳥聲替代電話鈴聲就大大地影響了每一個人。而且，鳥比電話服務便宜。終究，我們是在商言商。我們必須考慮到底線作為附加價值，鳥也會在新蓋的員工三溫暖館外的草坪上施點肥。

　　下一步，我們把電腦賣給 Stab、Grab、Grit 及 Nasty，這是附近的一家律師事務所。我們的電費馬上少很多。省太多了！這使老闆大為滿意。我們完全擁護書面科技。既然我們都使用鉛筆，亂畫情形不斷增加，並且手寫的品質也進步了。從本函我

的手寫筆跡你應該看得出來。還有，如果可行的話，請把這這張信紙寄還給我們。我們能擦掉筆跡重新使用。請把紙綁在瑪姬（鴿子名）的腳上，牠就知道要送去哪裡。

　　這裡現在非常寧靜。你會感覺到與先前有所差別。不再有大聲喋喋不休的講電話聲，我們聽到的只有鉛筆在紙上的摩擦聲、鴿子聲，以及紙摺飛機在各部門之間飛來飛去的聲音。太棒了，從小我就一直想要在保險公司上班。現在那太好了。

　　誠懇的，

　　伊蓮娜賴利

　　女發言人兼公司髮型師

　　ABC 活動保險：保障不必過勞

41. Which of the following best describes the life the author is leading?

　　下列哪一項最能描述作者導引的生活？

　　(A) A simple, slow-paced life.

　　　　單純，放慢腳步的生活。

　　(B) A life of hard work and security.

　　　　努力工作且有保障的生活。

　　(C) A religious, peasant-like life.

　　　　有宗教信仰，像農民一樣的生活。

　　(D) A life away from paper and pencils.

　　　　不用紙筆的生活。

解析

從答題關鍵的「All of us here think The International Institute of Not Doing Much is the best organization in the world. You know how to avoid unnecessary activities!」可看出，(A) 項的「A simple, slow-paced life.」才是正確選項。

42. Where is Eleanor's letter sent to?

　　伊蓮娜的信會寄去哪裡？

　　(A) Why Bother Magazine.

　　　　「不做太多」雜誌社。

　　(B) ABC Activity Insurance Company.

　　　　ABC 活動保險公司。

　　(C) Stab, Grab, Grit, and Nasty Law Firm.

　　　　Stab, Grab, Grit, and Nasty 律師事務所。

　　(D) The International Institute of Not Doing Much.

「不做太多」的國際機構。

解析

從答題關鍵的「The International Institute of Not Doing Much is the best organization in the world. You know how to avoid unnecessary activities!」可看出，(D) 項的「The International Institute of Not Doing Much.」才是正確選項。

43. Which of the following is practiced in the author's company?

下列哪一項在作者的公司實踐過？

(A) Replacing the manual work system with modern technology.

用現代技術替換手工做法。

(B) Turning off lights in the daytime to save electricity.

在白天關燈以省電。

(C) Recycling paper resources whenever possible.

隨時回收紙資源。

(D) Buying birds and pets as company for the staff.

買鳥和寵物與員工作伴。

解析

從答題關鍵的「By the way, if you can, please send this letter back to us. We can erase and reuse it.」可看出，(C) 項的「Recycling paper resources whenever possible.」才是正確選項。

44. What is true about **Maggie**?

關於瑪姬哪項為真？

(A) She works as a manager in the author's company.

她在作者的公司當經理。

(B) She sometimes helps fertilize the lawn outside the sauna.

她有時會在三溫暖間外面草坪施肥。

(C) She often helps with inter-office correspondence using e-mail.

她經常用電子郵件幫助傳遞部門之間的郵件。

(D) Her handwriting has improved a lot after entering the company.

進入公司後她的字寫得更好看。

解析

從答題關鍵的「Just tie it to Maggie's leg and she'll know where to take it.」可看出，(B) 項的「She sometimes helps fertilize the lawn outside the sauna.」才是正確選項。

45-48 為題組

The Galapagos Islands are the Pacific island paradise where Darwin's theory of evolution was born. They are places filled with giant tree lizards, sandy beaches, and tropical plants. Now they will be famous for one more thing: the world's first green airport.

This group of islands off the coast of Ecuador has recently contracted Argentine Corporacion America to manage the redevelopment of the airport on the island of Baltra. It is estimated that US$20 million is needed to complete **the project** by 2009. The new development has several important features: use of wind and solar energy, passive heating and cooling systems, as well as concrete runways in place of asphalt, which has a greater carbon footprint during its production cycle. This new development couldn't be coming at a better time for the Galápagos, which were added to an environmental "danger list" in 2007.

Pacific islands like the Galápagos, Easter Island, and Tahiti, have economies that are driven almost completely by tourism. However, some people think these are "unsustainable models of development." The number of visitors to the Galápagos rose more than 250% from 1990 to 2006, while the number of commercial flights to the area rose 193% from 2001 to 2006. These increases put great stress on the islands' resources and environment. Air travel is especially criticized for exhausting natural resources and causing environmental damage. Thus, efforts are being made to reduce the environmental impact of the tourism industry. The greening of airports is just one of these attempts.

加拉帕戈斯島是達爾文想出進化論的太平洋島國。在那裡充滿大型樹蜥蜴、沙灘和熱帶植物。他們將會因擁有世界第一個綠色機場而聞名。

這個在厄瓜多外海的群島最近與阿根廷公司簽約，以經營 Baltra 島的機場重新開發事宜。估計將需要 2,000 萬美元而會在 2009 年完工。新開發案有幾個重要的特色：使用風力與太陽能源、被動式冷暖系統，以及使用堅固的混凝土而不是瀝青，瀝青在生產期間所造成的碳跡較大。新開發案對加拉帕戈斯來說正是時候，該市在 2007 年被列入「環保危險名單」。

像加拉帕戈斯島、復活節島和大溪地等的太平洋群島，幾乎都是倚賴觀光事業。不過，有些人認為這些開發無法持續發展。在 1990～2006 年期間，到加拉帕戈斯的觀光客人數增加了 250%，而商業航班數量從 2001 年到 2006 年成長了 193%。這些發展給該島的資源和環境上，造成極大壓力。航空旅行因耗盡自然資源、造成環境污染，更是受到批評。因此，各部門都努力地降低旅遊業的環境影響。飛機場的綠化就是多種努力的一部分。

45. What is this article mainly about?

本文的主題是什麼？

(A) The problems of Darwin's theory.

達爾文理論的問題。

(B) The background of building a green airport.

建造綠色飛機場的背景。

(C) The history of the Galapagos Islands.

加拉帕戈斯島的歷史。

(D) The ease of transportation to the Pacific islands.

到太平洋群島的交通很方便。

解析

從整篇文章內容來看，是在說明該地要建綠色機場的始末，因此 (B) 項的「The background of building a green airport.」才是正確選項。

46. Where will the world's first green airport be built?

世界的第一個綠色機場將會建在哪裡？

(A) In Tahiti. 在大溪地。　　(B) In Argentina. 在阿根廷。

(C) In Baltra. 在Baltra。　　(D) In the United States. 在美國。

解析

從答題關鍵的「has recently contracted Argentine Corporacion America to manage the redevelopment of the airport on the island of Baltra」可看出，(C) 項的「In Baltra.」才是正確選項。

47. What is true about the Galapagos Islands?

關於加拉帕戈斯島哪項為真？

(A) They are located near Ecuador in the Pacific Ocean.

他們位在太平洋的厄瓜多附近。

(B) They have had a great increase in population since 2001.

從 2001 年起他們人口增加很多。

(C) They will invest US$20 million to promote their tourism.

他們將投資 2,000 萬美元推廣觀光。

(D) They have become one of the most dangerous places in the world.

他們已成為在世界上最危險的地方之一。

解析

從答題關鍵的「This group of islands off the coast of Ecuador」可看出，(A) 項的「They are located near Ecuador in the Pacific Ocean.」才是正確選項。

48. What does the project in the second paragraph refer to?

第二段文章內容與什麼有關？

(A) The plan to build a green airport.

計畫建造綠色機場。

(B) The research on the production of solar energy.

創造太陽能的的研究。

(C) The task of calculating a carbon footprint.

計算碳足跡的任務。

(D) The study on the exhaustion of natural resources.

在自然資源的竭盡上的研究。

解析

從整段文章內容來看，只提到建綠色機場之事，並無提到三選項的內容，因此 (A) 項的「The plan to build a green airport」才是正確選項。

49-52 為題組

According to popular folklore, many animals are smarter than they appear. Dogs bark before earthquakes; cattle predict rainfall by sitting on the ground. But cattle may have another hidden talent in telling which way is north.

Small animals such as mole rats living underground are known for the use of magnetism to navigate. Dr. Begall and her colleagues wanted to know whether larger mammals also have the ability to perceive magnetic fields. They investigated this possibility by studying images of thousands of cattle captured on Google Earth, a website that stitches together satellite photographs to produce an image of the Earth's surface.

Grazing animals are known to orient themselves in a way that minimizes wind chill from the north and maximizes the warmth of the sun when they are cold. The researchers therefore had to study a lot of cows grazing in lots of different places at different times of day, in order to average out these factors and see whether cattle could act like compass needles.

The researchers concluded that cattle do generally orient hemselves in a north-south direction. This north-south preference has also been noted in flies, termites and honeybees. But unfortunately, even the high resolution of Google Earth is not powerful enough to tell which end of the cow is its head, and which its tail. The researchers were therefore unable to answer their research questions of whether cattle prefer to look north or south, and whether that differs in the northern and southern hemispheres.

根據廣為流傳的民間傳說，很多動物比他們的外表看起來更聰明。狗會在地震發生前狂吠；牛會坐在地上來預測下雨。但是牛可能還有另一種隱藏的能力，牠會辨識北方。

小動物像是生活在地下的錢鼠，知道利用磁場認方向。Begall 與她的同事一直想知道大型哺乳動物是否有能力去感覺磁場。他們透過在「Google Earth」上捕捉的數千頭牛隻的圖像調查這種可能性，它是一個連結衛星照片的網站，可顯示地球表面的圖像。

草食動物被認為會調整自己的方向，把北方來的冷風減到最低，在天冷時，也會把太陽的熱能保持久一些。因此研究人員必須在每天的不同時間與地點觀察牛隻吃草的情形，以便平均出這些因素，也要看看牛隻會否像羅盤指針一樣的辨識方向。

研究人員的結論是，牛隻通常會站於南北向的方位。這種南北向的現象也會發生在蒼蠅，白蟻和蜜蜂等身上。但是令人遺憾，即使 GoogleEarth 的高解析度也無法分

辦牛隻的哪一端是頭，哪一端是尾巴。研究人員因此無法回答他們的研究問題，牛隻喜歡朝北還是朝南？另外，在北半球與南半球會不會不同？。

49. What is the article mainly about?

　本文大意為何？

　(A) The usefulness of Google Earth.

　　　Google Earth的實用。

　(B) Whether cattle are superior to other animals.

　　　是否牛隻優於其他動物。

　(C) Animals' sensitivity to natural disasters.

　　　動物對自然災害的敏感性。

　(D) Whether cattle behave like compass needles.

　　　是否牛隻行為像羅盤磁針。

　解析

　從整段文章談的都是牛隻與方向的問題，沒有提到其他三選項的內容，所以，(D) 項的「Whether cattle behave like compass needles.」才是正確選項。

50. Which of the following factors might affect Dr. Begall's research result?

　下列哪一項可能影響 Begall 博士的研究結果？

　(A) Rainfall 降雨。　(B) Earthquakes 地震。　(C) Location 位置。　(D) Cost 費用。

　解析

　從答題關鍵的「cattle do generally orient themselves in a north-south direction.」可看出，(C) 項的「Location」才是正確選項。

51. What is the major finding of Dr. Begall's study?

　博士的主要發現是什麼？

　(A) Cattle point north-south.

　　　牛隻朝向北方南方。

　(B) Magnetism can't be studied scientifically.

　　　無法用科學研究磁性。

　(C) Animals prefer to look south.

　　　動物喜歡向南方看。

　(D) Google Earth is a reliable research tool.

　　　Google Earth是一件可靠的研究工具。

　解析

　從答題關鍵的「The researchers concluded that cattle do generally orient hemselves in a north-south direction. This north-south preference has also been noted in flies, termites and honeybees. But unfortunately, even the high resolution of Google Earth is not powerful enough to tell which end of the cow is its head, and which its tail.」可看出，(A) 項的「Cattle point north-south.」才是正確選項。

52. Why couldn't the researchers get the answer to their research questions?

　　研究人員為什麼不能得到他們研究問題的答案？

(A) Many cattle in their study were sitting on the ground.

　　他們研究的很多牛隻坐在地上。

(B) The cattle constantly change directions to avoid wind chill.

　　牛隻經常改變方向以避免寒風。

(C) There is magnetic difference between the two hemispheres.

　　在兩個半球之間有磁性的差異。

(D) They couldn't tell a cow's head from its tail in the satellite pictures.

　　衛星畫面裡看不出牛的頭或尾巴。

解析

從答題關鍵的「even the high resolution of Google Earth is not powerful enough to tell which end of the cow is its head, and which its tail. The researchers were therefore unable to answer their research questions of whether cattle prefer to look north or south,」可看出，(D) 項的「They couldn't tell a cow's head from its tail in the satellite pictures.」才是正確選項。

53-56 為題組

　　Children normally have a distrust of new foods. But it's the parents' job to serve a variety of foods and expose their children to healthy dieting habits.

　　Some simple strategies can help even the pickiest eater learn to like a more varied diet. First of all, you don't have to send children out of the kitchen. With hot stoves, boiling water and sharp knives at hand, it is understandable that parents don't want children in the kitchen when they're making dinner. But studies suggest that involving children in meal preparation is an important first step in getting them to try new foods. In one study, nearly 600 children from kindergarten to sixth grade took part in a nutrition curriculum intended to get them to eat more vegetables and whole grains. The researchers found that children who had cooked their own foods were more likely to eat those foods in the cafeteria than children who had not. Kids don't usually like radishes, but if kids cut them up and put them in the salad, they will love the dish.

　　Another strategy is not to diet in front of your children. Kids are tuned into their parents' eating preferences and are far more likely to try foods if they see their mother or father eating them. Given this powerful effect, parents who are trying to lose weight should be careful of how their dieting habits can influence a child's perceptions about food and healthful eating. In one study of 5-year-old girls about dieting, one child noted that dieting involved drinking chocolate milkshakes, because her mother was using Slim-Fast drinks. Another child said dieting meant "you fix food but you don't eat it." By exposing young children to **erratic** dieting habits, parents may be putting them at risk for eating disorders.

　　孩子通常不相信新食品。提供不同食品且引導孩子吃健康食品的習慣，是父母親的工作。

　　一些簡單的策略能幫助或甚至是最愛挑食者，去學習喜歡不同的飲食。首先，你不必將孩子趕出廚房。有了熱爐、沸水和鋒利的刀在手上，可以理解雙親準備晚餐時，不要孩子跑來廚房。但是研究報告建議，讓孩子參與準備餐食是要他們嘗試新食品的重要的第一步。在一項研究，將近六百個孩子，從幼稚園到六年級生都有，參加目的要孩子多吃蔬菜與穀類營養課程。研究人員發現曾經自己烹飪的小孩，比不曾自己烹飪的小孩，比較會吃自助餐廳的食物。孩子通常不喜歡小蘿蔔，但如果孩子自己切蘿蔔，並放進沙拉，他們就會喜歡吃。

　　另一個策略就是，在你的孩子面前不要節食。如果孩子看見父母親吃某些食物，就更會想吃那些食物。有了這種強力效應，想減重的父母應該注意他們的忌食習慣會如何地影響孩子的想法。有關五歲女孩的節食研究裡，一個孩子注意到節食竟然可以吃熱巧克力奶昔，因為她母親使用「快瘦」飲料。另一個孩子說，節食的意思是「你準備食物，但你不吃它」。讓孩子養成怪異的節食習慣，父母可能已使小孩處於飲食失調的風險。

53. What is the main purpose of this article?

　　本文的主要用意是什麼？

(A) To explain what causes children's eating disorder.

　　解釋引起孩子亂吃的原因。

(B) To teach children about the meal preparation process.

　　教孩子餐食準備的過程。

(C) To advocate the importance of vegetables and whole grains.

　　提倡菜蔬和全穀類的重要性。

(D) To inform parents how they can help their children like varied foods.

　　告知父母他們怎樣幫助孩子喜歡不同的食物。

解析

從整篇文章的內容，談的都是父母親教孩子們不要挑挑食、親子共同準備晚餐等事情，可看出，(D) 項的「To inform parents how they can help their children like varied foods.」才是正確選項。

54. Which of the following groups will eat more balanced meals?

　　下列哪一項比較會吃均衡的飲食？

(A) The children who help cook food.

　　幫助烹飪的那些孩子。

(B) The children whose parents are on a diet.

　　有父母在節食的那些孩子。

(C) The children who do not love radishes.

　　不愛小蘿蔔的那些孩子。

(D) The children whose parents work in a cafeteria.

　　父母在自助餐廳工作的那些孩子。

解析

從答題關鍵的「The researchers found that children who had cooked their own foods were more likely to eat those foods in the cafeteria than children who had not. Kids don't usually like radishes, but if kids cut them up and put them in the salad, they will love the dish.」可看出，(A) 項的「The children who help cook food.」才是正確選項。

55. What does erratic in the last sentence imply?

　　最後一句的「erratic」是指何意？

(A) Obvious. 明顯。　(B) Healthful. 有益於健康。　(C) Dishonest. 不誠實。

(D) Inappropriate. 不適當。

解析

erratic 為古怪的、怪癖的之意，只有 (D) 項的「Inappropriate.」才是最接近選項。

56. Which of the following is true about Slim-Fast?

　　有關「快瘦」下列哪一項為眞？

(A) It is children's favorite food.

　　它是孩子最喜愛的食品。

(B) It looks like a chocolate milkshake.

　　它看起來像巧克力奶昔。

(C) It contains a variety of vegetables.

　　它含有多種菜蔬。

(D) It is intended for slim, fast people.

　　有意給快瘦的人。

解析

從答題關鍵的「one child noted that dieting involved drinking chocolate milkshakes, because her mother was using Slim-Fast drinks.」可看出，(B) 項的「It looks like a chocolate milkshake」才是正確選項。（選項 (D) 怎不能選？）

第貳部分：非選擇題（28分）

一、翻譯題（8分）

> 説明：1. 請將以下兩題中文譯成正確而通順達意的英文，並將答案寫在「答案卷」上。
> 　　　2. 請依序作答，並標明題號，每題僅能譯成一個英文句子。每題4分，共8分。

1. 大部分學生不習慣自己解決問題，他們總是期待老師提供標準答案。

解析

先將題句內相關字詞寫出中譯：

大部分學生 most students　不習慣 are not used to　自己解決問題 to solve their own problems 他們總是期待 they are expecting　老師提供標準答案 standard answer /solution from their teachers.

整句英譯

Most students are not used to solve their own problems, they are always expecting standard answers / solutions from their teachers.

2. 除了用功讀書獲取知識外，學生也應該培養獨立思考的能力。

解析

先將題句內相關字詞寫出中譯：

除了……外 besides　用功讀書 study hard　獲取知識 to get the knowledge　學生也應該 students should　培養 cultivate　獨立思考的能力 their thinking ability independently

整句英譯

Besides studying hard to get the knowledge, students should also cultivate their thinking ability independently.

二、英文作文（20分）

> 説明：1. 依提示在「答案卷」上寫一篇英文作文。
> 　　　2. 文長120個單詞（words）左右。

提示：請根據右方圖片的場景，描述整個事件發生的前因後果。文章請分兩段，第一段說明之前發生了什麼事情，並根據圖片內容描述現在的狀況；第二段請合理說明接下來可能會發生什麼事，或者未來該做些什麼。

解析

(1) 這種看圖說故事的作文很容易發揮，它並沒有固定的格式要求考生怎麼寫，只要寫出來的文章，不離圖意太遠、加上語句通順、文語法不要錯，都可得高分。

(2) 該圖看出來是一個簡陋房屋倒塌的圖片，內有一位背籮筐、戴斗笠的農人回到災難現場。只要圖上有的通通把它寫下來，最後再把所有的單句串聯起來就可以了。

相關字詞：從圖片推斷 an inference from the picture　倒塌的農舍或穀倉 collapsed farm house / barn　一位背籮筐戴斗笠農民 a farmer wearing a straw hat, and back-packed with a large basket　回到受災現場 returned to the site

To infer from what we see in the picture, it looks very much like a collapsed farm house stroke by the earthquack. You see the gravel all over, and you car hardly see what was in it before the house collapsed. There is no way of knowing whether the farmer has any family, or, perhaps he is alone.

Feeling sympathy for the farmer is one thing, to help him apply for aid from goverrment or private charity institute is another. The farmer should go directly to the town office seeking for any legal relief fund by the local government, there are so many different kinds of law concerning something so called "disaster relief fund", further more, there will be someone at the town offices to assist any illiterate citizen in filling up all kinds of forms.

99 年學測（學科能力測驗）

第壹部分：選擇題（72分）

一、詞彙（15分）

> 説明：第 1 至 15 題，每題選出最適當的一個選項，標示在答案卡之「選擇題答案區」。每題答對得 1 分，答錯不倒扣。

1. Mr. Lin is a very ＿＿＿＿＿ writer; he publishes at least five novels every year.
   林先生是一位非常 ＿＿＿＿＿ 作家，他每年最少出版五本小說。
   (A) moderate 適度的　(B) temporary 臨時的　(C) productive 多產的　(D) reluctant 勉強的

   解析
   (1)解題關鍵字在題目空格左、右方的「非常的」與「作家」二字。
   (2)四個答項中，只有選 (C) 項的「多產的」，才可有意義地連成「非常多產的作家」，也才符合後句的「每年出版五本小說」。

2. Using a heating pad or taking warm baths can sometimes help to ＿＿＿＿＿ pain in the lower back.
   利用電熱板或洗溫水澡，有助於 ＿＿＿＿＿ 下背部的疼痛。
   (A) polish 打蠟　(B) relieve 減輕　(C) switch 開關　(D) maintain 保持

   解析
   (1)解題關鍵字在題目空格左、右方的「有助於」與「疼痛」二字。
   (2)四個答項中，只有選 (B) 項的「減輕」，才可有意義地連成「有助於減輕疼痛」（下背部的疼痛）。

3. Peter stayed up late last night, so he drank a lot of coffee this morning to keep himself ＿＿＿＿＿ in class.
   彼德昨晚晚睡，所以他今早喝很多咖啡，可在課堂上使他保持 ＿＿＿＿＿ 。
   (A) acceptable 可接受　(B) amazed 驚奇的　(C) accurate 準確　(D) awake 清醒

   解析
   (1)答題關鍵在題目空格左方的「使他保持」。
   (2)四個選項中，只有選 (D) 項的「清醒」，才可有意義地連成「在課堂上使他保持清醒」。

4. Due to ＿＿＿＿＿＿ , prices for daily necessities have gone up and we have to pay more for the same items now.

由於 ＿＿＿＿＿＿ ，民生必須品的物價上升，而同樣的東西現在要付更多錢。

(A) inflation 通貨膨漲　(B) solution 解決辦法　(C) objection 反對　(D) condition 條件

解析

(1)答題關鍵在題目空格左、右方的「由於」與「民生必須品的物價上升」。

(2)四個選項中，只有選 (A) 項的「通貨膨漲」，才可有意義地連成「由於通貨膨漲，民生必須品的物價上升」。

5. The government is doing its best to ＿＿＿＿＿＿ the cultures of the tribal people for fear that they may soon die out.

政府正盡力在 ＿＿＿＿＿＿ 原住民文化以防其消失。

(A) preserve 保護　(B) frustrate 挫敗　(C) hesitate 猶豫　(D) overthrow 推翻

解析

(1)答題關鍵在題目空格右方的「原住民文化以防其消失」。

(2)四個選項中，只有選(A)項的「保護」，才可有意義地連成「保護原住民文化以防其消失」。

6. I could not ＿＿＿＿＿＿ the sweet smell from the bakery, so I walked in and bought a fresh loaf of bread.

我無法 ＿＿＿＿＿＿ 麵包店傳出的香味，所以我進去買了一條麵包。

(A) insist 堅持　(B) resist 抗拒　(C) obtain 獲得　(D) contain 包含

解析

(1)答題關鍵在題目空格左、右方的「無法」與「傳出的香味」。

(2)四個選項中，只有選(B)項的「抗拒」，才可有意義地連成「無法抗拒麵包店傳出的香味」。

7. Steve has several meetings to attend every day; therefore, he has to work on a very ＿＿＿＿＿＿ schedule.

史帝芬每天要參加好幾個會議，所以他要有一個非常 ＿＿＿＿＿＿ 工作表。

(A) dense 稠密的　(B) various 不同的　(C) tight 緊密的　(D) current 當前的

解析

(1)答題關鍵在題目空格左、右方的「一個非常」與「工作表」。

(2)四個選項中，只有選 (C) 項的「緊密的」，才可有意義地連成「他要有一個非常緊密的工作表」，也才能對應句前的「每天要參加好幾個會議」。

8. Michael Phelps, an American swimmer, broke seven world records and won eight gold medals in men's swimming ＿＿＿＿＿＿ in the 2008 Olympics.

麥可，一位美國游泳選手，在 2008 奧運男子游泳 ＿＿＿＿＿＿ 中，打破七次世界記錄並獲八面金牌。

(A) drills 鑽孔　(B) techniques 技術　(C) routines 例行事務　(D) contests 比賽

解析

(1)答題關鍵在題目空格左方的「男子游泳」。

(2)四個選項中，只有選 (D) 項的「比賽」，才可有意義地連成「在2008奧運男子遊泳比賽中，打破……」。

9. Those college students work at the orphanage on a _____ basis, helping the children with their studies without receiving any pay.

那些大學生以 _____ 方式，在孤兒院免費協助院童作功課。

(A) voluntary 志願的　(B) competitive 競爭的　(C) sorrowful 悲傷的　(D) realistic 現實的

解析

(1)答題關鍵在題目空格左方的「以」與「方式」。

(2)四個選項中，只有選 (A) 項的「志願的」，才可有意義地連成「以志願的方式，在孤兒院……」。

10. Studies show that asking children to do house _____ such as taking out the trash or doing the dishes, helps them grow into responsible adults.

研究調查顯示出，要求小孩做 _____ 像是倒垃圾或洗碗盤，有助於幫他們長大後更有責任感。

(A) missions 任務　(B) chores 家裡雜事　(C) approaches 接近　(D) incidents 事件

解析

(1)答題關鍵在題目空格左、右方的「做」與「像是」。

(2)四個選項中，只有選 (B) 項的「家裡雜事」，才可有意義地連成「要求小孩做雜事，像是倒垃圾……」。

11. John has been scolded by his boss for over ten minutes now. _____ she is not happy about his being late again.

約翰被老闆罵了十多分鐘。_____ 她是不高興他再次遲到。

(A) Expressively 表現地　(B) Apparently 顯然地　(C) Immediately 立即　(D) Originally 起初

解析

(1)答題關鍵在題目空格左、右方的「被老闆罵了十多分鐘」與「她是不高興……」。

(2)四個選項中，只有選 (B) 項的「顯然地」，才可有意義地連成「被老闆罵了 10 多分鐘。顯然地她是不高興……」。

12. Since the orange trees suffered _____ damage from a storm in the summer, the farmers are expecting a sharp decline in harvests this winter.

由於柳橙樹在夏天遭到暴風雨的 _____ 傷害，樹農們預期今年冬天的收成量

會劇減。

　(A) potential 潛力　　(B) relative 親戚　　(C) severe 嚴重的　　(D) mutual 互相

解析

(1)答題關鍵在題目空格右方的「傷害」。

(2)四個選項中，只有選(C)項的「嚴重的」，才可有意義地連成「遭到暴風雨的嚴重傷害」。

13. Typhoon Morakot claimed more than six hundred lives in early August of 2009, making it the most serious natural ＿＿＿＿＿＿ in Taiwan in recent decades.

　2009 年 8 月初的莫拉克颱風奪去 600 條人命，造成臺灣近十年來最嚴重的天然 ＿＿＿＿＿＿。

　(A) disaster 災難　　(B) barrier 障礙　　(C) anxiety 焦慮　　(D) collapse 倒塌

解析

(1)答題關鍵在題目空格左方的「天然」。

(2)四個選項中，只有選 (A) 項的「災難」，才可有意義地連成「造成臺灣近十年來最嚴重的天然災難」。

14. Robert was the only ＿＿＿＿＿＿ to the car accident. The police had to count on him to find out exactly how the accident happened.

　羅伯是車禍的唯一 ＿＿＿＿＿＿。警方指望他協助查出車禍是怎麼發生的。

　(A) dealer 業者　　(B) guide 導遊　　(C) witness 目擊者　　(D) client 客戶

解析

(1)答題關鍵在題目空格左、右方的「唯一」與「車禍」。

(2)四個選項中，只有選(C)項的「目擊者」，才可有意義地連成「車禍的唯一目擊者」。

15. Badly injured in the car accident, Jason could ＿＿＿＿＿＿ move his legs and was sent to the hospital right away.

　在車禍中嚴重受傷，傑森＿＿＿＿＿＿移動雙腿並立即送醫。

　(A) accordingly 依照　　(B) undoubtedly 肯定地　　(C) handily 熟練地　　(D) scarcely 幾乎不

解析

(1)答題關鍵在題目空格左方的「could」與「move his legs」。

(2)四個選項中，只有選(D)項的「幾乎不」，才可有意義地連成「傑森幾乎不能移動雙腿」。

(3)本題考副詞 hardly, scarcely 用法。could hardly, could scarcely 的中譯都是「幾乎不」之意。

二、綜合測驗（15分）

> 說明：第 16 至 30 題，每題一個空格，請依文意選出最適當的一個選項，標示在答案卡之「選擇題答案區」。每題答對得 1 分，答錯不倒扣。

　Anita was shopping with her mother and enjoying it. Interestingly, both of them

_____16_____ buying the same pair of jeans.

According to a recent marketing study, young adults influence 88% of household clothing purchases. More often than not, those in their early twenties are the more _____17_____ consumers. There isn't a brand or a trend that these young people are not aware of. That is why mothers who want to keep abreast of trends usually _____18_____ the experts－their daughters. This tells the retailers of the world that if you want to get into a mother's _____19_____ , you've got to win her daughter over first.

With a DJ playing various kinds of music rather than just rap, and a mix of clothing labels designed more for taste and fashion than for a precise age, department stores have managed to appeal to successful middle-aged women _____20_____ losing their younger customers. They have created a shopping environment where the needs of both mother and daughter are satisfied.

阿妮塔很高興地與她的母親上街購物。有趣的是，她們母女兩個 _____16_____ 都買了相同的牛仔褲。

根據新近的市場研究，年輕人影響了家人 88% 的衣物購買意願。通常，那些二十出頭的人是 _____17_____ 消費者。沒有一個品牌或者流行趨勢是這些年輕人不知道的。那就是為什麼想跟上趨勢的母親通常會 _____18_____ 專家──她們的女兒。這告訴世界上的零售商先要贏得女兒的認同才有辦法要母親 _____19_____ 。

一個 DJ 播放各種各樣的音樂而不是僅僅只有繞舌歌，不同的混合衣物商標是為品味與風尚而非為某一固定年齡層。百貨商店已經設法訴求於成功的中年婦女而 _____20_____ 失去他們家中的更年輕顧客。他們創造母親和女兒的需要且滿意的購物環境。

16. 題句：Interestingly, both of them _____16_____ buying the same pair of jeans.
　　　有趣的是，她們母女兩個 _____16_____ 都買了相同的牛仔褲。

　　　(A) gave up 放棄　(B) ended up 到最後　(C) took to 開始從事　(D) used to 過去的習慣

解析

依題意只有選(B)項的「到最後」才是正確選項。

**17. 題句：those in their early twenties are the more _____17_____ consumers.

選項：(A) informed 消息靈通的　(B) informative 情報的　(C) informal 非正式的　(D) informational 新聞的

解析

(1)答題關鍵在空格左方的「more」，其後一定要放形容詞。

(2)依題意只有選(A)項的「消息靈通的」才是正確選項。

(3) (B) 項的 informative 雖也有「見聞廣博」之意，但本篇短文是敘述購物，及對商品的流行、價位等，因此(A)項的「informed消息靈通的」才是正確選項。

18. 題句：That is why mothers who want to keep abreast of trends usually ____18____ the experts－their daughters.

那就是為什麼想跟上趨勢的母親通常會 ____18____ 專家——她們的女兒

選項：(A) deal with 交易　(B) head for 前往　(C) turn to 轉向　(D) look into 查資料

解析

依題意只有選(C)項的「轉向」（轉而向專家求助之意）才是正確選項。

19. 題句：This tells the retailers of the world that if you want to get into a mother's ____19____,

這告訴世界上的零售商先要贏得女兒的認同才有辦法要母親 ____19____。

選項：(A) textbook 教科書　(B) notebook 錢包、筆記本　(C) workbook 練習簿
(D) pocketbook 錢包

解析

依題意只有選 (D) 項的「錢包」才是正確選項。Get into a mother's pocketbook 為「讓母親掏錢」之意。

**20. 題句：department stores have managed to appeal to successful middle-aged women ____20____ losing their younger customers.

百貨商店已經設法訴求於成功的中年婦女而 ____20____ 失去他們家中的更年輕顧客。

選項：(A) in 之內　(B) while 當　(C) after 之後　(D) without 無、不、沒有

解析

對照空格前後兩句的題意，只有選 (D) 項的「without」才是正確選項。

Onions can be divided into two categories: fresh onions and storage onions. Fresh onions are available ____21____ yellow, red and white throughout their season, March through August. They can be ____22____ by their thin, light-colored skin. Because they have a higher water content, they are typically sweeter and milder tasting than storage onions. This higher water content also makes ____23____ easier for them to bruise. With its delicate taste, the fresh onion is an ideal choice for salads and other lightly-cooked dishes. Storage onions, on the other hand, are available August through April. ____24____ fresh onions, they have multiple layers of thick, dark, papery skin. They also have an ____25____ flavor and a higher percentage of solids. For these reasons, storage onions are the best choice for spicy dishes that require longer cooking times or more flavor.

洋蔥可以分成兩大類：新鮮洋蔥和儲存洋蔥。在 3 月到 8 月的洋蔥季節裡，它們的顏色 ____21____ 黃色、紅色和白色都有。從洋蔥的淺色薄皮可 ____22____ 它的好壞。它們比儲存洋蔥有較高的含水率，通常嘗起來甜一些也溫和一些。本身較高的含水率也使 ____23____ 較易碰傷。由於它的美味的口味，新鮮的洋蔥是沙

拉和其他輕煮食物理想的選擇。儲存洋蔥，另一方面，洋蔥可用期從 8 月到 4 月。
_____24_____ 新鮮洋蔥，有多層深色像紙的外皮，同時也有 _____25_____ 的味道和實心部分較多。由於這些原因，儲存洋蔥是需要長時間烹煮之辛辣菜餚的最佳選擇。

**21. 題句：Fresh onions are available _____21_____ yellow, red and white

　　選項：(A) from 從……　(B) for 為……　(C) in　(D) of

解析

依題意只有選(C)項的「in」才是正確選項。顏色之前的介係詞要用「in」。

22. 題句：They can be _____22_____ by their thin, light-colored skin.
　　　　　從洋蔥的淺色薄皮可 _____22_____ 它的好壞。

　　選項：(A) grown 成長　(B) tasted 嘗味道　(C) identified 識別、判斷　(D) emphasized 強調

解析

依題意只有選(C)項的「識別、判斷」才是正確選項。

**23. 題句：This higher water content also makes _____23_____ easier for them to bruise.
　　　　　本身較高的含水量也使 _____23_____ 較易碰傷。

　　選項：(A) such 如此　(B) much 多　(C) that 那個　(D) it 它

解析

依題意只有選(D)項的「it」才可有意義連成「makes it easier（使它更容易）」才是正確選項。

**24. 題句：_____24_____ fresh onions, they have multiple layers of thick, dark, papery skin.
　　　　　_____24_____ 新鮮洋蔥，有多層深色像紙的外皮。

　　選項：(A) Unlike 不像　(B) Through 經由　(C) Besides 在旁　(D) Despite 儘管

解析

依題意只有選(A)項的「Unlike不像」才可有意義連成「不像新鮮洋蔥……」，才是正確選項。

25. 題句：They also have an _____25_____ flavor and a higher percentage of solids.
　　　　　同時也有 _____25_____ 的味道和實心部分較多。

　　選項：(A) anxious 焦慮的　(B) intense 強烈的　(C) organic 有機的　(D) effective 有效率的

解析

依題意只有選(B)項的「強烈的」才是正確選項。

　　Many people like to drink bottled water because they feel that tap water may not be safe, but is bottled water really any better?

Bottled water is mostly sold in plastic bottles and that's why it is potentially health _____26_____ . Processing the plastic can lead to the release of harmful chemical substances into the water contained in the bottles. The chemicals can be absorbed into the body and _____27_____ physical discomfort, such as stomach cramps and diarrhea.

Health risks can also result from inappropriate storage of bottled water. Bacteria can multiply if the water is kept on the shelves for too long or if it is exposed to heat or direct sunlight. _____28_____ the information on storage and shipment is not always readily available to consumers, bottled water may not be a better alternative to tap water.

Besides these _____29_____ issues, bottled water has other disadvantages. It contributes to global warming. An estimated 2.5 million tons of carbon dioxide were generated in 2006 by the production of plastic for bottled water. In addition, bottled water produces an incredible amount of solid _____30_____ . According to one research, 90% of the bottles used are not recycled and lie for ages in landfills.

很多人喜歡喝瓶裝水因為他們覺得自來水可能不安全，但是瓶裝水真的更好嗎？

瓶裝水多數裝在塑膠瓶出售，那也就是它有潛在健康 _____26_____ 的原因。處理塑膠瓶會釋出有害的化學物質到瓶裝水。這些化學物質會被人體吸收並 _____27_____ 身體的不舒服，像是胃痙攣和腹瀉。

瓶裝水的不適當貯存也能引起健康風險。如果那些水被存放太久或者暴露高溫或受陽光直接照射，細菌都會倍數增加。 _____28_____ 消費者無法隨時得知關於貯存和運送瓶裝水的資訊，瓶裝水可能不是自來水以外的更好選擇。

除這些 _____29_____ 問題以外，瓶裝水有其他不利條件。它促使地球暖化。2006年在生產裝水的塑膠瓶時，估計產生約 250 萬公頓的二氧化碳。另外，瓶裝水產生極多的固體 _____30_____ 。根據一份研究，用過的瓶子有 90% 沒被回收處理，而是多年放在垃圾場裡。

26. 題句：Bottled water is mostly sold in plastic bottles and that's why it is potentially health _____26_____ .

那也就是它有潛在健康 _____26_____ 的原因。

選項：(A) frightening 害怕　(B) threatening 威脅　(C) appealing 上訴　(D) promoting 推廣

解析

依題意只有選 (B) 項的「威脅」才是正確選項。

**27. 題句：The chemicals can be absorbed into the body and _____27_____ physical discomfort,

這些化學物質會被人體吸收並 _____27_____ 身體的不舒服。

選項：(A) cause 導致　(B) causing（現在分詞）　(C) caused（過去式）　(D) to cause（不定詞）

解析

依題意只有選(A)項的「導致」才是正確選項。

**28. 題句：＿＿＿28＿＿＿ the information on storage and shipment is not always readily available to consumers,

　　　＿＿＿28＿＿＿ 消費者無法隨時得知關於貯存和運送瓶裝水的資訊。

　　選項：(A) Although 雖然　(B) Despite 不管　(C) Since 由於　(D) So 如此的

解析

依題意只有選(C)項的「由於」才能連成「由於消費者無法……」是正確選項。

29. 題句：Besides these ＿＿＿29＿＿＿ issues, bottled water has other disadvantages.

　　　除這些 ＿＿＿29＿＿＿ 問題以外，瓶裝水有其他不利條件。

　　選項：(A) display 展示　(B) production 生產　(C) shipment 裝運　(D) safety 安全

解析

依題意只有選(D)項的「安全」才是正確選項。

30. 題句：bottled water produces an incredible amount of solid ＿＿＿30＿＿＿ .

　　　瓶裝水產生極多的固體 ＿＿＿30＿＿＿ 。

　　選項：(A) waste 浪費　(B) resource 資源　(C) ground 地面　(D) profit 獲利

解析

依題意只有選(A)項的「浪費」才是正確選項。

三、文意選填（10分）

說明：第 31 至 40 題，每題一個空格，請依文意在文章後所提供的 (A) 到 (J) 選項中分別選出最適當者，並將其英文字母代號標示在答案卡之「選擇題答案區」。每題答對得 1 分，答錯不倒扣。

　　Football is more than a sport; it is also an invaluable ＿＿＿31＿＿＿ . In teaching young players to cooperate with their fellows on the practice ＿＿＿32＿＿＿ , the game shows them the necessity of teamwork in society. It prepares them to be ＿＿＿33＿＿＿ citizens and persons.

　　Wherever football is played, the players learn the rough-and-tumble lesson that only through the ＿＿＿34＿＿＿ of each member can the team win. It is a lesson they must always ＿＿＿35＿＿＿ on the field. Off the field, they continue to keep it in mind. In society, the former player does not look upon himself as a lone wolf who has the right to remain ＿＿＿36＿＿＿ from the society and go his own way. He understands his place in the team; he knows he is a member of society and must ＿＿＿37＿＿＿ himself as such. He realizes that only by cooperating can he do his ＿＿＿38＿＿＿ in making society what it should be. The man who has played football knows that teamwork is ＿＿＿39＿＿＿ in modern living. He is also aware that every citizen must do his part if the nation is to ＿＿＿40＿＿＿ . So he has little difficulty in adjusting himself to his role in family life and in the business world, and to his duties as a citizen.

　　足球是不僅是一種運動；它同時也是一名無價的 ＿＿＿31＿＿＿ 。在練習 ＿＿＿32＿＿＿ 它教年輕運動員與隊員合作，比賽也讓球員看到群體裡團隊合作的必要性。它使球員要成為 ＿＿＿33＿＿＿ 的公民和為人預作準備。無論在哪裡比賽，隊員們學習只有透過每球員間的 ＿＿＿34＿＿＿ ，在混戰中球隊才能獲勝。這是他們在球場上必須 ＿＿＿35＿＿＿ 的教訓。即使離開球場他們也都記住這個法則。在社會裡，老一輩的運動員不把自己看作是有權與社會 ＿＿＿36＿＿＿ 的孤獨份子。他在團隊裡能了解自己的立場，他知道他是社會的成員並且必須 ＿＿＿37＿＿＿ 良好。他意識到只有合作才能使他 ＿＿＿38＿＿＿ 而使社會祥和。踢足球的人都知道團隊合作在現代生活裡是 ＿＿＿39＿＿＿ 。他也意識到要使國家 ＿＿＿40＿＿＿ ，每位公民必須盡他的職責。因此他幾乎沒有困難地，可以在家庭與商場去適應他的角色，成為一個好國民。

(A) cooperation 合作　(B) prosper 繁榮　(C) teacher 教師　(D) behave 行為
(E) isolated 隔離　(F) essential 必要的　(G) better 更好的　(H) share 分享
(I) field 場地　(J) remember 記住

31. 題句：它同時也是一名無價的 ＿＿＿31＿＿＿ 。
解析
依題意只有選(C)項的「教師」才是正確選項。

32. 題句：在練習 ＿＿＿32＿＿＿ 它教年輕運動員與隊員合作。
解析
依題意只有選(I)項的「場地」才是正確選項。

33. 題句：它使球員要成為 ＿＿＿33＿＿＿ 的公民和為人預作準備。
解析
依題意只有選(G)項的「更好的」才是正確選項。

34. 題句：隊員們學習只有透過每球員間的 ＿＿＿34＿＿＿ ，在混戰中球隊才能獲勝。
解析
依題意只有選(A)項的「合作」才是正確選項。

35. 題句：這是他們在球場上必須 ＿＿＿35＿＿＿ 的教訓。
解析
依題意只有選(J)項的「記住」才是正確選項。

36. 題句：老一輩的運動員不把自己看作是有權與社會 ＿＿＿＿36＿＿＿＿ 的孤獨份子。
解析
依題意只有選(E)項的「隔離」才是正確選項。

37. 題句：他知道他是社會的成員並且必須 ＿＿＿37＿＿＿ 良好。
解析
依題意只有選(D)項的「行為」才是正確選項。

38. 題句：他意識到只有合作才能使他 ＿＿＿38＿＿＿ 而使社會祥和。
解析
依題意只有選(H)項的「分享」才是正確選項。

39. 題句：踢足球的人都知道團隊合作在現代生活裡是 ＿＿＿39＿＿＿ 。
解析
依題意只有選(F)項的「必要的」才是正確選項。

40. 題句：他也意識到要使國家 ＿＿＿40＿＿＿ ，每位公民必須盡他的職責。
解析
依題意只有選(B)項的「繁榮」才是正確選項。

四、閱讀測驗（32分）

說明：第 41 至 56 題，每題請分別根據各篇文章之文意選出最適當的一個選項，標示在答案卡之「選擇題答案區」。每題答對得 2 分，答錯不倒扣。

On the island of New Zealand, there is a grasshopper-like species of insect that is found nowhere else on earth. New Zealanders have given it the nickname *weta*, which is a native Maori word meaning "god of bad looks." It's easy to see why anyone would call this insect a bad-looking bug. Most people feel disgusted at the sight of these bulky, slow-moving creatures.

Wetas are nocturnal creatures; they come out of their caves and holes only after dark. A giant weta can grow to over three inches long and weigh as much as 1.5 ounces. Giant wetas can hop up to two feet at a time. Some of them live in trees, and others live in caves. They are very long-lived for insects, and some adult wetas can live as long as two years. Just like their cousins grasshoppers and crickets, wetas are able to "sing" by rubbing their leg parts together, or against their lower bodies.

Most people probably don't feel sympathy for these endangered creatures, but they do need protecting. The slow and clumsy wetas have been around on the island since the times of the dinosaurs, and have evolved and survived in an environment where they had no enemies until rats came to the island with European immigrants. Since rats love to hunt and eat wetas, the rat population on the island has grown into a real problem for many of the native species that are unaccustomed to **its** presence, and poses a serious threat to the native weta population.

在紐西蘭島上，有種長得像蚱蜢一樣、但在其他地方看不到的昆蟲。紐西蘭人給它取個綽號叫「唯它」，毛利語的意思是「醜陋之神」。要看出為什麼這種昆蟲被稱為難看昆蟲很容易。大多數人一看見這種龐大、移動緩慢的生物都會感到厭惡。

「唯它」是夜行性生物；只有天黑之後牠們才會從洞裡出來。大隻「唯它」能成長到超過 3 英寸，且重量多達 1.5 盎司，跳躍可高達兩英尺。牠們有些棲息在樹上，有些棲息在洞內。以昆蟲來說，牠們很長壽，一些成長的「唯它」能活兩年之久。就像牠們的表親蚱蜢和知了一樣，「唯它」會摩擦雙腿或用腿摩擦下半身來「唱歌」。多數人也許不會同情這些瀕臨絕種的生物，但是牠們的確需要保護。行動緩慢、笨拙的「唯它」從恐龍時期起就生長在島上，在老鼠跟著歐洲移民來島上之前，經演化的「唯它」在無天敵的環境中存活下來。由於老鼠喜歡吃「唯它」，島上的老鼠數量對本地的其他物種造成很大的麻煩，更大大威脅到本地「唯它」的生存。

41. From which of the following is the passage **LEAST** likely to be taken?

根據本文，哪一項是與本文最無關聯的？

(A) A science magazine.

一本科學雜誌。

(B) A travel guide.

旅遊指南。

(C) A biology textbook.

一本生物學教科書。

(D) A business journal.

一本生意雜誌。

解析

從整段文章內容來看，只有 (D) 項的「A business journal.」才是與本文最無關聯的選項。

42. According to the passage, which of the following statements is true?

根據本文，下列陳述哪一項為真？

(A) Wetas are unpleasant to the eye.

「唯它」長得不好看。

(B) The weta is a newly discovered insect species.

「唯它」是一種新發現的昆蟲物種。

(C) The Maoris nicknamed themselves "Wetas".

毛利人也把自己稱為「唯它」。

(D) The Europeans brought wetas to New Zealand.

歐洲人把「唯它」帶到紐西蘭。

解析

從答題關鍵的「New Zealanders have given it the nickname weta, which is a native Maori word meaning "god of bad looks." It's easy to see why anyone would call this insect a bad-looking bug. Most people feel disgusted at the sight of these bulky, slow-moving creatures.」可看出，(A) 項的「Wetas are unpleasant to the eye.」才是正確選項。

43. Which of the following descriptions of wetas is accurate?

下列哪一項有關「唯它」的描述是正確的？

(A) They are quick in movement

牠們行動快速。

(B) They are very active in the daytime.

牠們在白天很活躍。

(C) They are decreasing in number.

牠們的數量正在減少。

(D) They have a short lifespan for insects.

以昆蟲來看牠們的壽命很短。

解析

從答題關鍵的「Most people probably don't feel sympathy for these endangered creatures,」可看出，(C) 項的「They are decreasing in number.」才是正確選項。

44. Which of the following is the most appropriate interpretation of "**its**" in the last paragraph?

下列哪一項最能解釋最後一段落內容裡的「its」？

(A) The rat's. 老鼠。　　(B) The weta's. 唯它。

(C) The island's. 島。　　(D) The dinosaur's. 恐龍。

解析

從答題關鍵的「Since rats love to hunt and eat wetas, the rat population on the island has grown into a real problem for many of the native species that are unaccustomed to its presence,」可看出，(A) 項的「The rat's.」才是正確選項。

45-48 為題組

　　The high school prom is the first formal social event for most American teenagers. It has also been a rite of passage for young Americans for nearly a century.

　　The word "prom" was first used in the 1890s, referring to formal dances in which the guests of a party would display their fashions and dancing skills during the evening's grand march. In the United States, parents and educators have come to regard the prom as an important lesson in social skills. Therefore, proms have been held every year in high schools for students to learn proper social behavior.

　　The first high school proms were held in the 1920s in America. By the 1930s, proms were common across the country. For many older Americans, the prom was a modest, home-grown affair in the school gymnasium. Prom-goers were well dressed but not fancily dressed up for the occasion: boys wore jackets and ties and girls their Sunday dresses. Couples danced to music provided by a local amateur band or a record player.　After the 1960s, and especially since the 1980s, the high school prom in many areas has become a serious exercise in excessive consumption, with boys renting expensive tuxedos and girls wearing designer gowns. Stretch limousines were hired to drive the prom-goers to expensive restaurants or discos for an all-night extravaganza.

Whether simple or lavish, proms have always been more or less traumatic events for adolescents who worry about self-image and fitting in with their peers. Prom night can be a dreadful experience for socially awkward teens or for those who do not secure dates. Since the 1990s, alternative proms have been organized in some areas to meet the needs of particular students. For example, proms organized by and for homeless youth were reported. There were also "couple-free" proms to which all students are welcome.

高中畢業舞會是多數美國青少年第一個正式的社交活動。這也是差不多一個世紀以來年輕美國人的慶祝儀式。

「prom」一字首先是在十九世紀的九〇年代使用，像正式的舞會一樣，在大遊行時與會的貴賓會展示他們的時裝和跳舞技巧。在美國，父母和教育工作者認爲「舞會」是一門社交的重要課程。因此，中學校每年都會舉行高中畢業舞會來學習適當的社交行爲。

第一個高中畢業舞會是在二十世紀二〇年代的美國舉行。在二十世紀三〇年代，高中畢業舞會普及全國。對很多年長的美國人來說，學校體育館的高中畢業舞會是一種謙虛、國內才有的活動。參加舞會者穿得很正式但不是太花俏：男孩西裝領帶，而女孩則穿前往教堂所穿的服裝。成雙的舞者隨著一個本地業餘樂團或電唱機的音樂跳舞。在二十世紀六〇年代後，特別自八〇年代起，很多地區的高中畢業舞會已經成爲一種花大錢的嚴肅活動，男生租昂貴的晚禮服而女生則穿設計師設計的服裝。加長型轎車被租用來載與會者去昂貴餐廳或者狄斯可整晚狂歡。

無論簡單還是浪費，舞會或多或少一直都是青少年擔心形象與同學間之認同與否的心中之痛。舞會當晚可能是不擅社交的青少年，或沒有約會對象者的可怕經歷。從二十世紀九〇年代起，有些地方已有改良型的高中畢業舞會，以符合某些學生的需求。例如，報導說已有專爲無家可歸學生所組成的舞會。還有在「不需舞伴」的高中畢業舞會歡迎所有的學生。

45. In what way are high school proms significant to American teenagers?

高中畢業舞會對美國青少年代表的意義是什麼？

　(A) They are part of the graduation ceremony.

　　舞會是畢業典禮的一部分。

　(B) They are occasions for teens to show off their limousines.

舞會是青少年炫耀豪華轎車的場合。

(C) They are important events for teenagers to learn social skills.

　　舞會是青少年學習社交技巧的重要活動。

(D) They are formal events in which teens share their traumatic experiences.

　　舞會是青少年分享創傷經驗的正式活動。

解析

從答題關鍵的「In the United States, parents and educators have come to regard the prom as an important lesson in social skills.」可看出，(C) 項的「They are important events for teenagers to learn social skills.」才是正確選項。

46. What is the main idea of the third paragraph?

　　本文第三段的主要意思是什麼？

(A) Proper social behavior must be observed by prom-goers.

　　舞會參與者必須遵守適當的社會行為。

(B) Proms held in earlier times gave less pressure to teenagers.

　　早期的舞會給青少年較少壓力。

(C) Proms are regarded as important because everyone dresses up for the occasion.

　　舞會被認為是重要，因為每人都是盛裝參加。

(D) The prom has changed from a modest event to a glamorous party over the years.

　　多年來舞會已經從一般的活動轉變成有魅力的聚會。

解析

從答題關鍵的「For many older Americans, the prom was a modest, home-grown affair in the school gymnasium. Prom-goers were well dressed but not fancily dressed up for the occasion: boys wore jackets and ties and girls their Sunday dresses. Couples danced to music provided by a local amateur band or a record player. After the 1960s, and especially since the 1980s, the high school prom in many areas has become a serious exercise in excessive consumption,」可看出，(D) 項的「The prom has changed from a modest event to a glamorous party over the years.」才是正確選項。

47. According to the passage, what gave rise to alternative proms?

　　根據本文，為什麼會產生改良型的舞會？

(A) Not all students behaved well at the proms.

　　並非全部學生在舞會都很規矩。

(B) Proms were too serious for young prom-goers.

　　舞會對年輕的參與者來說太嚴肅了。

(C) Teenagers wanted to attend proms with their dates.

　　青少年想要與約會對象去參加舞會。

(D) Students with special needs did not enjoy conventional proms.

有特別需要的學生不喜愛傳統的舞會。

解析

從答題關鍵的「Since the 1990s, alternative proms have been organized in some areas to meet the needs of particular students. For example, proms organized by and for homeless youth were reported.」可看出，(D) 項的「Students with special needs did not enjoy conventional proms」才是正確選項。

48. Which of the following statements is true?

下列哪項陳述為真？

(A) Unconventional proms have been organized since the 1960s.

非傳統的舞會從二十世紀六〇年代就已經有了。

(B) In the 1980s, proms were held in local churches for teenagers to attend.

在二十世紀八〇年代，舞會在本地教堂舉辦給青少年參加。

(C) Proms have become a significant event in American high schools since the 1930s.

舞會從二十世紀三〇年代起在美國中學已經成為一種有意義的活動。

(D) In the 1890s, high school proms were all-night social events for some American families.

在十九世紀九〇年代的某些美國家庭來說，高中畢業舞會是整夜的活動。

解析

看完答題關鍵「By the 1930s, proms were common across the country.」後，可看出 (C) 項的「Proms have become a significant event in American high schools since the 1930s.」才是正確選項。

49-52 為題組

No budget for your vacation? Try home exchanges－swapping houses with strangers. Agree to use each other's cars, and you can save bucks on car rentals, too.

Home exchanges are not new. At least one group, Intervac, has been facilitating such an arrangement since 1953. But trading online is gaining popularity these days, with several sites in operation, including HomeExchanges. Founded in 1992, with some 28,000 listings, this company **bills** itself as the world's largest home exchange club, reporting that membership has increased 30% this year.

The annual fee is usually less than US$100. Members can access thousands of listings for apartments, villas, suburban homes and farms around the world. Initial contact is made via e-mail, with subsequent communication usually by phone. Before a match is made, potential swappers tend to discuss a lot.

However, the concept may sound risky to some people. What about theft? Damage? These are reasonable causes for concern, but equally unlikely. As one swapper puts it, "Nobody is going to fly across the ocean or drive 600 miles to come steal your TV. Besides, at the same time they're staying in your home, you are staying in their home."

Exchange sites recommend that swappers discuss such matters ahead of time. They may fill out an agreement spelling out who shoulders which responsibilities if a problem arises. It does not matter if the agreement would hold up in court, but it does give the exchangers a little satisfaction.

Generally, the biggest complaint among home exchangers has to do with different standards of cleanliness. Swappers are supposed to make sure their home is in order before they depart, but one person's idea of "clean" may be more forgiving than another's. Some owners say if they come back to a less-than-sparkling kitchen, it may be inconvenient but would not sour them on future exchanges.

你的渡假沒有預算嗎？試試住屋交換──與陌生人換房子住。同意使用彼此的汽車，並且你在租車部分也可省錢。住屋交換不是新事務，至少有一個組織，Intervac，從 1953 年起一直都有這樣的安排。但線上交易最近才開始普及，有幾個網站在營運中，包括「住屋交換」在 1992 年成立，有了大約 28,000 個會員，這公司在廣告中聲稱是世界上最大的換屋俱樂部，並報告說會員數已增加了 30%。

年費通常少於 100 美元。成員能造訪網上的數千間公寓、別墅、全世界的郊區和農家。一開始的接觸是透過電子郵件，有進一步的通訊則用電話聯絡。在撮合談成之前，準交換者之間的討論是多方面的。

不過，對某些人來說，概念可能聽起來有點風險。偷竊怎麼辦？這些是合理擔心的理由，但是同樣也是不太可能。一個交換者這麼說，「沒人會飛越海洋或開六百英里車去偷你的電視機。」此外，在同一時間，他們住在你們家、你們住在他們家。

換屋網站建議這類事情換屋者要事先討論。他們可能寫一份協議書，詳細說明一旦有事發生由誰負責。協議書是否送到法院並不重要，但如果有送，會使換屋者放心一些。

通常，在換屋者之間的最大抱怨，與清潔標準的不同認定有關。在出發之前，換屋者應該將房子保持井然有序，但是每個人對「乾淨」的看法不一樣。一些房屋所有人說，如果他們回來看到廚房不乾淨，也許這樣不太舒服，但是不會使他們排斥將來的換屋計畫。

49. What is the second paragraph mainly about?

第二個段落主要大意是什麼？

(A) How to exchange homes.

怎樣進行住屋交換。

(B) How home exchange is becoming popular.

為什麼住屋交換變得受歡迎？

(C) The biggest home exchange agency.

最大的住屋交換代理商。

(D) A contrast between Intervac and HomeExchange.

在 Intervac 和 HomeExchange 之間的一種差別。

解析

從本段落文章內容來看，都是在敘述交換住屋之事，所以 (B) 項的「How home exchange is becoming popular.」才是本段文章的主題。

50. Which of the following is closest in meaning to **"bills"** in the second paragraph?

在第二個段落裡的「bills」是指何意？

(A) advertises 做廣告　(B) dedicates 奉獻　(C) replaces 替換　(D) participates 參加

解析

Bill 另有「張貼廣告」之意，只有(A)項的「advertises」才是意思最接近的正確選項。

51. How do home exchangers normally begin their communication?

住屋交換者通常怎樣開始通訊？

(A) By phone. 用電話。　(B) By e-mail. 透過電子郵件。　(C) Via a matchmaker. 透過媒介者。　(D) Via a face-to-face meeting. 透過面對面的方法。

解析

從答題關鍵的「Initial contact is made via e-mail,」可看出，(B)項的「By e-mail.」才是正確選項。

52. What is recommended in the passage to deal with theft and damage concerns?

有關偷竊和損害部分本文如何建議？

(A) One can file a lawsuit in court.

提出訴訟。

(B) Both parties can trade online.

雙方在線上交易。

(C) Both parties can sign an agreement beforehand.

雙方能事先簽署一項協議。

(D) One can damage the home of the other party in return.

一個人可以損壞對方的房子做報復。

解析

從答題關鍵的「Exchange sites recommend that swappers discuss such matters ahead of time. They may fill out an agreement spelling out who shoulders which responsibilities if a problem arises. It does not matter if the agreement would hold up in court, but it does give the exchangers a little satisfaction.」可看出，(C)項的「Both parties can sign an agreement beforehand.」才是正確選項。

53-56 為題組

Bekoji is a small town of farmers and herders in the Ethiopian highlands. There, time almost stands still, and horse-drawn carts outnumber motor vehicles. Yet, it has consistently yielded many of the world's best distance runners.

It's tempting, when breathing the thin air of Bekoji, to focus on the special conditions of the place.　The town sits on the side of a volcano nearly 10,000 feet above sea level, making daily life a kind of high-altitude training. Children in this region often start running at an early age, covering great distances to fetch water and firewood or to reach the nearest school.　Added to this early training is a physical trait shared by people there－disproportionately long legs, which is advantageous for distance runners.

A strong desire burns inside Bekoji's young runners. Take the case of Million Abate.　Forced to quit school in fifth grade after his father died, Abate worked as a shoe-shine boy for years.　He saw a hope in running and joined Santayehu Eshetu's training program. This 18-year-old sprinted to the finish of a 12-mile run with his bare feet bleeding. The coach took off his own Nikes and handed them to him. To help Abate continue running, the coach arranged a motel job for him, which pays $9 a month.

Most families in Bekoji live from hand to mouth, and distance running offers the younger generation a way out. Bekoji's legend Derartu Tulu, who won the 10,000-meter Olympic gold medals in 1992 and 2000, is a national hero. As a reward, the government gave her a house. She also won millions of dollars in the races. They crowd the classrooms at Bekoji Elementary School, where Eshetu works as a physical-education instructor.

Motivated by such signs of success, thousands of kids from the villages surrounding Bekoji have moved into town. All these kids share the same dream: Some day they could become another Derartu Tulu.

Bekoji 是衣索比亞高地的農牧小鎮。那裡，時間幾乎不用，而且馬車數量多於機動車輛。然而，這個地方產生了多位世界最好的長跑選手。

這是很吸引人的，當呼吸 Bekoji 的稀薄空氣時，就必須專注於這個地方的特別條件。該鎮在近火山的海拔 10,000 呎之處，日常生活就是一種高海拔訓練。這個地區小孩很小就開始跑步，要跑很遠的地方去取水、撿木頭或是去上學。這種早期訓練使當地人有了共同的軀體特徵──不成比例的長腿，這對長跑選手特別有利。

一種強烈的願望在 Bekoji 的年輕賽跑者體內燃燒。以 Million Abate 案為例，在父親死後的五年級時被迫輟學，當擦鞋童多年。他看到長跑的希望並參加 Santayehu Eshetu 的培養訓練計畫。這位十八歲選手跑到 12 英里的終點時，光腳上都流了血。教練脫下自己的耐吉跑鞋交給他穿。為了幫助 Abate 繼續練跑，教練幫他安排一個汽車旅館的工作，每月薪資 9 美元。

在 Bekoji 裡多數家庭生活拮据，而長跑比賽提供年輕人一個出路。Bekoji 的傳奇人物 Derartu Tulu 在 1992 和 2000 年贏得 10,000 米的奧林匹克金牌，是一名國家英雄。作為一份獎勵，政府給她一所房子。她也在比賽中贏得數百萬美元。

受成功信念的驅使，Bekoji 鎮附近的數千個小孩都搬進鎮內。他們擠在 Bekoji 國小教室裡，在那裡 Eshetu 擔任體育教練。所有的孩子分享一個相同的夢想：有一天他們也能成為另外一個 Derartu Tulu。

53. Which of the following is NOT mentioned as a factor for the excellence of distance runners in Ethiopia?

有關衣索比亞的長跑運動員特佳原因，下列哪一項沒被提及？

(A) Well-known coaches.

著名的教練。

(B) Thin air in the highlands.

在高地的稀薄空氣。

(C) Extraordinarily long legs.

非常長的腿。

(D) Long distance running in daily life

日常生活中的長距離跑步。

解析

整段文章中都沒提到有關教練之事，所以 (A) 項的「Well-known coaches.」才是正確選項。

54. Which of the following is true about Bekoji?

關於 Bekoji 下列哪項為真？

(A) It's the capital of Ethiopia.

它是衣索比亞的首都。

(B) It has changed a lot over the years.

事過多年它已經改變了很多。

(C) It's located near a volcano.

它位於一座火山的附近。

(D) It has trouble handling car accidents.

它處理交通事故有困難。

解析

從答題關鍵的「The town sits on the side of a volcano nearly 10,000 feet above sea level,」可看出，(C) 項的「It's located near a volcano.」才是正確選項。

55. What is the goal of Bekoji's school kids?

Bekoji 的學校孩子的目標是什麼？

(A) To work as motel managers.

做汽車旅館經理。

(B) To win in international competitions.

在國際比賽中獲勝。

(C) To become PE teachers.

成為體育老師。

(D) To perform well academically at school.

在學校學業成績要好。

解析

從答題關鍵的「Motivated by such signs of success, thousands of kids from the villages surrounding Bekoji have moved into town.」可看出，(B) 項的「To win in international competitions」才是正確選項。

56. What can be inferred from this passage?

從本文可以推斷出什麼？

(A) More distance runners may emerge from Bekoji.

更多的長跑運動員可能來自 Bekoji。

(B) Nike will sponsor the young distance runners in Bekoji.

耐吉運動鞋將贊助在 Bekoji 的長跑運動員。

(C) Bekoji will host an international long-distance competition.

Bekoji 將舉辦國際長跑比賽。

(D) The Ethiopian government has spared no efforts in promoting running.

衣索比亞政府從未努力推廣跑步運動。

解析

從答題關鍵的「Motivated by such signs of success, thousands of kids from the villages surrounding Bekoji have moved into town.」可看出，(A) 項的「More distance runners may emerge from Bekoji.」才是正確選項。

第貳部分：非選擇題（28分）

一、翻譯題（8分）

說明：1. 請將以下兩題中文譯成正確而通順達意的英文，並將答案寫在「答案卷」上。
　　　2. 請依序作答，並標明題號。每題 4 分，共 8 分。

1. 在過去，腳踏車主要是作為一種交通工具。

解析

先將與題句內容相關字詞與中譯寫出：

在過去 in the past　腳踏車 bicycle　主要是 mainly　作為 used for　交通工具 transportation（本身已有運輸工具之意，其後不必畫蛇添足加上 tools）

整句英譯

In the past, bicycles are used mainly as one of the transportation.

說明

(1)在談到「以前如何如何」時，可用「in the past」這個說法。如果是說「過去三年來」或「這三年來」，英文就有「for the last three years」或「in the past three years」等說法。

2. 然而，騎腳踏車現在已經成為一種熱門的休閒活動。

解析

(1)先將與題句內容相關字詞與中譯寫出：

然而 However　騎腳踏車 bicycling　已經成為 has become　熱門的 popular　休閒活動 recreation
當今 nowadays

(2)bicycling 一字，現已成為「腳踏車運動」的專有名詞。

整句英譯

However, bicycling has become a popular recreation nowadays.

二、英文作文（20分）

說明：1. 依提示在「答案卷」上寫一篇英文作文。
　　　2. 文長至少 120 個單詞（words）。

提示：請仔細觀察以下三幅連環圖片的內容，並想像第四幅圖片可能的發展，寫出一個涵蓋連環圖片內容並有完整結局的故事。

解析

(1)這種看圖說故事的作文很容易發揮，它並沒有固定的格式要求考生怎麼寫，只要寫出來的文章，不離圖意太遠、加上語句通順、文語法不要錯，也不要寫中式英文，都可得高分。

(2)圖①的麵攤老闆娘與小男孩是什麼關係不重要，由考生隨意寫，寫成母子、姑姪……都可以。

甚至幫圖中人物取名字都可以，男孩叫 Tom，母親叫做 Sue，丟錢的人叫作 Jack 等等。

(3)接著把各圖裡的每一景象，用英文把它寫出來：

　圖①：there is a noodle stand 有一個麵攤

　　　　there is also a pricelist on the wall 牆上有個價目表

　　　　a woman is busy cooking something 有一位婦女在忙著煮東西

　　　　her boy is writing his homework 她兒子正在寫功課

　　　　a man with glasses is eating his noodle 一個戴眼鏡的男子在吃麵

　圖②：the man has gone

　　　　the boy and his mother open the bag

　　　　they found there was much money in the bag

　圖③：the man is now at the Hsin-chu train station

　　　　he suddenly realizes that he has lost the bag somewhere

　　　　he is so worried ,that's why he is perspiring a lot

　圖④：留下一個大問號，就是要考生再自由發揮，把你想要的結果寫出來，你可以說：那位男子立刻搭計程車回去麵攤去要回大包包

　　　　the man returned immediately to the noodle stand by taxi

　　　　也可以說母子二人在男子到麵攤前，已把大包包送去警察局

　　　　mother and son had turned in the bag to the police before the man came back to the stand.

　　　　也可以說，那些錢是該男子早上剛剛借來的

　　　　the man has just borrowed the money for his mother's hospital bill.

結尾：像以上的例句，考生要看到圖裡有什麼就寫什麼，這樣湊成幾十句之後，再把幾十個字句有意義的組合起來。成為以下的標準答案：

　　　There is a noodle stand in the street corner. It has also a nice looking price-list on the wall. One day, I saw a boy writing his homework at the stand. Later, a man with glasses came to the stand and ordered a bowl of soup noodle and something else. I saw the woman still busy cooking something while the man was eating the noodle. The man left a big bag on the stool between he and the boy. The man seemed enjoy eating the noodle, he finished the noodle and paid the money and left. However, the woman and her son found that the man had left a bag behind, obviously he forgot to take the bag alone when he left.

　　　By the time the man got to Hsin-chu Railway Station, he suddenly realized that he left the bag somewhere, it could possibily be at the noodle stand. He was worried so much about the bag because there was a lot of money in it, that was the money he borrowed this morning from the bank, it was supposed to be the money for his mother's hospital bill. He hurried to the noodle stand, but the woman told him that she had turned in the bag to the police just before he returned to her stand.

　　　However, the woman was so kind to help the man to claim his bag and money at the police station without any trouble.

100 年學測（學科能力測驗）

第壹部分：單選題（72分）

一、詞彙（15分）

1. All the new students were given one minute to _____ introduce themselves to the whole class.

   所有學生有一分鐘 _____ 向全班做自我介紹。

   (A) briefly 簡短地　(B) famously 著名地　(C) gradually 漸漸地　(D) obviously 顯然地

   解析
   (1)答題關鍵在題目空格左、右方的 _____「一分鐘」與「自我介紹」
   (2)四個選項中，只有選(A)項的「簡短地」，才可有意義連成「一分鐘簡短地自我介紹」。

2. His dark brown jacket had holes in the elbows and had _____ to light brown, but he continued to wear it.

   他棕色夾克手肘有破洞也已 _____ 至淺棕色，但他還是照樣穿。

   (A) cycled 回收　(B) faded 褪色　(C) loosened 鬆脫　(D) divided 已分離

   解析
   (1)答題關鍵在題目空格右方的「至淺棕色」。
   (2)四個選項中，只有選(B)項的「褪色」，才可有意義連成「已褪至淺棕色」。

3. Everyone in our company enjoys working with Jason. He's got all the qualities that make a _____ partner.

   公司所有人都想與傑生共事。他具有 _____ 伙伴的所有條件。

   (A) desirable 令人滿意的　(B) comfortable 舒適的　(C) frequent 時常的　(D) hostile 敵方的

   解析
   (1)答題關鍵在題目空格右方的「伙伴」。
   (2)四個選項中，只有選(A)項的「令人滿意的」，才可有意義連成「具有令人滿意伙伴的所有條件」。

4. Eyes are sensitive to light. Looking at the sun _____ could damage our eyes.
   眼睛對亮光很敏感 _____ 注視陽光會傷害到眼睛。
   (A) hardly 幾乎不　(B) specially 特別是　(C) totally 全部地　(D) directly 直接地

解析
(1)答題關鍵在題目空格左、右方的「注視陽光」與「傷眼睛」。
(2)四個選項中，只有(D)選項的「直接地」，才可有意義連成「直接注視陽光會傷眼睛」。

5. We were forced to _____ our plan for the weekend picnic because of the bad weather.
   由於壞天氣我們被迫 _____ 我們週末野餐的計畫。
   (A) maintain 維持　(B) record 記錄　(C) propose 提議　(D) cancel 取消

解析
(1)答題關鍵在題目空格左、右方的「被迫」與「我們……計畫」。
(2)四個選項中，只有選(D)項的「取消」，才可有意義連成「被迫取消……計畫」。

6. Three people are running for mayor. All three _____ seem confident that they will be elected, but we won't know until the outcome of the election is announced.
   有三人競選市長。三個 _____ 似乎都有信心會當選，但選舉結果未公布前誰也不知道。
   (A) particles 分子　(B) receivers 收件者　(C) candidates 候選人　(D) containers 容器

解析
(1)答題關鍵在題目空格左方的「競選市長」。
(2)四個選項中，只有選(C)項的「候選人」，才可有意義連成「三個候選人似乎都有信心」。

7. If you _____ a traffic law, such as drinking and driving, you may not drive for some time.
   如果你 _____ 交通法規像是酒駕，你就會有一陣子不能開車。
   (A) destroy 毀損　(B) violate 違反　(C) attack 攻擊　(D) invade 侵略

解析
(1)答題關鍵在題目空格右方的「交通法規」。
(2)四個選項中，只有選(B)項的「違反」，才可有意義連成「如果你違反交通法規」。

8. Applying to college means sending in applications, writing study plans, and so on. It's a long _____ , and it makes students nervous.
   向大學申請是指寄申請書寫就學計畫等。這個過程很長，學生也會緊張。
   (A) errand 差事　(B) operation 操作　(C) process 過程　(D) display 展示

解析
(1)答題關鍵在題目空格左方的「很長的」。

(2)四個選項中，只有選(C)項的「過程」，才可有意義連成「向大學申請……這個過程很長」。

9. Dr. Chu's speech on the new energy source attracted great ＿＿＿＿＿ from the audience at the conference.

朱博士的演講引起參加會議聽眾很大的 ＿＿＿＿＿ 。

(A) attention 注意　(B) fortune 財富　(C) solution 解決方法　(D) influence 影響

解析

(1)答題關鍵在題目空格左方的「引起很大的」。

(2)四個選項中，只有選(A)項的「注意」，才可有意義連成「引起（聽眾）很大的注意」。

10. Everyone in the office must attend the meeting tomorrow. There are no ＿＿＿＿＿ allowed.

公司每人都要參加明天的會議。不允許有 ＿＿＿＿＿

(A) exceptions 例外　(B) additions 附加　(C) divisions 分開　(D) measures 測量

解析

(1)答題關鍵在題目空格左、右方的「無」與「允許」。

(2)四個選項中，只有選(A)項的「例外」，才可有意義連成「不允許有例外」。

11. To make fresh lemonade, cut the lemon in half, ＿＿＿＿＿ the juice into a bowl, and then add as much water and sugar as you like.

要做新鮮檸檬水，將之切一半，把果汁 ＿＿＿＿＿ 進大碗內，加些糖水即可。

(A) decrease 減少　(B) squeeze 擠壓　(C) freeze 冰凍　(D) cease 停止

解析

(1)答題關鍵在題目空格右方的「果汁」與「進大碗內」。

(2)四個選項中，只有選(B)項的「擠壓」，才可有意義連成「把果汁擠進大碗內」。

12. Buddhism is the ＿＿＿＿＿ religion in Thailand, with 90% of the total population identified as Buddhists.

在泰國佛教是 ＿＿＿＿＿ ，有九成的人口是佛教徒。

(A) racial 種族的　(B) competitive 競爭的　(C) modest 謙虛　(D) dominant 占首位的、統治的

解析

(1)答題關鍵在題目空格右方的「宗教」。

(2)四個選項中，只有選(D)項的「占首位的」，才可有意義連成「在泰國它是占首位的」。

13. When I open a book, I look first at the table of ＿＿＿＿＿ to get a general idea of the book and to see which chapters I might be interested in reading.

打開一本書時，我先看它的 ＿＿＿＿＿ 初步了解書中內容或是要讀哪些章節。

(A) contracts 合約　(B) contents 目錄　(C) contests 比賽　(D) contacts 接觸

解析

(1)答題關鍵在題目空格左方的「table of」。

(2)四個選項中，只有選(B)項的「目錄」，才可有意義連成「書中目錄」。

14. The children were so ＿＿＿＿＿＿ to see the clown appear on stage that they laughed, screamed, and clapped their hands happily.

孩子們很高興看到臺上的小丑，大笑大叫也高興地拍手。

(A) admirable 令人欽佩的　(B) fearful 可怕的　(C) delighted 高興的　(D) intense 劇烈的

解析

(1)答題關鍵在題目空格左、右方的「孩子們」與「看到」。

(2)四個選項中，只有選(C)項的「高興的」，才可有意義連成「孩子們很高興看到臺上的……」。

15. Typhoon Maggie brought to I-lan County a huge amount of rainfall, much greater than the ＿＿＿＿＿＿ rainfall of the season in the area.

瑪姬颱風帶給宜蘭大量雨水，比該區整季的 ＿＿＿＿＿＿ 降雨量還多。

(A) average 平均　(B) considerate 體諒　(C) promising 有希望的　(D) enjoyable 快樂的

解析

(1)答題關鍵在題目空格右方的「降雨量」。

(2)四個選項中，只有選(A)項的「平均的」，才可有意義連成「比該區整季的平均降雨量還多」。

二、綜合測驗（15分）

説明：第16題至第30題，每題一個空格，請依文意選出最適當的一個答案，畫記在答案卡之「選擇題答案區」。各題答對得1分；未作答、答錯、或畫記多於一個選項者，該題以零分計算。

　　When it comes to Egypt, people think of pyramids and mummies, both of which are closely related to Egyptian religious beliefs. The ancient Egyptians believed firmly in life ＿＿16＿＿ death. When a person died, his or her soul was thought to travel to an underworld, where it ＿＿17＿＿ a series of judgments before it could progress to a better life in the next world. For the soul to travel smoothly, the body had to ＿＿18＿＿ unharmed. Thus, they learned how to preserve the body by drying it out, oiling and then ＿＿19＿＿ the body in linen, before placing it in the coffin. Egyptians also built pyramids as ＿＿20＿＿ for their kings, or pharaohs. The pyramid housed the pharaoh's body together with priceless treasure, which would accompany him into the next world.

　　當談論到埃及時，人們想起金字塔和木乃伊等，這兩者都與埃及宗教信仰密切相關。古埃及堅信人死 ＿＿16＿＿ 的生命。當一個人死時，他或她的靈魂被認為會旅行到地獄，在那裡它會 ＿＿17＿＿ 一系列的評判，來決定是否能前往下一個世界過

好的生活。為了讓靈魂能順利旅行，屍體必須 ＿＿＿＿18＿＿＿＿ 完整無傷。因此，埃及人學習怎樣使屍體先弄乾、上油然後用亞麻布 ＿＿＿19＿＿＿ 屍體，之後才放進棺材。埃及人也為他們的國王或法老建造金字塔當作 ＿＿＿20＿＿＿ 。他們會將無價之寶與法老一同放進金字塔，那些陪葬物將會伴隨法老進入下一個世界。

**16. 題句：The ancient Egyptians believed firmly in life ＿＿＿16＿＿＿ death.

　　　　古埃及堅信人死 ＿＿＿16＿＿＿ 的生命。

　選項：(A) for 為…… 　(B) by 被…… 　(C) after 之後 　(D) into 之內

解析

依題意只有選(C)項的「之後」才是正確選項。

17. 題句：where it ＿＿＿17＿＿＿ a series of judgments before it could progress to a better life in the next world.

　　　　在那裡它會 ＿＿＿17＿＿＿ 一系列的評判。

　選項：(A) went through 經歷過 　(B) made up 編造 　(C) changed into 變換 　(D) turned out 成為

解析

依題意只有選(A)項的「經歷過」才是正確選項。

18. 題句：For the soul to travel smoothly, the body had to ＿＿＿18＿＿＿ unharmed.

　　　　為了讓靈魂能順利旅行，屍體必須 ＿＿＿18＿＿＿ 完整無傷。

　選項：(A) remain 保留 　(B) remind 提醒 　(C) repair 修理 　(D) replace 取代

解析

依題意只有選(A)項的「保留」才是正確選項。

**19. 題句：to preserve the body by drying it out, oiling and then ＿＿＿19＿＿＿ the body in linen,

　　　　然後用亞麻布 ＿＿＿19＿＿＿ 屍體。

　選項：(A) wrapped 包裹（過去式） 　(B) wrapping （分詞片語） 　(C) to wrap （不定詞） 　(D) being wrapped （被動語態）

解析

依題意只有選(B)項的「wrapping」才是正確選項。

20. 題句：Egyptians also built pyramids as ＿＿＿20＿＿＿ for their kings, or pharaohs.

　　　　埃及人也為他們的國王或法老建造金字塔當作 ＿＿＿20＿＿＿ 。

　選項：(A) galleries 畫廊 　(B) landmarks 地標 　(C) companies 公司 　(D) tombs 墳墓

解析

依題意只有選(D)項的「墳墓」才是正確選項。

On March 23, 1999, the musical MAMMA MIA! made its first public appearance in London. It _____21_____ the kind of welcome it has been getting ever since. The audience went wild. They were literally out of their seats and singing and dancing in the aisles.

MAMMA MIA! has become a _____22_____ entertainment phenomenon. More than 30 million people all over the world have fallen in love with the characters, the story and the music. The musical has been performed in more than nine languages, with more productions than any _____23_____ musical. Its worldwide popularity is mainly due to its theme music, which showcases ABBA's timeless songs in a fresh and vital way _____24_____ retains the essence of both pop music and good musical theater. It has _____25_____ so many people that a film version was also made. To no one's surprise, it has enjoyed similar popularity.

在 1999 年 3 月 23 日，媽媽米亞音樂劇在倫敦首次公開露面。它 _____21_____ 的歡迎就像以前一樣。觀眾變得瘋狂。觀眾簡直無法在他們的座位上而是在走道又唱又跳。媽媽米亞已經成為一個 _____22_____ 的娛樂現象。超過三千萬人已經愛上劇中人物、劇情與音樂。這個音樂劇已被九種以上的語言唱過，比任何 _____23_____ 音樂劇有更多的相關產品問世。它以清新與充滿活力的方式，展現出 ABBA 劇團之隨時流行的歌曲，_____24_____ 保留流行音樂與好劇院的本質。它也 _____25_____ 世人，也製作了電影版本。沒有意外地，電影版本也同樣的流行。

**21. 題句：It _____21_____ the kind of welcome it has been getting ever since.
　　　　它 _____21_____ 的歡迎就像以前一樣。
　　選項：(A) is given 被給　(B) was given （過去式）　(C) has given （現在完成式）　(D) had given （過去完成式）

解析

依題意只有選(B)項的「被給予的」（也就是「所受到的歡迎」之意）才是正確選項。內容敘述發生時間為 1999 年，故應選 it was given ... 意指那時候被給予……。

22. 題句：MAMMA MIA! has become a _____22_____ entertainment phenomenon.
　　　　媽媽米亞已經成為一個 _____22_____ 的娛樂現象。
　　選項：(A) worthy 值得　(B) global 全球的　(C) sticky 黏的　(D) physical 軀體的

解析

依題意只有選(B)項的「全球的」才是正確選項。

**23. 題句：with more productions than any _____23_____ musical.
　　　　比任何 _____23_____ 音樂劇有更多的相關產品問世。
　　選項：(A) one 一　(B) thing 事物　(C) other 其他　(D) else 另外

解析

依題意只有選(C)項的「其他的」才是正確選項。

**24. 題句：which showcases ABBA's timeless songs in a fresh and vital way ___24___ retains the essence of both pop music and good musical theater

選項：(A) how 如何　(B) what 什麼　(C) where 哪裡　(D) that 那

解析

依題意，本題是考關係代名詞。句中的「a fresh and vital way」是前置詞，只有選(D)項的「that」作爲關代詞才是正確選項。

25. 題句：It has ___25___ so many people that a film version was also made.

它也 ___25___ 世人，也製作了電影版本。

選項：(A) appealed to 告知　(B) presented with 在場的　(C) resulted in 導至　(D) brought about 引起

解析

依題意只有選(A)項的「告知」才是正確選項。

　　Which is more valuable? Water or diamonds? Water is more useful to mankind than diamonds, and yet ___26___ are costlier. Why? Called the diamond-water paradox, this is a classic problem posed to students of economics.

　　The answer has to do with supply and demand. Being a rare natural resource, diamonds are ___27___ in supply. However, their demand is high because many people buy them to tell the world that they have money, ___28___ as *conspicuous consumption* in economics. In other words, the scarcity of goods is ___29___ causes humans to attribute value. If we ___30___ surrounded by an unending abundance of diamonds, we probably wouldn't value them very much. Hence, diamonds carry a higher monetary value than water, even though we find more use for water.

　　哪個更有價值？水或是鑽石？水比鑽石對人類更有用，然而 ___26___ 昂貴些。爲什麼？稱之爲鑽石與水的矛盾，這是給經濟學學生的最典型問題。

　　這個答案與供需有關。身爲稀有的天然資源，鑽石的供應是 ___27___ 。然而，人們對它的需求很高，因爲很多人買鑽石來告訴他人自己很有錢。在經濟學方面 ___28___ 「誇耀性消費」。換句話說，物質的缺乏是 ___29___ 導致人類去認定價值。如果我們 ___30___ 鑽石的無盡豐富包圍，我們或許將不太重視他們。因此，鑽石比水具更高的貨幣價值，即使我們認爲水更有用。

26. 題句：Water is more useful to mankind than diamonds, and yet ___26___ are costlier.

水比鑽石對人類更有用，然而 ___26___ 昂貴些。

選項：(A) the above 以上所述　(B) the former 前者　(C) the following 追隨　(D) the latter

後者

解析

依題意只有選(D)項的「後者」才是正確選項。

27. 題句：Being a rare natural resource, diamonds are _____27_____ in supply.
　　　　　身為稀有的天然資源，鑽石的供應是 _____27_____ 。
　　選項：(A) traded 交易的　(B) weakened 削弱　(C) limited 受限制的　(D) noticed 注意的

解析

依題意只有選(C)項的「受限制的」才是正確選項。

**28. 題句：many people buy them to tell the world that they have money, _____28_____ as conspicuous consumption in cconomics
　　　　　在經濟學方面 _____28_____「誇耀性消費」。
　　選項：(A) term 稱為　(B) termed （過去式）　(C) terms （三單現在式）　(D) was termed （被動過去式）

解析

依題意只有選(B)項的「稱為」才是正確選項。termed as 為「被稱為」之意，不能選(D)項的 was termed，除非它之前有 which。

**29. 題句：In other words, the scarcity of goods is _____29_____ causes humans to attribute value.
　　　　　換句話說，物質的缺乏是 _____29_____ 導致人類去認定價值。
　　選項：(A) what 什麼　(B) which 哪一　(C) why 為什麼　(D) how 為何

解析

依題意，空格後的 causes 是動詞，所以放入空格的必須是「主詞」。(A)項的「what」在此是代名詞，可當主詞用，才是正確選項。

**30. 題句：If we _____30_____ surrounded by an unending abundance of diamonds,
　　　　　如果我們 _____30_____ 鑽石的無盡豐富包圍。
　　選項：(A) be （原形動詞）　(B) being （現在分詞）　(C) to be （不定詞）　(D) were （過去式）

解析

(1)依題意只有選(D)項的「were」才是正確選項。
(2)在 if 之後的 be 動詞，其主詞不論人稱或單複數，皆須選 were。

三、文意選填（10分）

Popcorn is one of the snacks that rarely fail to make watching a movie more fun. However, the modern way of preparing this ___31___ snack may carry an unhappy secret. Research by the U.S. government now reports that microwave popcorn may contain substances that can cause health ___32___ .

Researchers found that commercial popcorn companies often coat their microwave popcorn bags with a ___33___ called perfluorooctanoic acid (PFOA) which has been found to cause both cancer and lung disease in laboratory animals. Making matters worse, the artificial butter substitute that generally ___34___ with microwavable popcorn contains a common food-flavoring substance. This substance, according to health scientists, is ___35___ for some serious lung diseases.

For an easy and ___36___ alternative, nutritionists suggest that we pop our own popcorn. All that is ___37___ a large, high pot, about four tablespoons of vegetable oil and a small handful of organic popcorn kernels. When the kernels start ___38___ , shake the pot to let the steam escape and to let the unpopped kernels fall to the bottom. As soon as the popping slows down, ___39___ the pot from the stove. Then pour the popcorn into a bowl and season with a small ___40___ of real butter or olive oil and natural salt. And the healthy and fun snack is ready to serve.

爆米花是使看電影更為有趣的點心之一。不過，準備這份 ___31___ 點心的現代做法可能有一個不愉快的祕密。美國政府的研究做出報告，微波爆米花可能含有引起健康 ___32___ 的物質。研究人員發現商業的爆米花公司經常給他們的微波爆米花袋塗上 ___33___ 叫 perfluorooctanoic 酸的（PFOA），而這物質已被發現是引起實驗室動物得癌症和肺病。更糟的是，人造奶油替代品通常 ___34___ 可微波爆米花而來，包含一種普通食品口味的物質。這種物質，根據健康科學家所言，要對一些嚴重的肺疾病 ___35___ 。

對一個簡單與 ___36___ 的選擇來說，營養學家建議我們自己做爆米花。 所 ___37___ 的只是一個大些高些的鍋，大約要四大匙植物油和一小把有機的玉米花果仁。當果仁開始 ___38___ 的時候，搖晃鍋子讓蒸汽跑出走並且讓未爆果仁掉至底部。當砰爆聲緩慢下來時，把鍋子 ___39___ 。然後把爆米花倒進一只大碗再用少 ___40___ 真正的奶油或者橄欖油和自然的鹽作調味。健康和有趣的點心就完成了。

(A) chemical 化學物質　(B) amount 數量　(C) popping 突出、爆出

(D) popular 受歡迎的　(E) comes 來　(F) healthy 健康

(G) needed 有需要　(H) responsible 負責　(I) remove 移開　(J) problems 問題

31. 題句：準備這份 ＿＿＿＿31＿＿＿＿ 點心的現代做法可能有一個不愉快的祕密。

解析

依題意只有選(D)項的「受歡迎的」才是正確選項。

32. 題句：微波爆米花可能含有引起健康 ＿＿＿＿32＿＿＿＿ 的物質。

解析

依題意只有選(J)項的「問題」才是正確選項。

33. 題句：爆米花公司經常給他們的微波爆米花袋塗上 ＿＿＿＿33＿＿＿＿ 叫 perfluorooctanoic 酸的（PFOA）。

解析

依題意只有選(A)項的「化學物質」才是正確選項。

34. 題句：the artificial butter substitute that generally ＿＿＿＿34＿＿＿＿ with microwavable popcorn ....

　　　人造奶油替代品通常 ＿＿＿＿34＿＿＿＿ 可微波爆米花而來。

解析

依題意只有選(E)項的「comes」才是正確選項。come with 指「伴隨而來」之意。

35. 題句：根據健康科學家所言，要對一些嚴重的肺疾病 ＿＿＿＿35＿＿＿＿ 。

解析

(1)依題意只有選(H)項的「responsible」才是正確選項。

(2)be responsible for 是「為……負責」之意，也就是「為某事的起因」。

36. 題句：對一個簡單與 ＿＿＿＿36＿＿＿＿ 的選擇來說。

解析

依題意只有選(F)項的「健康的」才是正確選項。

37. 題句：所 ＿＿＿＿37＿＿＿＿ 的只是一個大些高些的鍋。

解析

依題意只有選(G)項的「needed」才是正確選項。Is needed 為「所需的」之意。

38. 題句：當果仁開始 ＿＿＿＿38＿＿＿＿ 的時候。

解析

依題意只有選(C)項的「爆出」才是正確選項。

39. 題句：當砰爆聲緩慢下來時，把鍋子 _____39_____ 。

解析

依題意只有選(I)項的「移開」才是正確選項。

40. 題句：然後把爆米花倒進一只大碗再用少 _____40_____ 真正的奶油。

解析

依題意只有選(B)項的「量」才是正確選項。

四、閱讀測驗（32分）

說明：第 41 題至第 56 題，每題 4 個選項，請分別根據各篇文章之文意選出最適當的一個答案，畫記在答案卡之「選擇題答案區」。各題答對得 2 分；未作答、答錯、或畫記多於一個選項者，該題以零分計算。

41-44 題組

There is a long-held belief that when meeting someone, the more eye contact we have with the person, the better. The result is an unfortunate tendency for people making initial contact—in a job interview, for example—to stare fixedly at the other individual. However, this behavior is likely to make the interviewer feel very uncomfortable. Most of us are comfortable with eye contact lasting a few seconds. But eye contact which persists longer than that can make us nervous.

Another widely accepted belief is that powerful people in a society—often men—show their dominance over others by touching them in a variety of ways. In fact, research shows that in almost all cases, lower-status people initiate touch. Women also initiate touch more often than men do.

The belief that rapid speech and lying go together is also widespread and enduring. We react strongly—and suspiciously—to fast talk. However, the opposite is a greater cause for suspicion. Speech that is slow, because it is laced with pauses or errors, is a more reliable indicator of lying than the opposite.

很久以來就有人相信，當你與人見面時，越能注視對方的眼睛越好。在求職時的第一次面談時，這種結果是不利的。舉例來說，固定的凝視對方，不管怎樣，這種凝視對方的舉動可能使對方感到不舒服。我們多數人對幾秒鐘的眼光接觸不會感到不舒服，但是長於幾秒鐘的眼光接觸會使我們緊張。

另一種說法是，社會上有權勢的人，用各種不同的接觸方式來顯示自己的優越。實際上，研究顯示幾乎在所有情況下，位階低者先起動接觸。婦女比男性更會啟動接觸。

相信「說話快速和說謊常相隨而來」的人很普遍，對說話快速部分，我們反應強烈——也表示懷疑。不過，對方才是存疑的原因。說話慢是因為其中有暫停或錯誤，是對方說謊的更確實指標。

41. Which of the following statements is true according to the passage?

   根據本文，下列哪項為真？

   (A) Rapid speech without mistakes is a reliable sign of intelligence.

   　　沒有錯誤的快速說話是智力的可靠訊息。

   (B) Women often play a more dominant role than men in a community.

   　　在社區裡，婦女經常比男性更有支配欲。

   (C) Speaking slowly is more often a sign of lying than speaking quickly.

   　　講話慢比講話快才是說謊的表徵。

   (D) Touching tends to be initiated first by people of higher social positions.

   　　社會地位低的人比地位高的人會首先起動接觸。

   解析

   從答題關鍵的「Speech that is slow, because it is laced with pauses or errors, is a more reliable indicator of lying than the opposite.」可看出，(C) 項的「Speaking slowly is more often a sign of lying than speaking quickly.」才是正確選項。

42. What is true about fixing your eyes on a person when you first meet him/her?

   有關用眼睛凝視第一次會見的人，下列陳述哪項為真？

   (A) Fixing your eyes on the person will make him/her feel at ease.

   　　凝視他人會使對方很舒服。

   (B) It is more polite to fix your eyes on him/her as long as you can.

   　　凝視對方越久越有禮貌。

   (C) Most people feel uneasy to have eye contact for over a few seconds.

   　　多於幾秒鐘的凝視他人會使人感到不安。

   (D) It doesn't make a difference whether you fix your eyes on him/her or not.

   　　你是否凝視對方沒有差別。

   解析

   從答題關鍵的「However, this behavior is likely to make the interviewer feel very uncomfortable.」可看出，(C) 項的「Most people feel uneasy to have eye contact for over a few seconds.」才是正確選項。

43. Which of the following is **NOT** discussed in the passage?

   下列哪一項本文並未提及？

   (A) Facial expressions. 臉部表情。

   (B) Physical contact. 肢體接觸。

   (C) Rate of speech. 講話速度。

   (D) Eye contact. 眼光接觸。

解析

從整段文章並未提及臉部表情一事，所以 (A) 項的「Facial expressions.」才是未被提及的正確選項。

44. What is the main idea of the passage?

　　本文的大意是什麼？

(A) People have an instinct for interpreting non-verbal communication.

　　人們有詮釋非語言溝通的本能。

(B) We should not judge the intention of a person by his body language.

　　我們不應依他人的肢體語言去斷定一個人的意圖。

(C) A good knowledge of body language is essential for successful communication.

　　良好的肢體語言知識對成功的溝通是必要的。

(D) Common beliefs about verbal and non-verbal communication are not always correct.

　　一般關於語言或非語言溝通說法不是完全正確。

解析

從整段文章內容判斷，(D) 項的「Common beliefs about verbal and non-verbal communication are not always correct.」才是正確選項。

45-48 為題組

　　It is easy for us to tell our friends from our enemies. But can other animals do the same? Elephants can! They can use their sense of vision and smell to tell the difference between people who pose a threat and those who do not.

　　In Kenya, researchers found that elephants react differently to clothing worn by men of the Maasai and Kamba ethnic groups. Young Maasai men spear animals and thus pose a threat to elephants; Kamba men are mainly farmers and are not a danger to elephants.

　　In an experiment conducted by animal scientists, elephants were first presented with clean clothing or clothing that had been worn for five days by either a Maasai or a Kamba man. When the elephants detected the smell of clothing worn by a Maasai man, they moved away from the smell faster and took longer to relax than when they detected the smells of either clothing worn by Kamba men or clothing that had not been worn at all.

　　Garment color also plays a role, though in a different way. In the same study, when the elephants saw red clothing not worn before, they reacted angrily, as red is typically worn by Maasai men. Rather than running away as they did with the smell, the elephants acted aggressively toward the red clothing.

　　The researchers believe that the elephants' emotional reactions are due to their different interpretations of the smells and the sights. Smelling a potential danger means that a threat is nearby and the best thing to do is run away and hide. Seeing a potential threat without its smell means that risk is low. Therefore, instead of showing fear and running away, the elephants express their anger and become aggressive.

　　區分我們的朋友或敵人不難。但其他動物能這樣做嗎？大象能！牠們能利用視覺

和氣味去區別對他們有過威脅的人。

　　在肯亞，研究人員發現大象對馬賽族與堪巴族的穿著反應不同。年輕的馬賽人用矛刺動物，對大象有威脅；堪巴族主要是農人，對大象沒有危險。

　　在動物科學家負責的實驗中，大象之前放著乾淨的衣服，或者該二族人穿過五天的衣服。當大象偵測到馬賽人穿過衣服的氣味時，牠們迅速地不再聞了。但需稍長的時間才恢復平靜。

　　服裝顏色也有關係，雖然以不同模式做測試。在相同的研究裡，大象看到沒穿過的紅色衣服時，反應很憤怒，紅色通常是馬賽人的衣服顏色。大象向紅色衣服反應很具侵略性，而不是之前用聞的那樣。

　　研究人員相信大象的感情反應是來自對嗅覺與視覺有所不同。聞出潛在危險表示威脅就在附近，最好趕快逃走並且躲起來。看到而非聞到的潛在威脅表示危險很低。因此，大象表示了牠們的憤怒並變得有侵略性而不是害怕地逃走。

45. According to the passage, which of the following statements is true about Kamba and Maasai people?

根據本文，下列陳述哪一項關於堪巴人和馬賽人的為真？

(A) Maasai people are a threat to elephants.

　　馬賽人對象有威脅。

(B) Kamba people raise elephants for farming.

　　堪巴人飼養大象。

(C) Both Kamba and Maasai people are elephant hunters.

　　堪巴人和馬賽人都是獵象人。

(D) Both Kamba and Maasai people traditionally wear red clothing.

　　堪巴人和馬賽人傳統上穿紅色衣服。

解析

從答題關鍵的「從第一段內容『年輕的馬賽人用矛刺動物，對大象有威脅。』」可看出，(A) 項的「Maasai people are a threat to elephants.」才是正確選項。

46. How did the elephants react to smell in the study?

上項研究中，大象的嗅覺有何反應？

(A) They attacked a man with the smell of new clothing.

　　牠們攻擊有新衣服氣味的人。

(B) They needed time to relax when smelling something unfamiliar.

　　當聞出不熟悉之物，牠們需要時間恢復情緒。

(C) They became anxious when they smelled Kamba-scented clothing.

當聞到有堪巴人味道的衣服時，牠們變得焦慮不安。

(D) They were frightened and ran away when they smelled their enemies.

當牠們聞到敵人的味道時，牠們被嚇住並離開。

解析

從答題關鍵的「第五段內容：『Smelling a potential danger means ... run away and hide』」可看出，(D) 項的「They were frightened and ran away when they smelled their enemies.」才是正確選項。

47. What is the main idea of this passage?

本文的大意是什麼？

(A) Elephants use sight and smell to detect danger.

大象利用視覺與嗅覺偵測危險。

(B) Elephants attack people who wear red clothing.

大象攻擊穿紅衣服的人。

(C) Scientists are now able to control elephants' emotions.

科學家目前能夠控制大象的情感。

(D) Some Kenyan tribes understand elephants' emotions very well.

某些肯亞部落很能了解大象的情感。

解析

從整段內容可看出，(A) 項的「Elephants use sight and smell to detect danger.」才是正確選項。

48. What can be inferred about the elephant's behavior from this passage?

從本文內容可以推論出何種大象行為？

(A) Elephants learn from their experiences.

大象從經驗中學習。

(B) Elephants have sharper sense of smell than sight.

大象的嗅覺比視覺敏銳。

(C) Elephants are more intelligent than other animals.

大象比其他動物聰明。

(D) Elephants tend to attack rather than escape when in danger.

處於險境時，大象傾向於攻擊而不是逃走。

解析

從整段文章內容可看出，(A) 項的「Elephants learn from their experiences.」才是正確選項。

49-52 為題組

It was something she had dreamed of since she was five. Finally, after years of training and intensive workouts, Deborah Duffey was going to compete in her first high school basketball game. The goals of becoming an outstanding player and playing college ball were never far from

Deborah's mind.

The game was against Mills High School. With 1: 42 minutes left in the game, Deborah's team led by one point. A player of Mills had possession of the ball, and Deborah ran to guard against her. As Deborah shuffled sideways to block the player, her knee went out and she collapsed on the court in burning pain. Just like that, Deborah's season was over.

After suffering the bad injury, Deborah found that, for the first time in her life, she was in a situation beyond her control. Game after game, she could do nothing but sit on the sidelines watching others play the game that she loved so much.

Injuries limited Deborah's time on the court as she hurt her knees three more times in the next five years. She had to spend countless hours in a physical therapy clinic to receive treatment. Her frequent visits there gave her a passion and respect for the profession. And Deborah began to see a new light in her life.

Currently a senior in college, Deborah focuses on pursuing a degree in physical therapy. After she graduates, Deborah plans to use her knowledge to educate people how to best take care of their bodies and cope with the feelings of hopelessness that she remembers so well.

那是她五歲至今一直夢想的事。最後，在多年的密集訓練後，黛博拉・達菲將要參加她的第一次中學籃球比賽。黛博拉一心一意只想成爲傑出的運動員及參加大學校隊。那是與米爾中學的比賽。

在比賽剩下 1 分 42 秒時，黛博拉的球隊領先 1 分。一名米爾隊球員擁有控球權，而黛博拉跑去防範她。當黛博拉側面拖行以阻止該運動員，她的膝伸出時跌了一跤，當場疼痛萬分。就那樣，黛博拉的時機結束了。

在嚴重受傷之後，黛博拉發現有生以來的第一次，她無法控制自己。一場又一場的比賽，她除了在旁參觀別人打她最喜歡的比賽外，什麼也不能做。

在受傷後的五年內，她的膝蓋又受了三次傷，使她在球場比賽的時間大受限制。她必須接受很長時間的物理治療。她的頻繁進出門診中心使她對中心產生熱情並尊重他們的專業。黛博拉開始看到她生命中的一線曙光。

黛博拉目前是大學的高年級生，專心追求物理療法學位。在她畢業之後，黛博拉計畫用她的學識專長，教育人們怎樣最能照顧身體，並處理她不會忘懷的失落感問題。

49. What is the best title for this passage?

這段文章最佳主題是什麼？

(A) A Painful Mistake.

一個痛苦的錯誤。

(B) A Great Adventure.

大的冒險。

(C) A Lifelong Punishment.

一次終身處罰。

(D) A New Direction in Life.

在生命裡的新方向。

解析

從整段文章內容可看出，(D) 項的「A New Direction in Life.」才是正確選項。

50. How did Deborah feel when she first hurt her knee?

當她第一次受傷時，黛博拉感到怎樣？

(A) Excited. 令人激動。　(B) Confused. 干擾。　(C) Ashamed. 慚愧。　(D) Disappointed. 失望。

解析

從答題關鍵的「從文章第三段內容『在嚴重受傷之後，除了看人比賽之外，什麼也不能做』」可看出，(D) 項的「Disappointed.」才是正確選項。

51. What is true about Deborah Duffey?

關於黛博拉‧達菲哪一項為真？

(A) She didn't play on the court after the initial injury.

她在初次受傷後就沒再上球場打球。

(B) She injured her knee when she was trying to block her opponent.

她是在試圖阻止她的對手時，膝蓋受了傷。

(C) She knew that she couldn't be a basketball player when she was a child.

從小她就知道，她不會成為籃球選手。

(D) She refused to seek professional assistance to help her recover from her injuries.

她拒絕尋找專業協助來幫她從傷中恢復。

解析

從文章第二段內容可看出，(B) 項的「She injured her knee when she was trying to block her opponent.」才是正確選項。

52. What was the new light that Deborah saw in her life?

黛博拉在她的生命中看到的新曙光是什麼？

(A) To help people take care of their bodies.

幫助人們照顧自己的身體。

(B) To become a teacher of Physical Education.

成為一名體育教師。

(C) To become an outstanding basketball player.

成為一名傑出的籃球選手。

(D) To receive treatment in a physical therapy office.

　　接受物理療法部門的治療。

解析

從文章第五段內容可看出，(A)項的「To help people take care of their bodies.」才是正確選項。

53-56 為題組

　　Redwood trees are the tallest plants on the earth, reaching heights of up to 100 meters. They are also known for their longevity, typically 500 to 1000 years, but sometimes more than 2000 years. A hundred million years ago, in the age of dinosaurs, redwoods were common in the forests of a much more moist and tropical North America. As the climate became drier and colder, they retreated to a narrow strip along the Pacific coast of Northern California.

　　The trunk of redwood trees is very stout and usually forms a single straight column. It is covered with a beautiful soft, spongy bark. This bark can be pretty thick, well over two feet in the more mature trees. It gives the older trees a certain kind of protection from insects, but the main benefit is that it keeps the center of the tree intact from moderate forest fires because of its thickness. This fire resistant quality explains why the giant redwood grows to live that long. While most other types of trees are destroyed by forest fires, the giant redwood actually prospers because of them. Moderate fires will clear the ground of competing plant life, and the rising heat dries and opens the ripe cones of the redwood, releasing many thousands of seeds onto the ground below.

　　New trees are often produced from sprouts, little baby trees, which form at the base of the trunk. These sprouts grow slowly, nourished by the root system of the "mother" tree. When the main tree dies, the sprouts are then free to grow as full trees, forming a **"fairy ring"** of trees around the initial tree. These trees, in turn, may give rise to more sprouts, and the cycle continues.

　　紅杉樹是在地球上最高的植物，最高可長到一百公尺的高度。它們也以長壽聞名，通常會有五百年到一千年，也有些會超過兩千年。一億年以前的恐龍時期，紅杉在比較潮濕和北美洲的熱帶林裡很普遍。當氣候變得乾冷時，它們沿著北加州的太平洋沿岸形成狹窄的帶狀。

　　紅杉樹的樹幹非常堅固且通常形成一根筆直的柱子。它外層為美麗柔軟的海綿狀樹皮所覆蓋。這塊樹皮可能相當厚，成樹的樹皮都會有兩英尺以上的厚度。 樹皮的厚度可保護老樹免受昆蟲傷害，主要好處是，發生一般森林火災時，樹皮的厚度可使樹中心部位完好無傷。這種防火的品質就是紅杉木能長那麼高的原因。多數的其他樹種都被森林火災摧毀時，巨大的紅杉樹反而因他樹毀損而長得更好。一般的火災會燒光其他植物，而且升高的熱度會烤乾並打開紅杉的圓錐形毬果，把數以千計的種子散播在地上。

　　新樹經常長自於嫩芽、小樹、成為樹幹的基礎。這些嫩芽成長緩慢，由母樹的樹根系統提供養分。當主樹死亡時，這些樹芽就可獨立成長為全樹，形成環繞母樹的「仙女環」。這些樹，可能長出更多的樹芽，它的生命週期會循環下去。

53. Why were redwood trees more prominent in the forests of North America millions of years ago?

百萬年前在北美洲森林的紅杉樹為什麼更突出？

(A) The trees were taller and stronger.

樹更大更強壯。

(B) The soil was softer for seeds to sprout.

土壤更柔軟容易長出樹芽。

(C) The climate was warmer and more humid.

氣候更溫暖和更潮濕。

(D) The temperature was lower along the Pacific coast.

太平洋沿岸的溫度更低。

解析

從文章第一段內容「紅杉在比較潮濕和熱帶雨林很普遍」可看出，(C) 項的「The climate was warmer and more humid.」才是正確選項。

54. What does a "**fairy ring**" in the last paragraph refer to?

最後一段文章所提的「仙女環」是指什麼？

(A) Circled tree trunks.

環繞的樹幹。

(B) Connected root systems.

連結樹根系統。

(C) Insect holes around an old tree.

古樹周圍的昆蟲洞。

(D) Young trees surrounding a mature tree.

幼樹圍繞成樹。

解析

從文章末段內容「樹芽就可獨立成長……形成環繞母樹的仙女環」可看出，(D) 項的「Young trees surrounding a mature tree.」才是正確選項。

55. Which of the following is a function of the tree bark as mentioned in the passage?

下列內容哪項描述樹皮的功能？

(A) It allows redwood trees to bear seeds.

它讓紅杉樹生出種子。

(B) It prevents redwood trees from attack by insects.

它防止昆蟲攻擊紅杉樹。

(C) It helps redwood trees absorb moisture in the air.

它幫助紅杉樹吸收空氣中的水分。

(D) It makes redwood trees more beautiful and appealing.

它使紅杉樹更美麗、更動人。

解析

從文章第二段內容「樹皮的厚度可保護老樹免受蟲害」可看出，(B) 項的「It prevents redwood trees from attack by insects.」才是正確選項。

56. Why do redwood trees grow to live that long according to the passage?

根據本文紅杉樹為什麼會活那麼久？

(A) They have heavy and straight tree trunks.

它們有強壯和筆直的樹幹。

(B) They are properly watered and nourished.

它們接受正確地澆水與養分。

(C) They are more resistant to fire damage than other trees.

它們比其他樹種對火更有抵抗力。

(D) They produce many young trees to sustain their life cycle.

它們長出很多幼樹支援它們的生命週期。

解析

從文章第二段內容「這種防火的品質就是紅杉能長那麼高的原因」可看出，(C) 項的「They are more resistant to fire damage than other trees.」才是正確選項。

第貳部分：非選擇題（28分）

一、中譯英（8分）

> 說明：1. 請將以下中文句子譯成正確、通順、達意的英文，並將答案寫在「答案卷」上。
>
> 　　　2. 請依序作答，並標明題號。每題 4 分，共 8 分。

1. 臺灣的夜市早已被認為足以代表我們的在地文化。

解析

先將題句內相關字詞寫出中譯：

臺灣的夜市 night markets in Taiwan　被認為 is thought to be　足以代表 to represent　我們的在地文化 our local culture

整句英譯

The night markets in Taiwan are thought to be to represent our local culture.

2. 每年它們都吸引了成千上萬來自不同國家的觀光客。

解析

先將題句內相關字詞寫出中譯：

每年 every year　它們都吸引了 the night markets attract　成千上萬 hundreds of thousands　來自不同國家的觀光客 tourists from all over the world

整句英譯

Night markets in Taiwan attract hundreds of thousands tourists from all over the world.

二、英文作文（20分）

説明：1. 依提示在「答案卷」上寫一篇英文作文。
　　　2. 文長約 100 至 120 個單詞（words）。

提示：請仔細觀察以下三幅連環圖片的內容，並想像第四幅圖片可能的發展，寫出一個涵蓋連環圖片內容並有完整結局的故事。

解析

⑴這種看圖説故事的作文很容易發揮，它並沒有固定的格式要求考生怎麼寫，只要寫出來的文章，不離圖意太遠、加上語句通順、文語法不要錯，都可得高分。

⑵接下來把每一幅圖畫的細節寫出來：

　圖①：那是一場化妝舞會 a boy and a girl were in a costume party

　　　　男生帶著眼罩　　the boy ware a blindfold

　　　　女生化妝成選美女王 the girl was playing a role of beauty queen

丘比特愛心之箭射向女生 Cupid's arrow was shooting toward the girl

酒杯裡還剩有酒　there was still some wine left in the glass

圖②：圖中有星星月亮 表示是晚上 it was a night time scene

男生在女生住家外面的樹旁 the boy was playing a guitar and singing outside the girl's residence

要唱給那位女生聽　the boy was doing it for the girl

圖③：不久就有人開窗出來抗議 there were some people complaining about the loud noise

三樓的那位還是滿臉狐疑，不知發生什麼事 the man on the third floor was wondering what was going on

圖④：這時考生就可以開始自己編繼續下去的情節：

這個男生向大家抱歉 the boy apologized for the loud music

在這個檻尬的時刻，那位女生也跑出來 at this embarrassing moment, the girl came out

兩人一起散步到附近的小公園繼續純聊天 the boy and the girl both walked to the park nearby and made a happy ending

　　There were a boy and a girl attended a costume party one evening, the boy could not see anything because he was wearing a blindfold while the girl was playing a role of beauty queen. The boy's Cupid's arrow was shooting toward the girl, means he had a crush on the girl. Next evening the boy stood outside the girl's house, and was playing a guitar and singing a song at the same time, he was doing it for the girl. Before long, there were some people complaining about the loud music. the man on the third floor was wondering what was going on. Finally, the boy apologized for the loud noise.However, at this embarrassing moment, the girl came out she didn't even bother to say "Hello" to her neighbors, took the boy to the park nearby and made a happy ending on this passage. （約153字）

101<small>年統測</small>（四技二專考試）

I. 字彙題

1. All city council members decided to _____ a percentage of their income to the poor.
   (A) rebuild　(B) bribe　(C) finish　(D) donate

2. Due to the hard economic times, we can expect a _____ in job vacancies.
   (A) decline　(B) capacity　(C) sketch　(D) balance

3. Mary started her _____ as a high school teacher as soon as she graduated from college, and is still in love with her job at this moment.
   (A) vacation　(B) motto　(C) career　(D) homework

4. The patient's chronic illness has _____ her so much that she has difficulty walking.
   (A) weakened　(B) strengthened　(C) lightened　(D) broadened

5. Patrick has just got a next-week _____ for a comedy movie and he looks very happy right now.
   (A) attraction　(B) audition　(C) applicant　(D) appendix

6. The manager decided to offer a bargain price to increase sales and discourage _____.
   (A) designers　(B) roosters　(C) competitors　(D) scholars

7. A relief team rescued 500 villagers from mudslides caused by the typhoon, but there were still five people who _____ into thin air and were never seen again.
   (A) transformed　(B) survived　(C) explored　(D) vanished

8. In August 2011 Steve Jobs wrote, "Unfortunately, that day has come." Then he knew he could no longer _____ the expectations of his position as the CEO of the company.
   (A) cherish　(B) fulfill　(C) dominate　(D) spare

9. The road to the border was closed, and the soldiers were forced to alter their plans.

(A) miss   (B) keep   (C) change   (D) recover

10. A computer program will be used to assess the quality of language education.

(A) compose   (B) evaluate   (C) remind   (D) offend

11. More than two million birds migrate south to the lake each fall for food.

(A) travel   (B) progress   (C) drop   (D) float

12. Driving in stressful conditions, he is suffering from fatigue and wants to go to bed early.

(A) belt   (B) return   (C) handle   (D) tiredness

13. The tree in the front yard makes the room dark. We should get it trimmed.

(A) fit   (B) cut   (C) revised   (D) marked

14. The chairperson's late arrival postponed the start of the committee meeting.

(A) hurried   (B) supported   (C) delayed   (D) recovered

15. The lawyer's evidence proved to be false although it looked convincing when first presented.

(A) minor   (B) excited   (C) unlikely   (D) believable

II. 對話題

第 16 至 25 題，請依對話內容，選出一個最適合的答案，使其成為有意義的對話。

16. James: Do you know anything about "Lohas"?

Amy: Well, it stands for people who enjoy "lifestyles of health and sustainability".

James: _____

Amy: People from this group prefer to live an environmentally friendly and healthy life.

(A) Where are they going?   (B) When do they go to work?

(C) How about those who are not rich?   (D) What do they do?

17. Student A: Shall I lock the chemistry lab now before I go home?

Student B: _____ I'll check it myself later.

Student A: Then, you have a nice weekend!

(A) What a pity!   (B) It's fantastic.   (C) Don't bother.   (D) No, I won't.

18. Jack: What are you going to do for this weekend?

Tom: I am going to the park for a party.

Jack: A party in the park? _____

Tom: There will be a musical concert featuring Mozart. I love his music.

(A) Is the park going to be big?　(B) It's a piece of cake, isn't it?

(C) What do you mean?　(D) How far is the park from here?

19. Jack: Finally, my job is done.

Tom: What do you think of it?

Jack: At the first sight, I believe it is terrific. But...

Tom: _____

(A) But the boss is about to take it as a jewel.

(B) But the boss thinks it still has a lot to be desired.

(C) But the boss likes it very much.

(D) But the boss will have no regrets about it.

20. Jack: What do you think is the best way to start making friends?

Tom: I believe that a proper joke can break the ice.

Jack: Telling a joke? _____ And I'll try it later.

(A) Don't be silly!　(B) It makes sense.

(C) I won't count on it.　(D) I can't stand it any longer.

21. Jack: I am looking for a new apartment.

Tom: My building has some vacancies. _____

Jack: Yes. Let me know more details.

(A) Will you be interested in them?　(B) Could you show me around?

(C) Where do you go for laundry?　(D) Are you saying it is rent-free?

22. Interviewer: Do you think yourself a talent, winning all these games?

Jeremy Lin: No. It's just incredible. I don't think anyone, including myself, saw this coming.

Interviewer: _____

Jeremy Lin: Basketball's so fun when you play on a team where people pitch in and work through tough times.

(A) How do you like the game?

(B) Would you like to talk about baseball?

(C) How much money do you make?

(D) When will you retire?

23. Tim: The next slide shows sales over the past six months.

Kevin: _____

Tim: Yes, we did.

Kevin: Any idea what caused this drop in sales?

(A) Gee! We hit quite a slump.　　(B) Anything I can do to help.

(C) Let's take a break first.　　(D) That was a good thing.

24. (On the phone...)

Secretary: Mr. Hubbard's office. How may I help you?

Client: Yes, I'd like to speak to Mr. James, please?

Secretary: _____

Client: This is Mrs. Stone from Sandhill.

(A) Who is calling, please?　　(B) May I ask what this call is about?

(C) How do you find us?　　(D) Where are you going?

25. Customs Officer: May I see your passport and landing card?

Thomas: _____

Customs Officer: Do you have anything to declare?

Thomas: Oh, nothing special.

(A) I don't need my passport.　　(B) Sure. Here you are.

(C) They're not real.　　(D) Be focused.

III. 綜合測驗

以下三篇短文，共有 15 個空格，為第 26 至 40 題，每題有四個選項，請依各篇短文文意，選出一個最適合該空格的答案。

▲下篇短文共有 5 個空格，為第 26-30 題，請依短文文意，選出一個最適合該空格的答案。

　　CouchSurfing has developed into a new craze for the travel community since it began in 1999. CouchSurfing, usually ____26____ as CS, offers a great way for budget conscious travelers to travel the world in a far less expensive way. CS works when travelers find people who are willing to open up their homes to them and have spare couches for them to sleep on. ____27____ saving money on accommodation, CS provides travelers ____28____ a unique opportunity to encounter local perspectives from the area in which they are traveling, ____29____ various cultural, political, and religious viewpoints and lifestyles. Do you have a limited travel budget? Are you comfortable spending time with strangers? Do you want to experience different outlooks from other parts of the world? ____30____ *CouchSurfing.org*, a popular social networking site for both surfers and hosts, to gain a better understanding of how to find and contact potential hosts and begin your journey today. You won't be disappointed.

26. (A) abbreviated　(B) lengthened　(C) knew　(D) became

27. (A) In order to　(B) Because of　(C) In addition to　(D) In case of

28. (A) with　(B) from　(C) to　(D) of

29. (A) excluding　(B) having　(C) consisting　(D) including

30. (A) To visit　(B) Visit　(C) Visiting　(D) Visited

▲下篇短文共有 5 個空格，為第 31–35 題，請依短文文意，選出一個最適合該空格的答案。

A few interesting similarities can be found between the two great philosophers: Confucius and Socrates. They indicated that virtue can cause happiness in life. Using their own lives as ＿＿＿31＿＿＿, they tried to tell their followers that acting virtuously is the way to success in life. Another common point between Confucius and Socrates is their emphasis on the importance of education. ＿＿＿32＿＿＿ education, it is difficult to build up the virtue of wisdom. They considered self-knowledge important. Self-knowledge refers to the ability to know what we know and what we do not know. With the awareness of our own knowledge and ＿＿＿33＿＿＿, we are able to succeed and avoid errors. They believed that careful self-examination can analyze and ＿＿＿34＿＿＿ our personal characters, aims, methods and attitudes. For both Confucius and Socrates, ＿＿＿35＿＿＿ learning and wisdom with other virtues, one can have a good and productive life. They pointed out that wisdom obtained from learning can be used as guidance for all good deeds.

31. (A) manners　(B) models　(C) masses　(D) measurements

32. (A) Without　(B) With　(C) Like　(D) For

33. (A) illustration　(B) invasion　(C) ignorance　(D) interruption

34. (A) improved　(B) improving　(C) improves　(D) improve

35. (A) inferring　(B) integrating　(C) inhabiting　(D) imposing

▲下篇短文共有 5 個空格，為第 36–40 題，請依短文文意，選出一個最適合該空格的答案。

A computer addict uses a computer all the time-playing online games, browsing websites, e-mailing friends, and so on. He is annoyed when he has no ＿＿＿36＿＿＿ to the computer. As soon as he turns it on, he feels ＿＿＿37＿＿＿ again. Computer addiction is a social and physical problem. Socially, a person with a computer addiction thinks his "Cyber friends" are important, so he spends less time with his family and friends. Physically, a computer addict can ＿＿＿38＿＿＿ symptoms such as dry eyes, headaches, and backaches after he hasn't eaten and slept properly for some time. If you are a computer addict, you need to help yourself. First, ＿＿＿39＿＿＿ that you have a problem. Then, talk to your family about it and limit your computer use. For example, ＿＿＿40＿＿＿ an alarm clock before using a computer. Turn the computer off when the clock rings. Take action now, or the computer will take a full control of you.

36. (A) track　(B) input　(C) route　(D) access

37. (A) relieved　(B) distressed　(C) stressed　(D) preserved

38. (A) lend　(B) develop　(C) expose　(D) drop

39. (A) edit　(B) owe　(C) intend　(D) admit

40. (A) put   (B) set   (C) turn   (D) keep

IV. 閱讀測驗

以下有兩篇短文，共有 10 個題目，為第 41 至 50 題，請於閱讀短文後，選出最適當的答案。

▲閱讀下文，回答第 41-45 題

For those who think of straws as nothing but animal feed, materials for the roof, natural fertilizers or occasional medical herbs, I would suggest that they take a trip to Snugburys. Snugburys, an ice cream maker in the U.K., has had a plan to construct a sculpture every year in their farm field to celebrate the coming of summer. This year, they have a GIANT polar bear-a statue which has 3 tons of straws inside. The steel-skeleton-straw-stuffed replica of the animal from the arctic region is attracting interest from tourists, visitors or ice cream buyers while keeping guard at this ice cream destination beside A51 Chester Road. The animal is approximately four times as big as a real adult male polar bear: standing 38 feet tall and weighing in at 9 tons. The sculpture will stay there for about half a year. "Ex-straw-dinary!" uttered one of my friends. The concept started in 1998 with a huge Millennium Dome sculpture and, since then, on the list of the works of art are replicas of the Big Ben Clock, a windmill, the Lovell telescope, a rocket, an angel from the West, a dinosaur as well as last year's meerkat. Speaking about this year's design, Mr. Sadler, the business owner, responded with a smile: "There's no real reason why we chose a polar bear but we think that they're cool and ice cream is cool so I guess that's a good enough explanation!" A certain part of all sales from the shop's "Polar Bear Cones" will be given away to The Children's Adventure Farm Trust which provides holidays for the kids in need: ill at a terminal stage, disabled, disadvantaged and the like.

41. Which of the following items is NOT mentioned as the use of straws?

   (A) An alternative therapy.   (B) Fertilizers.

   (C) Farming tools.   (D) Roofing materials.

42. Which of the following is NOT on the Snugburys' list of the structures made of straws?

   (A) A polar bear.   (B) A rocket.   (C) A locomotive.   (D) A meerkat.

43. Why is the polar bear taken as the theme for this year's structure?

   (A) It's cool.   (B) It's in grave danger.

   (C) It's of significant value.   (D) It's snow-white.

44. Why does the author offer the suggestion of taking a trip to Snugburys?

   (A) To do research on a herbal remedy.

   (B) To enjoy the urban atmosphere.

   (C) To enhance the business chance.

   (D) To learn an artistic display of straws.

45. According to the passage, which of the following statements is true?

(A) Snugburys is a famous ice cream manufacturer in the U.S.A.

(B) A charity unit for the kids has offered to promote the straw shows.

(C) "Ex-straw-dinary" is used here to express praise and admiration.

(D) An average adult male polar bear stands 38 feet tall and weighs in at 9 tons.

▲閱讀下文，回答第 46-50 題

　　Michael Hart, founder of Project Gutenberg, invented eBooks in 1971 and continued to inspire the creation of eBooks and related technologies today. He announced that the greatest value created by computers would not be computing, but the storage, retrieval and searching of what was stored in our libraries. There are three categories of the Project Gutenberg Library: Light Literature-such as *Alice in Wonderland, Through the Looking-Glass, A Christmas Carol, Peter Pan, Aesop's Fables*, etc; Heavy Literature-such as the Bible or other religious documents, *Shakespeare, Moby Dick, Paradise Lost, Heart of Darkness*, etc; References-such as Roget's Thesaurus, almanacs, dictionaries, encyclopedias, etc. The Light Literature Collection is designed to get people to the computer in the first place, whether a preschooler or a great-grandparent. We(Project Gutenberg team) love to hear about kids or grandparents taking each other to an Etext to *Peter Pan* when they come back from watching *HOOK* at the movies, or when they read *Alice in Wonderland* after seeing **it** on TV. Nearly every Star Trek movie has quoted current Project Gutenberg Etext releases. This was a primary concern when we chose the books for our libraries.

46. In which of the following categories can encyclopedias be found?

(A) References.　(B) Heavy Literature.　(C) Journals.　(D) Light Literature.

47. Which of the following is considered Heavy Literature?

(A) *Through the Looking-Glass*.　　(B) *A Christmas Carol*.

(C) *Heart of Darkness*.　　(D) *Peter Pan*.

48. What does the word **it** in line 11 refer to?

(A) *Shakespeare*.　(B) *Moby Dick*.　(C) *Paradise Lost*.　(D) *Alice in Wonderland*.

49. What is the passage mainly about?

(A) How to buy and sell literary works through Gutenberg.

(B) The selection and the goal of Project Gutenberg Etexts.

(C) Project Gutenberg publishes copyrighted literary works.

(D) Project Gutenberg promotes intellectual property rights.

50. About Project Gutenberg, which of the following is mentioned in the passage?

(A) The Etexts should cost so little that no one will care how much they are.

(B) The Etexts should be so easily used that one can read and search them.

(C) Michael Hart was trying to take over the entire publishing industry.

(D) Project Gutenberg aims to encourage people to read Etexts from computers.

101年統測解答

題號	1	2	3	4	5	6	7	8	9	10	11	12	13	14	15	16	17	18	19	20
答案	D	A	C	A	B	C	D	B	C	B	A	D	B	C	D	D	C	C	B	B
題號	21	22	23	24	25	26	27	28	29	30	31	32	33	34	35	36	37	38	39	40
答案	A	A	A	A	B	A	C	A	D	B	B	A	C	D	B	D	A	B	D	B
題號	41	42	43	44	45	46	47	48	49	50										
答案	C	C	A	D	C	A	C	D	B	D										

101 年學測（學科能力測驗）

第壹部分：單選題（占72分）

一、詞彙（占15分）

說明：第1題至第15題，每題有4個選項，其中只有一個是正確或最適當的選項，請畫記在答案卡之「選擇題答案區」。各題答對者，得1分；答錯、未作答或畫記多於一個選項者，該題以零分計算。

1. The ending of the movie did not come as a ＿＿＿＿＿＿ to John because he had already read the novel that the movie was based on.
　(A) vision　(B) focus　(C) surprise　(D) conclusion

2. In order to stay healthy and fit, John exercises ＿＿＿＿＿＿ He works out twice a week in a gym.
　(A) regularly　(B) directly　(C) hardly　(D) gradually

3. Traveling is a good way for us to ＿＿＿＿＿＿ different cultures and broaden our horizons.
　(A) assume　(B) explore　(C) occupy　(D) inspire

4. The story about Hou-I shooting down nine suns is a well-known Chinese ＿＿＿＿＿＿, but it may not be a true historical event.
　(A) figure　(B) rumor　(C) miracle　(D) legend

5. According to recent research, children under the age of 12 are generally not ＿＿＿＿＿＿ enough to recognize risk and deal with dangerous situations.
　(A) diligent　(B) mature　(C) familiar　(D) sincere

6. Helen let out a sigh of ＿＿＿＿＿＿ after hearing that her brother was not injured in the accident.
　(A) hesitation　(B) relief　(C) sorrow　(D) triumph

7. Research suggests that people with outgoing personalities tend to be more _____, often expecting that good things will happen.

(A) efficient (B) practical (C) changeable (D) optimistic

8. No one could beat Paul at running. He has won the running championship _____ for three years.

(A) rapidly (B) urgently (C) continuously (D) temporarily

9. If you fly from Taipei to Tokyo, you'll be taking an international, rather than a _____ flight.

(A) liberal (B) domestic (C) connected (D) universal

10. Jack is very proud of his fancy new motorcycle. He has been _____ to all his friends about how cool it looks and how fast it runs.

(A) boasting (B) proposing (C) gossiping (D) confessing

11. The ideas about family have changed _____ in the past twenty years. For example, my grandfather was one of ten children in his family, but I am the only child.

(A) mutually (B) narrowly (C) considerably (D) scarcely

12. The chairperson of the meeting asked everyone to speak up instead of _____ their opinions among themselves.

(A) reciting (B) giggling (C) murmuring (D) whistling

13. Although Mr. Chen is rich, he is a very _____ person and is never willing to spend any money to help those who are in need.

(A) absolute (B) precise (C) economic (D) stingy

14. If you want to know what your dreams mean, now there are websites you can visit to help you _____ them.

(A) overcome (B) interpret (C) transfer (D) revise

15. The memory _____ of the new computer has been increased so that more information can be stored.

(A) capacity (B) occupation (C) attachment (D) machinery

二、綜合測驗（占15分）

說明：第16題至第30題，每題一個空格，請依文意選出最適當的一個選項，請畫記在答案卡之「選擇題答案區」。各題答對者，得1分；答錯、未作答或畫記多於一個選項者，該題以零分計算。

Kizhi is an island on Lake Onega in Karelia, Russia, with a beautiful collection of wooden churches and houses. It is one of the most popular tourist ____16____ in Russia and a United Nations Educational, Scientific, and Cultural Organization (UNESCO) World Heritage Site.

The island is about 7 km long and 0.5 km wide. It is surrounded by about 5,000 other islands, some of ____17____ are just rocks sticking out of the ground.

The entire island of Kizhi is, ____18____, an outdoor museum of wooden architecture created in 1966. It contains many historically significant and beautiful wooden structures, ____19____ windmills, boathouses, chapels, fish houses, and homes. The jewel of the architecture is the 22-domed Transfiguration Church, built in the early 1700s. It is about 37 m tall, ____20____ it one of the tallest log structures in the world. The church was built with pine trees brought from the mainland, which was quite common for the 18th century.

16. (A) affairs　(B) fashions　(C) industries　(D) attractions

17. (A) them　(B) that　(C) those　(D) which

18. (A) in fact　(B) once again　(C) as usual　(D) for instance

19. (A) except　(B) besides　(C) including　(D) regarding

20. (A) make　(B) making　(C) made　(D) to make

There was once a time when all human beings were gods. However, they often took their divinity for granted and ____21____ abused it. Seeing this, Brahma, the chief god, decided to take their divinity away from them and hide it ____22____ it could never be found.

Brahma called a council of the gods to help him decide on a place to hide the divinity. The gods suggested that they hide it ____23____ in the earth or take it to the top of the highest mountain. But Brahma thought ____24____ would do because he believed humans would dig into the earth and climb every mountain, and eventually find it. So, the gods gave up.

Brahma thought for a long time and finally decided to hide their divinity in the center of their own being, for humans would never think to ____25____ it there. Since that time humans have been going up and down the earth, digging, climbing, and exploring-searching for something already within themselves.

21. (A) yet　(B) even　(C) never　(D) rather

22. (A) though　(B) because　(C) where　(D) when

23. (A) close　(B) apart　(C) deep　(D) hard

24. (A) each　(B) more　(C) any　(D) neither

25. (A) look for　(B) get over　(C) do without　(D) bump into

In the fall of 1973, in an effort to bring attention to the conflict between Egypt and Israel, *World Hello Day* was born. The objective is to promote peace all over the world, and to ____26____ barriers between every nationality. Since then, *World Hello Day*-November 21st of every year- ____27____ observed by people in 180 countries.

Taking part couldn't be ____28____. All one has to do is say hello to 10 people on the day. However, in response to the ____29____ of this event, the concepts of fostering peace and harmony do not have to be confined to one day a year. We can ____30____ the spirit going by communicating often and consciously. It is a simple act that anyone can do and it reminds us that communication is more effective than conflict.

26. (A) skip over　(B) come across　(C) look into　(D) break down
27. (A) is　(B) has been　(C) was　(D) had been
28. (A) quicker　(B) sooner　(C) easier　(D) better
29. (A) aim　(B) tone　(C) key　(D) peak
30. (A) push　(B) keep　(C) bring　(D) make

三、文意選填（占10分）

説明：第31題至第40題，每題一個空格，請依文意在文章後所提供的(A)到(J)選項中分別選出最適當者，並將其英文字母代號畫記在答案卡之「選擇題答案區」。各題答對者，得1分；答錯、未作答或畫記多於一個選項者，該題以零分計算。

　　Generally there are two ways to name typhoons: the number-based convention and the list-based convention. Following the number-based convention, typhoons are coded with _____31_____ types of numbers such as a 4-digit or a 6-digit code. For example, the 14th typhoon in 2003 can be labeled either as Typhoon 0314 or Typhoon 200314. The _____32_____ of this convention, however, is that a number is hard to remember. The list-based convention, on the other hand, is based on the list of typhoon names compiled in advance by a committee, and is more widely used.

　　At the very beginning, only _____33_____ names were used because at that time typhoons were named after girlfriends or wives of the experts on the committee. In 1979, however, male names were also included because women protested against the original naming _____34_____ for reasons of gender equality.

　　In Asia, Western names were used until 2000 when the committee decided to use Asian names to _____35_____ Asians' awareness of typhoons. The names were chosen from a name pool _____36_____ of 140 names, 10 each from the 14 members of the committee. Each country has its unique naming preferences. Korea and Japan _____37_____ animal names and China likes names of gods such as Longwang (dragon king) and Fengshen (god of the wind).

　　After the 140 names are all used in order, they will be _____38_____. But the names can be changed. If a member country suffers great damage from a certain typhoon, it can _____39_____ that the name of the typhoon be deleted from the list at the annual committee meeting. For example, the names of Nabi by South Korea, and Longwang by China were _____40_____ with other names in 2007. The deletion of both names was due to the severe damage caused by the typhoons bearing the names.

(A) request　　(B) favor　　(C) disadvantage　(D) composed　(E) recycled

(F) practice　　(G) replaced　(H) raise　　　(I) various　　(J) female

四、閱讀測驗（占32分）

説明：第41題至第56題，每題請分別根據各篇文章之文意選出最適當的一個選項，請畫記在答案卡之「選擇題答案區」。各題答對者，得2分；答錯、未作答或畫記多於一個選項者，該題以零分計算。

41-44為題組

The kilt is a skirt traditionally worn by Scottish men. It is a tailored garment that is wrapped around the wearer's body at the waist starting from one side, around the front and back and across the front again to the opposite side. The overlapping layers in front are called "aprons." Usually, the kilt covers the body from the waist down to just above the knees. A properly made kilt should not be so loose that the wearer can easily twist the kilt around the body, nor should it be so tight that it causes bulging of the fabric where it is buckled. Underwear may be worn as one prefers.

One of the most distinctive features of the kilt is the pattern of squares, or sett, it exhibits. The association of particular patterns with individual families can be traced back hundreds of years. Then in the Victorian era (19th century), weaving companies began to systematically record and formalize the system of setts for commercial purposes. Today there are also setts for States and Provinces, schools and universities, and general patterns that anybody can wear.

The kilt can be worn with accessories. On the front apron, there is often a kilt pin, topped with a small decorative family symbol. A small knife can be worn with the kilt too. It typically comes in a very wide variety, from fairly plain to quite elaborate silver-and jewel-ornamented designs. The kilt can also be worn with a sporran, which is the Gaelic word for pouch or purse.

41. What's the proper way of wearing the kilt?

(A) It should be worn with underwear underneath it.

(B) It should loosely fit on the body to be turned around.

(C) It should be long enough to cover the wearer's knees.

(D) It should be wrapped across the front of the body two times.

42. Which of the following is a correct description about setts?

(A) They were once symbols for different Scottish families.

(B) They were established by the government for business purposes.

(C) They represented different States and Provinces in the 19th century.

(D) They used to come in one general pattern for all individuals and institutions.

43. Which of the following items is **NOT** typically worn with the kilt for decoration?

(A) A pin.　(B) A purse.　(C) A ruby apron.　(D) A silver knife.

44. What is the purpose of this passage?

(A) To introduce a Scottish garment.　(B) To advertise a weaving pattern.

(C) To persuade men to wear kilts.　(D) To compare a skirt with a kilt.

45-48為題組

Wesla Whitfield, a famous jazz singer, has a unique style and life story, so I decided to see one of her performances and interview her for my column.

I went to a nightclub in New York and watched the stage lights go up. After the band played an introduction, Wesla Whitfield wheeled herself onstage in a wheelchair. As she sang,

Whitfield's voice was so powerful and soulful that everyone in the room forgot the wheelchair was even there.

At 57, Whitfield is small and pretty, witty and humble, persistent and philosophical. Raised in California, Whitfield began performing in public at age 18, when she took a job as a singing waitress at a pizza parlor. After studying classical music in college, she moved to San Francisco and went on to sing with the San Francisco Opera Chorus.

Walking home from rehearsal at age 29, she was caught in the midst of a random shooting that left her paralyzed from the waist down. I asked how she dealt with the realization that she'd never walk again, and she confessed that initially she didn't want to face it. After a year of depression she tried to kill herself. She was then admitted to a hospital for treatment, where she was able to recover.

Whitfield said she came to understand that the only thing she had lost in this misfortunate event was the ability to walk. She still possessed her most valuable asset-her mind. Pointing to her head, she said, "Everything important is in here. The only real disability in life is losing your mind." When I asked if she was angry about what she had lost, she admitted to being frustrated occasionally, "especially when everybody's dancing, because I love to dance. But **when that happens** I just remove myself so I can focus instead on what I can do."

45. In which of the following places has Wesla Whitfield worked?

(A) A college.　(B) A hospital.　(C) A pizza parlor.　(D) A news agency.

46. What does "**when that happens**" mean in the last paragraph?

(A) When Wesla is losing her mind.

(B) When Wesla is singing on the stage.

(C) When Wesla is going out in her wheelchair.

(D) When Wesla is watching other people dancing.

47. Which of the following statements is true about Wesla Whitfield's physical disability?

(A) It was caused by a traffic accident.

(B) It made her sad and depressed at first.

(C) It seriously affected her singing career.

(D) It happened when she was a college student.

48. What advice would Wesla most likely give other disabled people?

(A) Ignore what you have lost and make the best use of what you have.

(B) Be modest and hard-working to earn respect from other people.

(C) Acquire a skill so that you can still be successful and famous.

(D) Try to sing whenever you feel upset and depressed.

49-52為題組

Forks trace their origins back to the ancient Greeks. Forks at that time were fairly large with two tines that aided in the carving of meat in the kitchen. The tines prevented meat from twisting or moving during carving and allowed food to slide off more easily than it would with a knife.

By the 7th century A.D., royal courts of the Middle East began to use forks at the table for dining. From the 10th through the 13th centuries, forks were fairly common among the wealthy in Byzantium. In the 11th century, a Byzantine wife brought forks to Italy; however, they were not widely adopted there until the 16th century. Then in 1533, forks were brought from Italy to France. The French were also slow to accept forks, for using them was thought to be awkward.

In 1608, forks were brought to England by Thomas Coryate, who saw them during his travels in Italy. The English first ridiculed forks as being unnecessary. "Why should a person need a fork when God had given him hands?" they asked. Slowly, however, forks came to be adopted by the wealthy as a symbol of their social status. They were prized possessions made of expensive materials intended to impress guests. By the mid 1600s, eating with forks was considered fashionable among the wealthy British.

Early table forks were modeled after kitchen forks, but small pieces of food often fell through the two tines or slipped off easily. In late 17th century France, larger forks with four curved tines were developed. The additional tines made diners less likely to drop food, and the curved tines served as a scoop so people did not have to constantly switch to a spoon while eating. By the early 19th century, four-tined forks had also been developed in Germany and England and slowly began to spread to America.

49. What is the passage mainly about?

(A) The different designs of forks.

(B) The spread of fork-aided cooking.

(C) The history of using forks for dining.

(D) The development of fork-related table manners.

50. By which route did the use of forks spread?

(A) Middle East→Greece→England→Italy→France

(B) Greece→Middle East→Italy→France→England

(C) Greece→Middle East→France→Italy→Germany

(D) Middle East→France→England→Italy→Germany

51. How did forks become popular in England?

(A) Wealthy British were impressed by the design of forks.

(B) Wealthy British thought it awkward to use their hands to eat.

(C) Wealthy British gave special forks to the nobles as luxurious gifts.

(D) Wealthy British considered dining with forks a sign of social status.

52. Why were forks made into a curved shape?

　　(A) They could be used to scoop food as well.

　　(B) They looked more fashionable in this way.

　　(C) They were designed in this way for export to the US.

　　(D) They ensured the meat would not twist while being cut.

53-56為題組

　　Animals are a favorite subject of many photographers. Cats, dogs, and other pets top the list, followed by zoo animals. However, because it's hard to get them to sit still and "perform on command," some professional photographers refuse to photograph pets.

　　One way to get an appealing portrait of a cat or dog is to hold a biscuit or treat above the camera. The animal's longing look toward the food will be captured by the camera, but the treat won't appear in the picture because it's out of the camera's range. When you show the picture to your friends afterwards, they'll be impressed by your pet's loving expression.

　　If you are using fast film, you can take some good, quick shots of a pet by simply snapping a picture right after calling its name. You'll get a different expression from your pet using this technique. Depending on your pet's mood, the picture will capture an interested, curious expression or possibly a look of annoyance, especially if you've awakened it from a nap.

　　Taking pictures of zoo animals requires a little more patience. After all, you can't wake up a lion! You may have to wait for a while until the animal does something interesting or moves into a position for you to get a good shot. When photographing zoo animals, don't get too close to the cages, and never tap on the glass or throw things between the bars of a cage. Concentrate on shooting some good pictures, and always respect the animals you are photographing.

53. Why do some professional photographers **NOT** like to take pictures of pets?

　　(A) Pets may not follow orders.

　　(B) Pets don't want to be bothered.

　　(C) Pets may not like photographers.

　　(D) Pets seldom change their expressions.

54. What is the use of a biscuit in taking pictures of a pet?

　　(A) To capture a cute look.

　　(B) To create a special atmosphere.

　　(C) To arouse the appetite of the pet.

　　(D) To keep the pet from looking at the camera.

55. What is the advantage of calling your pet's name when taking a shot of it?

　　(A) To help your pet look its best.

　　(B) To make sure that your pet sits still.

　　(C) To keep your pet awake for a while.

　　(D) To catch a different expression of your pet.

56. In what way is photographing zoo animals different from photographing pets?

(A) You need to have fast film.

(B) You need special equipment.

(C) You need to stay close to the animals.

(D) You need more time to watch and wait.

第貳部分：非選擇題（占28分）

一、中譯英（占8分）

說明：1.請將以下中文句子譯成正確、通順、達意的英文，並將答案寫在「答案卷」上。

2.請依序作答，並標明題號。每題4分，共8分。

1. 近年來，許多臺灣製作的影片已經受到國際的重視。

2. 拍攝這些電影的地點也成為熱門的觀光景點。

二、英文作文（占20分）

說明：1.依提示在「答案卷」上寫一篇英文作文。

2.文長至少 120 個單詞（words）。

提示：你最好的朋友最近迷上電玩，因此常常熬夜，疏忽課業，並受到父母的責罵。你（英文名字必須假設為 Jack 或 Jill）打算寫一封信給他/她（英文名字必須假設為 Ken 或 Barbie），適當地給予勸告。

請注意：必須使用上述的 Jack 或 Jill 在信末署名，**不得使用自己的真實中文或英文名字**。

101年學測解答

題號	1	2	3	4	5	6	7	8	9	10	11	12	13	14	15	16	17	18	19	20
答案	C	A	B	D	B	B	D	C	B	A	C	C	D	B	A	D	D	A	C	B
題號	21	22	23	24	25	26	27	28	29	30	31	32	33	34	35	36	37	38	39	40
答案	B	C	C	D	A	D	B	C	A	B	I	C	J	F	H	D	B	E	A	G
題號	41	42	43	44	45	46	47	48	49	50	51	52	53	54	55	56				
答案	D	A	C	A	C	D	B	A	C	B	D	A	A	A	D	D				

附錄一
統測、學測、指考等之重點文法

　　雖然沒有正式統計數據，但幾乎可以說，在臺灣，有為數不少的人對「英文文法」很排斥。作者教了幾十年英文，每逢有人問起「英文文法重不重要」時，我都會給兩個答案：

　　1.不參加英文考試時，英文文法不那麼重要。
　　2.要參加英文考試時，英文文法就會很重要。

　　諷刺的是，很多人排斥英文文法，但它卻是英文考試得分的重要關鍵。因為，英文文法的所有規定都是死板的、固定的，考生只要記熟這些規定，加上本書中〈重點文法篇〉的「解題技巧」協助，要考高分並不難。

　　相較之下，字彙測驗的範圍就大得多。因為字彙題的「單字量」是無限寬廣的，不像「英文文法」，尤其是初級、中級的英文文法，其範圍是固定的，準備起來就輕鬆多了。

　　了解「英文文法」的唯一步驟，就應從「英文八大詞類」說起。以下僅就在八大詞類部分，選擇與考試得分有關，也就是「各層級英文考題較常出現的文法項目」舉例說明如下：

名詞

1.不可數名詞的「數量」

　　中文裡常說「數量」二字，即「數」與「量」的意思。在英文裡，「可數名詞的多寡」是用「數」的多少表示；反之，「不可數名詞的多寡」是用「量」的多少表示。

　　例句：Can I have two books?（可數名詞）

　　　　　Can I have two cups of tea / glasses of water ?（不可數名詞）

重點提醒：在不可數名詞前的「計量名詞」，如「cups of」、「glasses of」等，不可漏掉其後的介系詞「of」。

2.人稱所有格，有一種形式→Tom is her friend.

　　非人稱所有格，有一種形式→The cover of the book.（用「of」來代表所有格）

3.雙重所有格，有兩種形式

　　→Tom is a friend of Bob's.（用「of」與「 's」，表示雙重所有格）

　　→Tom is a friend of my brother's.（用「of」與「 's」，表示雙重所有格）

代名詞

　　1.代名詞所有格：共有my、our、your、his、her、its、their等七個，其後必需加名詞。

　　2.所有代名詞：共有mine、ours、yours、his、hers、its、theirs等七個，其後不可加名

詞。

上述兩項詞稱不同，用法就不同。

前項詞稱是「所有格」，所以其後必加名詞，不可不加。如my car、our school、his friends……等。

後項詞稱是「代名詞」，其後不可加名詞。如a friend of mine、a book of hers、a car of his……等。

3.such a nice ～　　　　　It is such a nice book.　They are such nice books.

　so nice a ～　　　　　It is so nice a book..　　　　The books are so nice.

重點提醒：這兩個用法固定，不要混淆。考生要注意的是形容詞（nice）的不同位置。

such as＋多個名詞→He enjoys sports, such as swimming, diving and skiing.

重點提醒：such as，中譯為「像是、諸如」之意，其後大多接複數。

4.both 的三種用法

　⑴(Both A and B) → Both Tom and Mary are from Paris.

　⑵(Both of them...)→Both of them　　　　are from Paris.

　⑶(They both) → 　They both　　　　　　are from Paris.

重點提醒：用both的前提，只限在「兩者之間」，三者以上不適用。

5.either兩者任一皆～　Either girl can dance.（兩位女生中的任何一個都會跳舞。）

　neither兩者任一皆不～　Neither girl can dance.（兩位女生中的任何一個都不會跳舞。）

重點提醒：

⑴neither屬於「否定」字，本身已含否定字義，其後同句內不可有「not、no」等字出現。其他常用否定字有：never、seldom、rarely、hardly、scarcely等。

⑵用either, neither的前提，只限在「兩者之間」，三者以上皆不適用。

⑶請考生注意，either、neither二字，也可當副詞，例如：

　I like this book, too.（肯定句的「也」用「too」作副詞）

　I don't like this book, either（否定句的「也」，用「either」作副詞）

6.關係代名詞：who、which、what等三字，位於句中時稱為「關係代名詞」，例句：

　Tom is the student who called yesterday.

　Tom is the student whom I met yesterday.

　Tom is the student whose father is a doctor.

重點提醒：題目空格處要選who、whom或whose，取決於空格右方的字，該字是「動詞」時，需選主格的who；該字是「人稱主格」（如Tom、Mary、you、I、they）時，選受格的whom；該字是「一般名詞」時，選所有格的whose。

7.關係副詞：when、where、why、how等四字位於句中時，稱為「關係副詞」，例句：

　Last Tuesday was the day when he returned to Taipei.

　Hualien is the place where his parents live.

Financial problem is the reason <u>why</u> he stole the money.

Going by metro is the way <u>how</u> he goes to work.

重點提醒：考題空格內要選擇哪一個關係副詞，取決於空格前的先行詞，代表「時間」的用when，代表「地方」的用where，代表「原因」的用why，代表「方法」的用how。

8.不能省略的介系詞──有些片語組內的介系詞，在關係代名詞的使用不能省略。例句：

Tom was the person whom <u>I talked with</u> yesterday.

=Tom was the person <u>with whom</u> I talked yesterday.

This is issue <u>of which</u> they <u>spoke</u> a week ago.

This is issue which they <u>spoke of</u> a week ago.

重點提醒：片語的末字為介系詞，用在關係代名詞或關係副詞時，介系詞不可省略。

9.連接詞用法：

位於兩個子句中的七個疑問詞都是連接詞。另外，最常用的連接詞還有who、which、what、when、where、why、how、that、before、after、because、whether、if、unless、in case、as soon as、as long as……等。

重點提醒：

(1)連接詞後的「從屬子句」，不可倒裝。例句：

(○) I know <u>who you are</u>.

(x) I know who are you.

(2)連接詞後的「從屬子句」，不用否定句。例句：

(○) I <u>don't think</u> he is coming.

(x) I think he is not coming.

形容詞

1.形容詞的後位形容：

名詞 + 現在分詞片語 The man <u>sitting by the tree</u> came from New York..

　　　　　　　　 = The man <u>who is sitting by the tree</u> came from New York.

名詞 + 過去分詞片語 This is the book <u>published by ABC Co.</u> last week.

　　　　　　　　 =This is the book <u>which was published by ABC Co.</u> last week.

重點提醒：名詞後加現在分詞片語或過去分詞片語，在許多考題上常出現。它等於關係代名詞後的「形容詞片語」。換言之，是上述例句內的「sitting by the tree = who is sitting by the tree」。

2.形容詞三級

級別	原級	比較級	最高級
單音節時	tall	taller	tallest
多音節	expensive	more expensive	most expensive

⑴單音節的「比較級」，是在原級字後加「er」；「最高級」，是在原級字後加「est」。

⑵多音節的「比較級」，是在原級字前加「more」；「最高級」，是在原級字前加「most」。

⑶不論單音節或多音節的最高級，都需在字前加「the」，如the tallest、the most expensive。

動詞

1. 英文動詞分「有限類動詞」與「非限類動詞」兩大類。

⑴有限類動詞：包括「普通動詞」與「特別動詞」兩種。

⑵英文動詞字後未加s、es、ed、ing等，統稱爲「普通動詞」。

⑶特別動詞只有六組（24個）（請參閱P.241「英文動詞字群（表一）」）。24個特別動詞外的成千上萬個動詞，都稱爲「普通動詞」。

⑷不論特別動詞或普通動詞，一定是句子中的第一個動詞。而24個特別動詞，在句中的位階都比普通動詞高。

例句：He goes to school every day.

He did not go to school yesterday.

He will go to school tomorrow.

（第一句為「現在式」，句中第一個動詞goes，因為不在24個特別動詞內，所以是普通動詞。第二句為「未來式」，因文法公式，在原句第一個動詞goes前加入will。此時will才是句中第一個動詞，原有的goes變成句中第二個動詞。既然不再是第一個動詞，所以它只好恢復原形，成為「原形動詞」。）

2. 一個英文句子如果有兩個以上的動詞時，特別動詞之後可接哪些動詞，依表二規定（見P.241表二）。

⑴99%的普通動詞之後加「不定詞」。例句：

I want to go home to study English and to take a shower.

⑵1%的普通詞詞之後加「動名詞」。例句：

I enjoy reading.

Keep talking.

Don't stop singing.

換言之，

⑴其後需加動名詞的這1%普通動詞，有mind、enjoy、avoid、finish、keep、stop、deny、quit、resent、delay、admit、consider、begin……。

⑵其後需加動名詞的，還有兩個形容詞busy、worth。

⑶其後需加動名詞的，還有片語組 be sued to、be accustomed to、look forward to、according to、be up to、be capable of、feel like、have fun、it's no use、end up等的所

有介系詞之後。

3. 簡單過去式與現在完成式的差別在於：

簡單過去式（有明顯的過去時間副詞）→Tom bought a new car last week.

現在完成式（不可有明顯的過去時間副詞）→Tom has bought a new car.

4. 現在完成式與現在完成進行式的差別在於：

現在完成式，指「至今為止的狀態」　　He has been sick for two days.

　　　　　　　　　　　　　　　　　I have just finished my homework.

現在完成進行式，指「持續的動作」　　He has been playing the game for two hours.

　　　　　　　　　　　　　　　　　He has been standing there all morning.

5. 過去進行式與過去完成式的差別在於：

過去進行式：主要子句用「was, were +Ving + 連接詞 + 從屬子句用過去式動詞」

I　　　　was reading a report　　　　when　　　　Peter came in..

= When Peter came in , I was reading a report.

過去完成式：主要子句用「had + pp（過去分詞）＋ 連接詞 + 從屬子句用過去式動詞」

I　　　had finished the tet　　　　before　　　　I left school.

The manager had left　　　　when　　　　I arrived at his office.

6. 時間或條件子句時，從屬句用現在式動詞　Give this letter to Joe when he comes.

從屬子句作受詞時，用未來式動詞　　　　I don't know when he will come

7. 附帶問句用法：

⑴ 肯定句用否定附帶 He is nice, <u>isn't he</u> ?

　　　　　　　　　 He has been here before, <u>hasn't he</u> ?

⑵ 否定句用肯定附帶 She always comes early, <u>doesn't she</u> ?

　　　　　　　　　 She was late yesterday, <u>didn't she</u> ?

重點提醒：

⑴ 這種句子的應答技巧，在於句中第一個動詞。前句是用哪一個特別動詞，附帶句就用同一個特別動詞答回去。

⑵ 前句的第一個動詞如果是用普通動詞說，附帶句就只能用 do 組的 do、does、did 的某一個答回去。

⑶ 此外，考生還要注意：不管上述否定附帶或肯定附帶，它的前半句與後半句都是相反的。

8. 原形動詞的省略：

want to, hope to, like to, try to,　　Do you want to go ?　　　　No, I don't want to.

have to, be going to,　　　　　　　Do you have to write it ?　　Yes, I have to.

9. 原形動詞的位置：

⑴ 在下列 14 個特別動詞之後 do, does, did, can, could, may, might, shall, should, will, would, must, need, dare

Do you want...?　Does she like...?　Did they say...?　Can you sing ...?　May I speak....?　Shall we go...?　Will you be....?　Would you like...?　He must go.　You need not go.　He dare not say that.

⑵ 在感官動詞see, hear之後

I hear her sing every morning.

I see her sell watches every day.

⑶ 在下列使役動詞或成語之後 make, let, have, had better, would rather, do nothing but, can not but,

Don't make me laugh

Let's go

You had better leave before I change my mind.

10.常用聯結動詞有三組，後加原級形容詞

⑴ be 動詞組　am, are, is, was, were　　　　She is beautiful.

⑵ 感官動詞組feel, look, smell, sound, taste　The hat looks nice on you.

⑶ 其他組 become, get, grow, seem, keep,　　The culture remain strong.
　　　　　Appear, remain

11.分詞構句

Judging from ～ 由～判斷　　　　Judging from his accent, he must be English.

Speaking of ～ 說到～　　　　　Speaking of the devil, here comes Tom..

Generally speaking 一般而言　Generally speaking, he is a good person.

12.現在分詞與過去分詞作為形容詞

The baby is sleeping

The wounded soldier needs help.

13.試題四選項裡怎應選 Ved 或 Ving？

The movie is embarrassing　還是 This movie is embarrassed?

I am / feel bored.　　　　　　還是 I am / feel boring.

重點提醒：embarrassing 與 embarrassed 都當形容詞。要看句中主詞來決定用哪一個。

⑴ 主詞為事或物時，用 embarrassing 只形容該事或物如何如何。

⑵ 主詞為人時，用 embarrassed 來說明主詞這個人的「感覺」如何如何。

14.have ＋人時，後接原形動詞　I will have Tom mail the letter.

have ＋物時，後接過去分詞　　　I had my house painted last week.

重點提醒：have 後面是人 Tom，所以接原形動詞 mail

　　　　　had 之後是物 house，所以接過去分詞 painte

used to + 原形動詞　　　　My friend Bob used to come here every week.

be used to 名詞 / 動名詞　I am used to my wife's nagging.

get used to　　　　　　　You'd better get used to his bad temper if you want this high salary.

重點提醒：

⑴ 空格右邊是動詞 come，所以空格內選 used to。

⑵ 空格右邊是名詞 my wife's，所以空格內選 be used to。

⑶ 空格右邊是名詞 his bad temper，所以空格內選 get used to。

15. if 之後如果選 be 動詞，只能選 were I wouldn't say that if I <u>were</u> you.

He talks as if he <u>were</u> the manager of the department

16. 倒裝題的解題

試題開頭，如果有 never, hardly, only, no 等相關字（no sooner, on no account...等），選項要倒裝：

Not only <u>did we lost</u> the money, but we also got lost.

Only if you have a visa <u>can you</u> enter the country.

英文動詞字群（表一）

第一類動詞：一定是句子中第一個動詞，字形隨主詞作變化。
1. 特別動詞　24 個
2. 普通動詞　N 個（24 個特別動詞外的所有動詞原式）
說明：
⑴ 特別動詞後接的動詞，應依（表二）規定
⑵ 普通動詞後接的動詞，規定如下：
① 99%普通動詞＋不定詞
② 1%普通動詞＋動名詞
第二類動詞：不可做為句子中第一個動詞，字形不隨主詞作變化。
1. 原形動詞：不加 s、es、ed、ing 等動詞原形。如 come、go 等。
2. 不定詞：原形動詞前加 to 者，如 to come、to go 等。
3. 動名詞：原形動詞後加 ing 者，如 coming、going 等。
4. 現在分詞：原形動詞後加 ing 者，如 coming、going 等。
5. 過去分詞：規則變化時，原形後加 ed；不規則時，字形不定。

特別動詞 ＋ 第二類動詞（表二）

組別	特限類動詞	非限類動詞	
Be	Am　Are　Is　Was　Were	＋現在分詞＝進行式	例句1
		＋過去分詞＝被動語態	例句2
		＋不定詞　＝表目的	例句3
Have	Have　Has　　Had	＋過去分詞＝完成式	例句4
		＋不定詞　＝表必須	例句5

Do	Do　Doe　　Did		例句6
Can	Can May　　Could Might	＋原型動詞	例句7
Shall	Shall Will　　Should Would		例句8
Must	Must　Need　Dare		例句9
Ought	Used	＋不定詞	例句10

1. They <u>are</u> <u>having</u> a meeting at the moment.

2. All students <u>are told</u> <u>to stand</u> in line at the ticket counter.

3. We <u>are</u> <u>to study</u> European history today.

4. She <u>has</u> <u>passed</u> her final exam at school.

5. You don't <u>have</u> <u>to take</u> this job if you don't want to.

6. <u>Do</u> you <u>want</u> me to wake you up in the morning ?

7. <u>Can</u> I <u>use</u> the pay-phone there ?

8. I <u>will</u> <u>call</u> you sometime tomorrow.

9. You <u>mustn't</u> <u>leave</u> now, we are in the middle of the meeting

10. You <u>ought</u> <u>to do</u> what your mother says.

　　They <u>used</u> <u>to come</u> here every week.

附錄二
重要片語、俚語之補充
（學測、指考、統測）

A

a stone's throw/cast　短距離

annoyed at　惱怒

at a premium　高價

at a snail's pace　緩慢

at all cost　不計代價

at any rate　無論如何

at finger's ends　精通

at issue　爭論中

at length　最後 詳細的

at sixes and sevens　七嘴八舌

at the risk of　冒險

aware of　知道

B

be opposed to　相對立

behind time　過期

blame for　責備

bound for　開往

break out　爆發

bring about　引起

by fours and fives　三五成群

by means of　用～方法

by no means　決沒有

by virture of　由於

C

carry on　繼續

carry out　進行

charge with　控訴

comparable with　可比較

correspond with　符合

count on / rely on　倚賴

crucial for　至關重要

D

deal with　處理

deprive of　剝奪

derive from　從～得到

devote to　奉獻

different from　不同於

distant from　遠的

distinct from　與不同

distinguish from　辨別

divided into　分開

donkey's years　很長時間

F

famous for　因～出名

free from　沒有

G

get away with　僥倖做到

give in　屈服

give up　放棄

H

hear from　到～訊息

hinder from　妨礙

I

identify with　認同

in care of　由～轉交

in case of　如果

in charge of　負責

in lieu of　代替

in the lion's paws　處於險境

inquire into　查究

interfere with　干擾　妨礙

K

keep house　管理家務

L

live a dog's life　過悲慘生活

M

meet the demand　滿足需求

mistaken for　誤為

N

not a dog's chance　毫無機會

O

on a razor's edge　處險境

on account of　因為

on all fours　吻合　爬行

on behalf of　代表

one's hearts' content　心滿意足

out of order　故障

out of question　毫無疑問

P

persuade of　說服

prevent from　防止

provide with　提供

put off　延遲

R

remind of　提醒

responsible for　對～負責

result from　起因於

result in　導致

S

separate from　與～分開

set about　開始

set in　開始

show off　炫耀

show up　出現

six of one and half a dozen　差不多

stir up a hornet's nest　自找麻煩

straight from the horse's mouth　來自可靠消息

substitute for　代替

T

take for　認為

take off　起飛　脫下

take on　呈現

ten to one　十之八九

to one's advantage　對～有利

to sum up　總之

turn out　變成

turn out　變成

turn up　出現

two by four　微不足道的

twos and threes　三三兩兩

U

under the circumstances　在此情況下

W

with a view to　為了～

附錄三
重要字彙補充
（學測、指考、統測）

A

accuracy　準確
achievement　成就
administration　管理
aggressive　積極
agriculture　農業
alternative　選擇
amateur　業餘
ambitious　有雄心
analyze　分析
anniversary　週年日
announcement　公告
anxious　焦慮不安
applause　掌聲
appliance　器具
appropriate　合適
aquarium　水族館
architecture　建築
artificial　人造
assassinate　暗殺
athelete　運動員
atmosphere　氣氛
attractive　有吸引力
autobiography　自傳

B

bacteria　細菌
bankrupt　破產
bargain　講價
behavior　行為
beneficial　受益
budget　預算
bulletin board　佈告牌

C

campaign　活動
candidate　候選人
canyon　峽谷
capacity　能力
casualty　傷亡
celebrate　慶祝
ceremony　典禮
certificate　證明書
characteristic　特性
circulation　流通
civilization　文明
classify　分類
climax　高潮
clumsy　笨拙
coincidence　巧合
collapse　瓦解
colleague　同事
combination　結合
comfortable　舒適
commission　委托
communication　通訊
community　社區
competitor　競爭者
complicated　複雜
comprehension　理解
concentrate　集中
conference　會議
confidence　信任
congratulate　祝賀
connection　連接
consequence　後果
conservative　保守

constitution　憲法

construction　建設

consumer products　消費產品

contemporary　當代

continental　大陸

contribution　貢獻

convenience　便利

convention　傳統

convince　使確信

courtesy　禮貌

crash　碰撞

creature　動物

criminal　犯罪

criticize　批評

cultivate　培養

curiosity　好奇

cyclist　騎車者

D

deadline　期限

decade　十年

declaration　宣告

decoration　裝飾

defend　防衛

definition　定義

delegate　代表

democracy　民主

demonstration　遊行示威

depression　沮喪

describe　描述

deserve　應得的

destination　目的地

destroy　破壞

destructive　有破壞性

determination　決心

development　發展

device　小設備

devote　奉獻

digestion　消化

digital　數據化

disappointed　失望

disaster　災難

discipline　紀律

disguise　偽裝

disgust　厭惡

domestic　國內

dominate　支配

drawbacks　缺點

dynamic　動力

E

editorial　社論

efficiency　效率

elementary　初步

eliminate　消除

emphasize　強調

energetic　充滿活力

enlarge　擴大

entertainer　演員

enthusiasm　熱情

entitle　有資格

environment　環境

equipment　設備

escalator　電扶梯

essential　必要的

establish　建立

estimate　估計

evaluate　評價

eventually　終於

evidence　證據

exaggerate　誇大

excellent　極好

excursion　旅行

executive　執行

exhaust　筋疲力盡

exhibition　展覽會

experiment　實驗

extreme　極端

F

facility　能力
faithful　忠實
familiar with　熟悉
farewell party　惜別會
fatal　致命
feedback　回饋
financial　金融
forecast weather　預報天氣
fortunately　幸好
frequenly　經常
frightened　嚇住
frustrate　受挫
function　起作用

G

genuine　真實
gigantic　龐大
glorious　光榮
gradually　逐漸
greenhouse　溫室
grocery　雜貨店
guarantee　保證
guardian　守護人

H

habitual　習慣
hairdresser　理髮師
handicap　障礙
hardship　艱難
harmony　和諧
harvest　收成
headquaters　總部
hesitate　猶豫
hijack　劫持
historical　歷史
horizon　地平線
humanity　人類
humidity　濕度
hurricane　颶風

hydrogen　氫

I

identification　鑑定
identity　身分
ignore　忽視
imagination　想像
immediately　立即
impact　影響
impression　印象
increasing　增加
independent　獨立於
inevitable　不可避免
inflation　通貨膨脹
informal　非正式
ingredient　成分
inhabitant　居民
injection　注射
injured　使受傷
innocence　清白
inquiry　詢問
inspector　檢查員
inspire　鼓舞
institution　機構 學院
intellectual　智慧
intensify　加強
interact　相互作用
interfere　干涉
internal　內部
interpret　解釋
intruder　入侵者
invade　侵入
invention　發明
investment　投資
invisible　看不見

J

journey　旅行

K

kidnap　拐走
knowledge　知識

L

landmark　地標
landscape　風景
landslide　山崩
language barrier　語言障礙
latitude　緯度
launch　發動　開始～
lavatory　洗手間
league　聯盟
lecture　演講
legendary　傳奇
leisure　休閒
liberate　解放
literature　文學
loyalty　忠實
luxurious　豪華

M

magnet　磁鐵
majority　多數
manageable　可管理
manufacture　製造
marathon　馬拉松
margin profit　最低利潤
mature　成熟
measurement　測量
memorandum　備忘錄
mineral　礦物質
ministry　部會
minority　少數
miracle　奇跡
miserable　痛苦
moderate　適度
moisture　水分
monument　紀念碑
mortgage　抵押

motivation　動機
multiple　倍數
mystery　神祕

N

negotiate　談判
novelist　小說家
nuclear　核子
numerous　許多
nutrition　營養

O

obedient　服從
observe　觀察
obviously　顯而易見
occasion　場合
occupy　佔用
offensive　冒犯
opposition　反對
oral　口頭
orchestra　管弦樂隊
organic　有機
orphanage　育幼院
outstanding　傑出
overcome　克服
overthrow　推翻
oxygen　氧

P

panic　恐慌
paragraph　段落
parliament　議會
participate　參加
particular　特別
partnership　合夥
patriotic　愛國
peculiar　獨特
penalty　懲罰
penguin　企鵝
performance　表現

perfume　香水

pernanent　永久

persist　堅持

persuade　説服

phenomenon　現象

philosopher　哲學家

physical　物理

pilgrim　朝拜者

pioneer　開發者

pirate　海盜

poetry　詩

poisonous　有毒

politics　政治

portable　可攜帶

portrait　肖像

postpone　延遲

potential　潛能

practical　實際

predict　預言

preferable　更好

pregnant　懷孕

presentation　説明會

prevent　防止

previous　之前

primary　主要

privacy　隱私

privilege　特權

procedure　程序

profitable　有利潤

progressive　進步

prohibit　禁止

promote　推廣

prompt　迅速

proper　適當

proportion　比例

proposal　提議

prosperous　繁榮

protective　保護

psychology　心理學

publicity　宣傳

punctual　準時

pursuit　追逐

Q

qualification　資格

quantity　數量

quotation　報價

R

racial　種族

radiation　輻射

rank　職級

reaction　反應

realistic　實際

recession　衰退

recognize　認出

recommend　推薦

recreation　娛樂

reduction　減少

reference　參考

reflection　反射

refugee　難民

registration　登記

rehearsal　排練

relative　有關

relax　放鬆

reliable　可靠

relief　舒緩疼痛

religion　宗教

remarkable　驚人

remind　提醒

reputation　名聲

requirement　要求

research　研究

resemble　相像

reservation　預定

resignation　辭職

S

sacrifice　犧牲

sanctions　國際制裁

satellite　衛星

satisfy　滿足

scenery　風景

scheme　計畫

scholarship　獎學金

scold　訓斥

scratch　抓癢

sculpture　雕刻品

security　安全

seize　抓住

sensitive　敏感

settlement　解決

sexual　性

significance　意義

similarity　相似

skyscraper　摩天大廈

slighly　稍微

sociable　愛交際

sorrow　悲哀

specific　具體　明確

spiritual　精神

splendid　壯觀

sportsmanship　運動員風格

squeeze　擠壓

stadium　體育場

starve　飢餓

stimulate　刺激

strategy　策略

structor　指導者

structure　架構

stubborn　頑固

substance　物質

suburbs　市郊

suffer　遭受

sufficient　足夠

suicide　自殺

summarize　總結

superior　優良

supervisor　監督人

supreme court　最高法院

survival　生存

suspect　懷疑

suspend　中止

suspicious　疑心

symbolize　象徵性

sympathy　同情

symphony　交響樂

symptom　症狀

T

talent　才能

technical　技術

temporary　暫時

terminal　終端

territory　領土

tolerate　容忍

tornado　龍捲風

tortoise　烏龜

tragedy　悲劇

transform　改變

tremendous　驚人地

typical　典型

U

unconscious　無意識

underweight　重量不足

unfortunately　令人遺憾

urge　呼籲

urgent　緊急

V

vacant　空位空房

vegetarian　素食者

victom　受害者

vigor　活力

visual　視覺

vital　至關重要

voluntary　自願

voyage　航行

W

wages　工資

wander　徘徊

welfare　福利

widespread　廣泛

worthwhile　值得

Note

Note

國家圖書館出版品預行編目資料

97～101年英文科統測・學測等歷屆試題解
析應考破題技巧大公開／黃惠政著. －－二
版.－－臺北市：文字復興，2013.01
　面；　公分
ISBN 978-957-11-6937-8（平裝）
1.英語　2.問題集　3.中等教育　4.技職教育
524.38　　　　　　　　　　101015721

WX07　　升大學06

97～101年英文科統測・學測等歷屆試題解析
應考破題技巧大公開

作　　者 ― 黃惠政 (302.5)

發 行 人 ― 楊榮川

總 編 輯 ― 王翠華

主　　編 ― 黃惠娟

責任編輯 ― 盧羿珊

封面設計 ― 黃聖文

出 版 者 ― 文字復興有限公司

地　　址：106台北市大安區和平東路二段339號4樓

電　　話：(02)2705-5066　傳　　真：(02)2706-6100

網　　址：http://www.wunan.com.tw

電子郵件：wunan@wunan.com.tw

劃撥帳號：01068953

戶　　名：文字復興有限公司

台中市駐區辦公室/台中市中區中山路6號

電　　話：(04)2223-0891　傳　　真：(04)2223-3549

高雄市駐區辦公室/高雄市新興區中山一路290號

電　　話：(07)2358-702　傳　　真：(07)2350-236

法律顧問　元貞聯合法律事務所　張澤平律師

出版日期　2013年 1 月二版一刷

定　　價　新臺幣280元